NEW ENGLAND

Pretty Evil

NEW ENGLAND

TRUE STORIES
OF VIOLENT VIXENS AND
MURDEROUS MATRIARCHS

SUE COLETTA

Globe
Pequot
GUILFORD, CONNECTICUT

Globe
Pequot

An imprint of The Rowman & Littlefield Publishing Group, Inc.
4501 Forbes Blvd., Ste. 200
Lanham, MD 20706
www.rowman.com

Distributed by NATIONAL BOOK NETWORK

British Library Cataloguing in Publication Information available

Library of Congress Cataloging-in-Publication Data

Names: Coletta, Sue, 1967- author.
Title: Pretty evil New England : true stories of violent vixens and murderous matriarchs / Sue Coletta.
Description: Guilford, Connecticut : Globe Pequot, [2020] | Summary: "Nineteenth century New England was the hunting ground of five female serial killers: Jane Toppan, Lydia Sherman, Nellie Webb, Harriet E. Nason, and Sarah Jane Robinson. In Pretty Evil New England, true crime author Sue Coletta tells the story of these five women, from broken childhoods, to first brushes with death, and she examines the overwhelming urges that propelled these women to take the lives of a combined total of more than one-hundred innocent victims. The murders, investigations, trials, and ultimate verdicts will stun and surprise readers"—Provided by publisher.
Identifiers: LCCN 2020026162 (print) | LCCN 2020026163 (ebook) | ISBN 9781493052332 (paperback ; alk. paper) | ISBN 9781493052349 (epub)
Subjects: LCSH: Murder—New England—Case studies. | Women murderers—New England—Case studies.
Classification: LCC HV6533.N22 C65 2020 (print) | LCC HV6533.N22 (ebook) | DDC 364.152/3092520974—dc23
LC record available at https://lccn.loc.gov/2020026162
LC ebook record available at https://lccn.loc.gov/2020026163

∞™ The paper used in this publication meets the minimum requirements of American National Standard for Information Sciences—Permanence of Paper for Printed Library Materials, ANSI/NISO Z39.48-1992

CONTENTS

CONTENTS

To honor the victims and their families,
I offer a poem by New England native
Edgar Allan Poe.

A Dream

In visions of the dark night
I have dreamed of joy departed—
But a waking dream of life and light
Hath left me broken-hearted.
Ah! what is not a dream by day
To him whose eyes are cast
On things around him with a ray
Turned back upon the past?
That holy dream—that holy dream,
While all the world were chiding,
Hath cheered me as a lovely beam
A lonely spirit guiding.
What though that light, thro' storm and night,
So trembled from afar—
What could there be more purely bright
In Truth's day-star?

PART I:
JANE TOPPAN

1
UNKNOWINGLY TEMPTING FATE

In 1887, thirty-six-year-old Amelia Phinney survived the surgery for a uterine ulcer in Cambridge Hospital, a procedure done via cauterization with nitrate of silver—only to come face-to-face with New England's most prolific female serial killer, whose body count reached well into the double digits. Post-op the following evening, Amelia tossed and turned on the cot in her room, the abdominal pain so severe it prevented her from falling asleep.

A shadowy figure emerged through the golden smolder of a bedside oil lamp. The dark-haired, dark-eyed nurse hovered over her bed with a peculiar intensity. When Amelia met her gaze, the stranger asked how she was feeling. The surgery, although successful, left her in a state of suffering. Amelia pleaded with the portly nurse to summon her doctor.

"There is no need for that." The nurse's voice remained soft, caring. "I have something to make you feel better. Here." She slid her arm under Amelia's shoulders and raised her far enough off the pillow to sip from the glass pressed to her lips. "Drink this."

After swallowing a foul-tasting liquid, a numbness branched throughout Amelia's torso and limbs. Her mouth and throat grew dry and scratchy, her eyelids weighted as she faded into a semi-conscious state. Someone pulled down the bedclothes. The cot creaked and the thin mattress sagged beneath the weight of a person climbing into bed with her.

The nurse cuddled and groped Amelia, stroking her hair, tenderly kissing her cheeks, forehead, and chin; her voice was soft, whispering that soon everything would be all right. Then the stranger rose to her knees. Hovering over Amelia, the nurse flipped Amelia's eyelids inside-out and leaned in—a determined stare, eye-to-eye.

Was this really happening?

The nurse's breathing accelerated into a heavy pant. Hot breath pummeled the side of Amelia's face as though her suffering excited the stranger.

"Come, dear." The nurse pressed the glass to Amelia's bottom lip again, urging her to swallow more of the bitter medicine. "Drink just a little more."

Unwilling to obey, Amelia clamped her mouth closed and rolled her face to the opposite side of her pillow like a petulant toddler refusing to eat vegetables. Wooden clogs pattering down the hall outside the room startled the nurse, and she leaped off the bed and bustled out the door.

The next morning, a trainee named McCutcheon shook Amelia awake. When she opened her eyes her stomach acid sloshed in protest, a queasiness rising to her throat. For several hours she fought through a drug-induced haze. Once she'd regained her faculties, she thought it best not to share the story of the bizarre encounter from the night before. The incident was so crazy it must have been a bad dream; a nightmare brought on by the pain reliever.

Or had a mystical guardian angel saved her life?

It would take fourteen years for her to discover the truth.

According to FBI behaviorists, the best way to survive a male serial killer's attack is to let him get to know you on a personal level. By humanizing yourself, you'll ruin his fantasy of you as a victim.

This won't work with a female serial killer. They already know you.

Another scorching summer day, another unexplained death.

In 1901 on Cape Cod, seagulls squawked over the catch of the day in fishermen's nets, osprey nested along marshlands and sandy beaches, waves lapping against miles and miles of shorelines on the eastern, western, and southern tips of the Massachusetts peninsula, where horse-drawn carriages kicked up sorrel dust clouds, iron-shoed hooves clomping against pressed-gravel streets. Salt scented the air for miles. But by August 15 of that year, something evil veiled the peaceful seaside community of Cataumet.

Jane Toppan vacationed in the area for the first time in 1897. As a trained nurse and Cambridge Hospital graduate, Jane looked the part in every line of her face, every curve of her ample figure, every movement and mannerism. At that time she stayed at the Davis cottage with the prominent family of L. W. Ferdinand of Cambridge, next door to a rambling seasonal hotel called Jachin House. Guests from the city would congregate on Jachin House's wide wrap-around porches to relax, rocking away the evening hours, cooled off by crisp ocean breezes sweeping in from Buzzards Bay.

The Davis family owned both properties. Alden Davis, considered by many to be Cataumet's most influential citizen due to his reorganization

Jachin House *Courtesy of Bourne Public Library*

of the railroad system so the train stopped at the Cape, worked as the town's postmaster, station agent, and had a successful marble business. He also ran the general store across from Depot Square. Some say he founded the town.

Most of the headstones in the local cemetery were engraved by Alden Davis's hand, a fact that seems ominous in hindsight.

Jane Toppan fell in love with Cape Cod. So much so, she returned to Jachin House year after year to spend the summer, thereby avoiding the hustle and bustle of city life. During one such summer, in late August of 1889, Jane's foster sister,

Jane Toppan *Public Domain*

Elizabeth Brigham, decided to come down from Lowell to visit Jane—a little "girl time" for the two women to reconnect.

Jane had something else planned for their reunion.

Over the years Jane had maintained a cordial relationship with Elizabeth, but deep down she harbored resentment. Twenty years her senior, Elizabeth represented everything Jane wasn't. Not only was Elizabeth pampered by her biological mother, Ann Toppan, while Jane was treated as the family slave, Elizabeth was also wealthy, attractive, and married to Oramel A. Brigham (known as "O. A."), a well-liked, highly regarded deacon of the First Trinitarian Congregational Church in Lowell and depot master for the Boston & Maine Railroad.

When Ann Toppan, Jane's foster mother, died she excluded Jane from the will. And Jane touched on this in her confession:

I felt rather bitter against Mrs. [Elizabeth] Brigham after Mother Toppan's death, because I always thought she destroyed the will that

5

left me some of the old lady's property. Mrs. [Elizabeth] Brigham came down to visit me at Cataumet on Buzzards Bay, where I was spending the Summer of 1899 in one of the Davis cottages. That gave me a good chance to have my revenge on her.

On August 26, the day after Elizabeth arrived on the Cape, Jane suggested a picnic on the beach might lift her foster sister's spirits. For several weeks Elizabeth had been suffering with a mild but persistent case of melancholia (known today as depression).

Weaved picnic basket in hand, Jane escorted Elizabeth down to Scotch House Cove, where the two women spent several hours chatting away the day while munching on cold corned beef and taffy. Salted ocean breezes swept its fingers through their hair as they basked in the summer sun. But deep within Jane a volcano of resentment was about to erupt.

She was really the first of my victims that I actually hated and poisoned with a vindictive purpose. So I let her die slowly, with griping tortures. I fixed mineral water so it would do that and then added the morphia to it.

All that sun drained Elizabeth of energy, so she retired early to her upstairs bedroom. The following morning, Jane called Elizabeth down for breakfast. When she didn't respond, Jane rushed to the home of her landlord, Alden Davis, and asked if he could summon the doctor because "her sister had taken sick." Jane then telegrammed O. A. in Lowell, informing him that his wife was in grave condition.

Alarmed, O. A. took the first available train to Cape Cod. By the time he arrived the next morning, Monday, August 28, Elizabeth had fallen into a coma. She died in the early morning hours of August 29. The doctor said Elizabeth had suffered a stroke of apoplexy (cerebral hemorrhage or stroke).

But Jane knew better.

I held her in my arms and watched with delight as she gasped her life out.

As O. A. packed up his wife's belongings, he only found five dollars in her pocketbook, which was odd since he and Elizabeth agreed that she should take "no less than fifty dollars" for her trip. When he asked Jane about the missing money, she feigned innocence. As far as she knew, Elizabeth arrived with only a few dollars. If money went missing, Jane assured him, she didn't know anything about it.

Taking Jane at her word, O. A. continued to pack Elizabeth's belongings when Jane rested a soothing hand on his forearm. Just before slipping into a coma, she said, Elizabeth expressed the desire to leave Jane her gold watch and chain. Touched by his wife's kind gesture, O. A. fulfilled Elizabeth's final wish.

As the years rolled by, the folks in Cataumet village witnessed a different side of Jane, who was often spotted in a white dress and pinstriped sailor cap, hand-in-hand with a human chain of children, skipping down to the beach at Scotch House Cove or below the bluffs on Squiteague Bay. The kids carried picnic baskets stuffed with food for yet another fun-filled day with "Jolly Jane."

No one could figure out how she afforded these outings. Did it matter? Everyone adored Jane, with her kind, jovial, fun-loving personality, and her uncanny ability of winning her way into the hearts of everyone she met.

During those summers, however, Jane signed several notes for unpaid rent and personal loans totaling thousands, five hundred dollars of which remained outstanding. The Davis family was so fond of Jane that no one pressured her for the money, until June 25, 1901, when Mattie Davis's generosity had run out.

When Mattie woke on the morning of June 25, the temperature had already risen to a balmy seventy degrees by early dawn. The summer day promised to be another scorcher, but nothing could persuade her to forego her trip to Cambridge to confront Jane. Good friend or not, she and Alden had been patient long enough. Besides, her daughter, Genevieve Gordon, was visiting in-laws in Somerville, Massachusetts, all the way from her home in Chicago. Mattie could kill two birds, so to speak, and visit with Genevieve once Jane paid the past-due notes. She also needed to find out if Jane wanted to reserve a room at Jachin House that summer or rent the Davis cottage again.

In poor health from diabetes, exacerbated by the heat and humidity, Mattie didn't move fast enough that morning. The 6:45 a.m. train to Boston was due any minute. To help his wife, Alden volunteered to run over to the depot and ask the conductor to hold the train. The hotel stood only three hundred feet from the station. He made it just in time to catch the locomotive and two passenger cars as they squealed across the tracks to the platform.

While Alden chatted with the conductor, Charles F. Hammond, Mattie clambered down the long flight of stairs from the Davis cottage. Hustling down the hill to the depot, she tripped and sailed through the air, landing face-first on the ground in front of all the passengers.

Through the train window Alden spotted his wife sprawled out on the grass and rushed to her aid. But by the time he reached her, Mattie was already back on her feet, moaning and limping toward the platform.

Disheveled, badly shaken, her face flushed from embarrassment, Mattie clung to her husband's arm as he assisted her to the rear of the second car. Hammond then took over, guiding her through the baggage compartment and into her seat before collecting tickets from the other passengers. One of Mattie's fellow passengers was a man named George Hall, a representative of a Boston meat and provision house, who witnessed the accident. Leaning aside to his friend in the next seat, he said he wouldn't be surprised if the fall turned out to be Mrs. Mattie Davis's "death blow."

If only that were true. Dying of complications from a fall would've been a blessing compared to the agony Mattie would soon endure.

By the time the train left the station, Mattie had more or less steadied her nerves. Another passenger, Willard Hill, who'd also witnessed the fall, sat in the seat across from Mattie and asked if she was okay.

"Nothing hurt but my dignity," she said.

They continued to chitchat during the train ride, Mattie sharing the reason for her trip to Cambridge. Mr. Hill acted appalled when he learned Nurse Toppan had been so lax in paying her overdue notes. Knowing "Jennie" (as close friends and family called Jane) as well as he did, he'd always thought so highly of her. But clearly, she'd taken advantage of the Davis family. He told Mattie it was time to get tough with her. If he were in Mattie's position, he wouldn't leave Cambridge until Jane Toppan paid her debts.

Disembarking from the train in Cambridge, Mattie made her way to 31 Wendell Street, the home of ex-city councilman Melvin Beedle and his wife, Eliza, with whom Jane was boarding. Mattie hoped her good friend "Jennie" would understand the urgency to get the notes squared away. Or would Jane view Mattie's visit as confrontational?

What Mattie Davis failed to realize was that even the most patient and gentle animals might attack when cornered. For someone like Jolly Jane, Mattie showing up on her doorstep, unannounced, likened to slandering her good name in front of the town crier.

2

AN UNFLINCHING WALTZ WITH DEATH

Before boarding with Mr. and Mrs. Beedle, Jane lived down the road at 19 Wendell Street, the home of Israel and Lovey Dunham. "Mr. Dunham was getting pretty old—about seventy-seven—and was feeble and fussy," she would later confess. "I thought a little morphia would do him good, but I gave him too much and he never woke up. It was just as well for him."

Israel Dunham died on May 26, 1895. The doctors misdiagnosed the cause of death as heart failure.

> I continued to live in the same place, and two years later I found Mrs. Dunham rather troublesome. She was old and cranky, so I gave her the same dose as her husband, and she passed away [on] September 19, 1897.

After murdering the Dunhams, Jane moved in with Mr. and Mrs. Beedle. They, however, employed a live-in housekeeper named Mary Sullivan. As far as Jane was concerned, Mary's services were no longer required. So, she drugged the young woman into a stupor with morphia. When Jane beckoned Mrs. Beedle up to Mary's room on the second floor, the housekeeper lay spread-eagle on the bed. Jane insisted Mary had a drinking problem, probably sneaking alcohol during work hours, too. Mrs. Beedle fired her housekeeper on the spot.

Jane sniggered. The plan had worked better than expected.

Now with full control of the household, Jane poisoned the Beedles on a whim. She only gave enough of her deadly cocktail to cause gastrointestinal upset. Perhaps this was *her* way of reminding Mr. and Mrs. Beedle just how helpful and convenient a live-in nurse could be, thereby securing a warm place to sleep without the threat of eviction hanging over her head.

As Mattie Davis knocked at the Beedles' front door that June evening, the family was just sitting down to dinner. Eliza Beedle insisted that Mattie join them. Jane hustled into the kitchen and returned to the dining room with a glass of Hunyadi (a medicinal mineral water) for her friend.

"You must be very thirsty after your trip," she said as she passed Mattie the glass.

During dinner, Mattie told the embarrassing story of falling in full view of everyone on the train. By the end of the meal she'd drained the last drop of mineral water. Jane suggested they walk to the bank so she could withdraw the funds to pay her overdue balance. Since Mattie needed to deposit cash anyway, she agreed. But when she rose from the table, the room spun off its axis. Woozy, Mattie slapped a hand on the back of her chair.

"Perhaps it was that fall," suggested Jane. "Should we wait for a while?"

"No, no, I'm fine." Mattie couldn't let her condition stand in her way, not with being so close to achieving her goal. After all, collecting the money from Jane was the main reason she'd traveled to Cambridge in the first place. Her family had waited long enough for payment.

Once Mattie stepped outside into the sultry night air, she let out a groan and crumbled to the street.

With no one else around, Jane bent down to wrangle Mattie to her feet. Perhaps she added too much morphia to the Hunyadi water. Now she had to practically carry Mattie into the house. Thank goodness she hadn't gotten far before she collapsed.

Grunting, Jane heaved the lethargic woman back inside. Melvin Beedle jogged over to assist in carrying a limp Mattie Davis up the stairs to the guest bedroom. When Melvin dashed back down the stairs to fetch a cold glass of water for Mattie, who looked like she'd fainted from the heat, Jane darted into her own bedroom and swiped a hypodermic needle from her bag. Back in the guest room, low whimpers escaped Mattie's lips.

So I gave her another small dose of morphia. And that quieted her.

Later that night, Jane sent an urgent telegram to Alden Davis, explaining that his wife had arrived at the house "dazed" and was now quite ill. She also telegraphed Mattie's daughter, Genevieve, who was growing increasingly more worried by the minute.

The following afternoon, Wednesday, June 26, Genevieve arrived at the Beedles' home to find her mother lying unconscious in a darkened room hung with ice sheets; Nurse Toppan sat by her mother's sickbed. Even though Jane said she could care for Mattie without assistance, Genevieve insisted on calling a physician to take a look at her. But the blistering eastern heat wave of 1901—the most destructive disaster of its type in US history—caused many to flee the city. Finding a doctor wasn't easy under these circumstances.

After telephoning four different general practitioners, the Beedles finally reached Dr. John T. G. Nichols—the same man who misdiagnosed arsenic poisoning fifteen years earlier in the Sarah Jane Robinson case. Now, he would be called to the bedside of another victim of a female serial killer. Would he redeem himself or cause this patient to perish by misdiagnosing her symptoms? And more importantly, allow "Jolly Jane" to keep on killing?

Only time would tell.

Unfortunately for him and Mattie Davis, Dr. Nichols had no idea who he was up against. Jane introduced herself as "Nurse Toppan, an old friend of the Davis family." Then she informed Dr. Nichols that Mattie was a diabetic. Earlier, Mattie had refused to heed Jane's warnings and treated herself to a nice slice of Mrs. Beedle's white-frosted velvet cake at dinnertime, Jane claimed, collapsing shortly thereafter, probably due to her overindulgence. There was no need for the doctor to take more urine; Jane had collected a sample for him to test before he arrived.

By all accounts, Jane appeared to be a competent caretaker. With no reason to suspect Nurse Toppan of anything nefarious, how could he have known she'd tampered with the sample?

Under the watchful eyes of Dr. Nichols, Genevieve Gordon, and Mr. and Mrs. Beedle, Jane toyed with Mattie Davis, reveling in her control over life and death. By varying the doses of atropine, a derivative of belladonna, which counteracted the effects of the morphine she'd also administered, Jane produced a wide range of symptoms. If Jane lessened the dose of narcotic, Mattie would shake out of the foggy haze of partial consciousness. She even allowed Mattie to rise to full lucidity, as though to offer the family a glimmer of hope before plunging her back into a medicinally induced coma.

> I always had my own way. I would not allow either the doctors or members of the family where I was working to dictate to me. They usually liked me, though, because I was so jolly, and didn't mind my bossing them.

After "playing" with her patient for a solid week, Jane administered the fatal dose on the Fourth of July, and Mattie died.

No one in Cataumet was particularly surprised by the news of Mattie's passing. The eastern heat wave of 1901 claimed the lives of 9,500 men, women, and children that year. Mattie Davis, the townsfolk said, really hadn't been well for quite some time. Genevieve in no way suspected Nurse Toppan; in fact, she begged Jane to return to Cataumet with her. She couldn't bear to take her mother's body back alone.

Reluctantly, Jane agreed.

There were many friends of the family who had come down from Cambridge to attend the funeral. I thought to myself and I wanted to say to them: 'You had better wait and in a little while I will have another funeral for you. If you wait it will save your going back and forth.'

The funeral took place on another sizzling hot day. After the service, the mourners gathered at Jachin House.

Well, we laid Mrs. [Mattie] Davis away in the Cataumet Cemetery and I took up my home with [Alden] Davis and his daughters, Mrs. Harry Gordon [Genevieve] and Mrs. Irving Gibbs [Minnie], in the big roomy Jachin cottage.

The previous summer, when Jane lived in Cataumet and worked at the local Woods Holl Summer School, she went into debt by lavishing her friends with gifts. She was exceedingly reticent about her affairs but told an intimate friend that she had invested in railroad and electric securities.

"Who knows?" she said. "But I may make a fortune," indicating that she might be speculating on the stock market. Jane also spent to excess, like paying the tab for guests who visited her at one of the Davis cottages. When asked what she had done with all her money, she laughed. "No one can say that I spent it on clothes." And indeed, rarely, if ever, did Jane shop for herself.

I had borrowed a good deal of money of [Alden] Davis and his daughters and had given them my notes. The thought occurred to me: If I should burn up this house all those papers would be destroyed. One night I kindled up some papers in a closet near the fireplace, so it might appear the chimney had caught fire. When the smoke began to fill the halls [Alden] Davis rushed out of his room in his night clothes and started to put out the flames.

I danced with delight in my room—but when [Alden Davis] began to call for help I ran out and aided him to throw water on the fire so as to avoid suspicion. I was hoping all the while that the house would burn up, but it didn't.

With so much mishap in such a short period of time, Genevieve Gordon was growing "pale and worn." And soon, with a little nudge from Jolly Jane in the form of doused Hunyadi water, she too complained of not feeling well. Jane had already announced to the family that she must return to Cambridge on the next train, stating "nursing engagements" as the reason.

In the face of Genevieve's grave condition, Alden Davis pleaded with Jane to stay. Once again, she agreed.

Then I made up my mind to kill Mrs. [Genevieve] Gordon. Poor thing, she was grieving herself to death over her sickly child. So life wasn't worth living anyway. I was sorry, though, for the poor, unfortunate child, Genevieve [named after her mother]. I love the little one very much. . . . I thought with Mrs. [Genevieve] Gordon out of the way I could be a mother to her child and get [her husband] Harry Gordon to marry me.

Was that the real reason or another lie?

Yes, it was for love of him and the child that made me poison her. "I followed Mrs. [Genevieve] Gordon to the bathroom one night and gave her mineral water with morphia in it, telling her she needed some medicine."

Later that night, Minnie Gibbs, Genevieve's sister, called to Jane. "Jennie, what's the matter with Genevieve?"

Jane leaped out of bed. To not arouse suspicion, she examined Genevieve to make the others think she was trying to help. Confiding in Minnie, Jane said that days earlier she'd overheard Genevieve threatening to commit suicide; she also hinted she may have poisoned herself with an insecticide

Minnie Gibbs, one of Jane Toppan's victims *Courtesy of the Francis A. Countway Library of Medicine at Harvard University*

called Paris green—made of arsenic and copper—which the Davises kept in the shed. At the same time, she sent word to Genevieve's husband, Harry Gordon, informing him that his wife had threatened to take her own life.

Like with Mattie Davis, Genevieve lingered through that blistering hot July. Sometimes it appeared as though her health was improving, other times she took a turn for the worse.

"But she kept sinking till the evening of July 29," Jane confessed.

Official reports state Genevieve died on July 31, not July 29. Her gravestone confirmed this death date. After murdering an entire family in one summer, perhaps it's understandable how Jane could be off a day or two in her confession.

"I went to the funeral and was as jolly as can be," Jane gloated, "and nobody thought anything of it."

Afraid that Alden Davis would find out she'd murdered his wife and daughter, Jane set her sights on him next.

> At first after his wife's death I thought [Alden] would marry me, but I had found out he wouldn't, but might leave me some of his property in his will. He went to Boston one hot day, and when he came back he was pretty tired and almost prostrated. I saw my chance then, for I could say, if any one suggested that he was poisoned,

16

that he got the drug in Boston and committed suicide out of grief for his wife.

As Alden lounged on the horsehair sofa in Jachin House, Jane ambled into the sitting room, her kind eyes and downturned mouth full of sympathy and concern. "You need some medicine."

Alden waved her away.

"Now"—she shoved the glass toward him—"now!"

At her professional insistence, Alden drank the Hunyadi water. It was easier than arguing with her.

On the morning of August 5, Minnie's father-in-law, Captain Paul Gibbs, a tall, retired old sailor with a snowy-white Van Dyke, drove over to the tiny hamlet of Cataumet in the town of Bourne to offer whatever consolation he could. When he reached Jachin House, he would later report, it took "only one glance at Nurse Toppan to know something dreadful had happened."

"There's been more trouble, terrible trouble," Jane said. "During the night, Mr. Davis died. When [Alden] failed to come down for breakfast this morning, I went up and found him. The doctor has just left. He tells me it was a cerebral hemorrhage."

Town residents weren't all that surprised by Alden's death, either. According to the locals,

The cross of grief he's been bearing, it's no wonder.

They had no idea Jolly Jane had struck again. In her words,

I made it lively for the undertakers and gravediggers. Three graves in a little over three weeks in one lot in the cemetery. Then I turned my attention to the last surviving member of the Davis family, Mrs. Minnie Gibbs.

Alden and Mattie Davis, taken from Dr. Stedman's scrapbook
Courtesy of the Francis A. Countway Library of Medicine at Harvard University

Minnie Gibbs, Jane admitted, was one of her dearest friends.

Murdering those "near and dear" is typical for female serial killers. Males hunt, females gather. Meaning, rather than troll for victims like male serial killers often do, females gather their victims around them, usually attend the funerals, and comfort surviving family members.

In the case of Jane Toppan, her nursing career was the perfect cover. Who would suspect a professional and highly regarded caregiver of using one's sickbed as a honey trap? If Jane had stopped, or at least slowed down after Alden Davis's murder, she might never have gotten caught. But "poisoning had become a habit" in her life. So much so, that her greatest ambition was to "kill more people—helpless people—than any other man or woman who ever lived."

3

ONE FATAL MISTAKE

With another funeral behind them, Captain Paul Gibbs, who looked like a typical New England seaman in style, dress, and stoicism, tried to persuade Minnie to go back to Pocasset with her two young sons and await her husband's return from the sea. Captain Irving Gibbs was out on his schooner, *Golden Ball*, which Captain Paul had custom-made and sailed for two years, when in 1862,

I put my son in charge and retired from the sea.

Minnie refused to follow her father-in-law's advice. "I'd like to," she said, "but there is just too much to do to settle things here." After her mother, father, and sister had all died without warning, someone had to deal with the estate. "Nurse Jane has agreed to stay on a little while longer, and Cousin Beulah [Jacobs] is coming down from Cambridge to be with me."

Genevieve's widowed husband, Harry Gordon, also offered to help. After traveling from Chicago upon receiving Jane's urgent message, staying for a few more days to assist Minnie was not a problem.

Nothing Captain Paul said could change Minnie's mind. Satisfied that with Beulah Jacobs, Harry Gordon, and Nurse Toppan on hand his daughter-in-law would be well cared for, he agreed to babysit his grandsons, his namesake Paul and his younger brother Jesse, at his Pocasset home. It'd be easier to settle family matters without two active younglings underfoot.

Minnie seemed to be holding up okay. Brokenhearted, yes, but otherwise in fine health. Certainly not ill.

19

Toward mid-August Captain Paul received an urgent message to return to Cataumet. And so, he raced to the Jachin House—now operating as a family home rather than a hotel—and jogged up the stairs to Minnie's bedroom. When he peered into the darkened room, his heart sank in his chest. Minnie lay comatose, gasping for air.

He ran to her, spoke to her, but she didn't respond. How could this happen?

As he leaned over the bed a shadowy figure moved in his peripheral vision, and he startled. When he glanced up, Nurse Toppan filled the doorway.

Jane rushed to the invalid's side, injecting a hypodermic needle into Minnie's arm. In a determined tone, she said, "The doctor has ordered Mrs. Gibbs to be kept absolutely quiet." She waved a dismissive hand toward the door. "I must ask you to leave immediately."

Jane told Captain Paul that Minnie had gone shopping in Falmouth for the day and when she returned she hadn't felt well. Perhaps the heat and emotional distress were just too much for her, the poor dear. Not to worry, Jane assured him, she'd take good care of her.

He had no reason to doubt her. Everyone adored Jennie, with her expert nursing skills, professionalism, and bubbly personality. So, he followed her advice under the assumption that he was leaving his daughter-in-law in more than capable hands.

The following day he returned. Minnie looked even worse, practically "death struck." Before she reached the point of no return, he summoned Dr. Latter, the family physician, who lived five miles away at Monument Beach.

When the doctor arrived, he asked Nurse Toppan, "What is the problem?"

"I think she is just all tired out."

"She's very pale." The doctor ran a gentle palm across Minnie's sweaty forehead. "She needs rest. Make sure she is perfectly quiet."

Captain Paul piped up, "What's the matter with her, Doctor?"

Shaking his head, his gaze never left his patient. "I don't know. [Her condition] looks funny to me."

Another physician, Dr. Frank P. Hudnut of Boston, was vacationing in North Falmouth (in the northern part of the peninsula, locally known as the

"Upper Cape"). Harry Gordon asked him to hurry over to Jachin House, but by the time he arrived Minnie's complexion had turned even more pallid and dry, her pupils dilated. Neither he nor Dr. Latter could offer any answers for Captain Paul. Both physicians seemed puzzled by her condition.

At 4 p.m. on August 13, Mary gasped her final breath. She was only thirty-nine years old.

After the death certificate was duly signed and the doctors left, the undertaker arrived, to whom the captain announced, "I think there should be an autopsy."

Indignant, Jane disagreed. "There is no need of an autopsy. There were no suspicious circumstances. No reason why there should have been, and if it were necessary, Dr. Latter would have ordered one. There was no vomiting, no convulsions."

Something still didn't sit right with the old sea captain. Within forty-one days the entire Davis family had been erased.

Jane's response to the rapid succession of deaths was frank. "Coincidence. Alden died of severe heart failure, and his wife had diabetes."

Dr. Latter had offered no concrete explanation for Minnie's sudden death. But he did, however, mention an off-the-wall diagnosis which showed his confusion about the case. "If such a thing exists, [Minnie] might have died of a broken heart."

Nurse Toppan scoffed at that remark. "People don't die of broken hearts."

On the death certificate Dr. Latter listed "diabetes" as the primary cause and "exhaustion" as the immediate cause, neither of which satisfied Captain Paul. How would he explain Minnie's passing to his son and grandchildren? He sent an urgent message to the *Golden Ball*, now docked in Virginia, informing Irving of the terrible news.

On Thursday, August 15, mourners once again trekked to the quaint white-shingled Methodist church, like they had done three times before. The congregation sang "Lead" and "Kindly Light." Beneath the scorching summer sun men perspired through dark double-breasted suits and stiff collars, the women in whalebone corsets and full-length dresses, cinched at the waist. After the service, pallbearers carried Minnie's coffin across the gravel road to Cataumet Cemetery.

Captain Paul choked back his emotions as he clutched his precious grandsons to his side. As they set Minnie's coffin next to the other Davis family graves, any lingering doubt about Jane Toppan's innocence washed away like footprints in the sand at high tide.

Word of Minnie's death rocked the seaside village of Cataumet. Rumors flooded sun-drenched streets—the Davis family must be cursed! This line of thinking was not without reason. More than two decades earlier, the Davises were involved in one of the most grisly and sensationalized murders in New England history.

In the late 1870s, Alden and Mattie Davis and many of their neighbors split from the Methodist Church to join a new Christian sect called the Second Adventist Church. Cape residents weren't the only parishioners to make the switch. This new religion swept across all six New England states like the bubonic plague. Charles Freeman, a dear friend of Alden Davis, led the Cataumet congregation.

Freeman obsessed over the notion that God was testing him. During a violent thunderstorm on the evening of April 30, 1879, he swore he heard the voice of God telling him to sacrifice one of his family members, like Abraham in the Old Testament. Grappling with this holy quest, he tucked his two daughters into the bed they shared and kissed them goodnight.

They never seemed so dear to me as then.

Around 2:30 a.m. he woke from a dead sleep and shook his wife's arm. "The Lord has appeared to me," he said. "I know who the victim must be— my pet, my idol, my baby Edith."

Hattie, his wife, begged him to reconsider.

Steadfast in his beliefs, Freeman ignored the mother's pleas to spare her child. "The Lord has said it is necessary."

After a long, teary-eyed conversation, Hattie finally conceded (why remains a mystery). "If it is the Lord's will, I am ready for it."

That one sentence signaled the beginning of the end.

With no one standing in his way, Freeman climbed out of bed and got dressed. Singing the Lord's praises, he stalked into the shed where he stored a large sheath knife—a dagger-like blade sheathed in leather—then strode back inside the house. He lit the oil lamp and padded into his daughters' bedroom. His eldest, Bessie, woke up when he entered the room, and he told her to get in bed with her mother.

Freeman set the oil lamp on a nearby chair and drew the blankets down off four-year-old Edith. Dropping to his knees, he steepled his fingers, praying his daughter would sleep through the sacrifice. He also prayed for God to stay his hand at the last moment, like he did for Abraham.

He raised the knife high above his head, waited a beat for God to stop him, but his prayers went unanswered. So, he drove the blade into Edith's side.

The little girl's eyes flashed wide. "Oh, Papa," she gasped. Then died.

Freeman curled his body around his precious daughter, rocking her in his arms till dawn. After an initial "good deal of agony of mind," a sensation of peace washed over him. Triumphant, he'd been tested by God and prevailed. Surely, he would be rewarded for such a faithful act.

Come morning, Freeman called twenty-five of his fellow Second Adventists to gather in his Pocasset home (a thirty-minute walk from the Davis cottage and Jachin House), where he proudly unveiled the lifeless body of little Edith—proclaiming, God would resurrect his daughter in three days!

Although Alden Davis was out of town at the time, Mattie Davis was in attendance, along with eight-year-old Genevieve, seventeen-year-old Minnie, and the Davises' two other children, twelve-year-old Henry and nine-year-old Bessie.

Later that afternoon, Minnie was visited in her home by a potential suitor, the town's constable, Seth Redding. The tearful teenager told Redding about what she'd witnessed earlier in the day. The following morning police arrested Freeman and his wife. News of the couple's arrest flooded local and national newspapers.

At Edith's funeral, Alden Davis made one fatal mistake. Unscathed by Freeman's actions—or blinded by loyalty—he faced the crowd of two hundred mourners, and said, "I can vouch that there [has] never lived a purer man than Charles Freeman."

Those words almost incited a riot.

The rumor mill churned with gossip and muffled whispers about Alden Davis—since they buried Edith before the resurrection could take place, it might be necessary to sacrifice another child, perhaps one of his own. According to reports, a weepy-eyed Minnie wandered through the streets of Cataumet, terrified that her father might try to kill her.

Consistent with early nineteenth century beliefs, any man who could sacrifice his own daughter must be insane, so authorities sent Freeman directly to the lunatic asylum in Danvers, Massachusetts. Alden Davis voluntarily followed, though only stayed for a brief period before returning to Cataumet to operate his hotel and cottages by the shores of Buzzards Bay.

Four years later, officials transferred Freeman to the Barnstable County Courthouse. On May 1, 1883, which happened to fall on the anniversary of Edith's murder, the court ordered him held at the jail until the next grand jury meeting when they would decide if he should stand trial.

Captain Paul Gibbs sat on that grand jury.

Two weeks later, Alden and Mattie lost their only son, Henry. And two weeks after that, their youngest daughter, Bessie, also died unexpectedly—as though Freeman's return had cursed the entire Davis family.

On December 5, 1883, Freeman stood trial for murdering little Edith. The jury found him not guilty by reason of insanity. Even though the asylum doctors swore under oath that he'd regained complete control of his faculties, the court sentenced him to return to the State Lunatic Hospital at Danvers (known today as Danvers State Hospital) for the rest of his natural life.

Ever since that time rumors about "the Davis family curse" wafted through Cataumet's gravel streets like unsettled spirits.

If the curse wasn't to blame for all the deaths in the Davis family, maybe something was wrong with the plumbing in Jachin House. Could the old drains emit toxins into the air?

The bereaved returned to Jachin House after Minnie's funeral; the hotel-turned-family-home barely held all the mourners, most of whom praised Jane Toppan for all her hard work in nursing each member of the Davis family. It could not have been easy dealing with all that death.

Suspicions continued to grow within Captain Paul. After his son, Irving, received the message about his wife, he rushed back to Cataumet, where his father shared his misgivings about Nurse Toppan.

"When your wife was dying, she couldn't talk, but she tried to," he said. "And she acted scared every time Jane came near her."

Captain Irving pleaded for an autopsy to confirm the cause of death, but Minnie's body was already buried in the graveyard, along with the rest of the Davis family.

Jane left the Cape shortly after the funeral. At the train station, she told well-wishers she doubted that she would ever return to the area because the peaceful village of Cataumet held "too many bad memories." Too many ghosts.

Minnie's death gnawed at Captain Paul. His son, Irving, was understandably devastated by his wife's death, and his two young sons missed their mom.

Compelled to clear his conscience about this woman they'd welcomed into their family, Captain Paul met with Dr. Latter. "Somehow, I feel there's something wrong. I feel there's something wicked about Jane Toppan. I should never have left the house that afternoon when she told me to go."

Dr. Latter said he also found the case unusual. "But not without precedence. Although [Minnie's] case has puzzled me, I have not a shred of evidence against Nurse Toppan."

"Nor have I. But that last day I was at the house—when [Minnie] seemed unconscious—watching Nurse Toppan give her the injection gave me the shivers, I'm frank to say."

With a bewildered stare at Captain Paul, Dr. Latter said in deadpan tone, "I didn't order an injection."

4

A GAME OF CAT
AND MOUSE

<hr>

Dr. Ira Cushing rode the same train as Alden Davis on August 7. He didn't think much of it at the time, but after learning about Alden's death the following day, he found the circumstances "fishy." By all outward appearances Alden looked perfectly healthy on the train. But now that Alden's daughter, Minnie, had also died, Dr. Cushing longed for Captain Paul Gibbs to act on behalf of the Davis family.

Unfortunately, he didn't know Captain Paul well enough to approach him on such a sensitive matter. Instead, he urged a mutual friend, Captain Ed Robinson, to speak with Captain Paul about the possibility that arsenic poisoning might be to blame. The request to open an inquiry into the poisoning deaths of the entire Davis family would be better received coming from a close friend and fellow sailor.

Although Captain Paul agreed, he found himself in a quandary. Dr. Latter had died of natural causes shortly after Minnie. Without the family physician's statement to back up his claim, he had no corroborating evidence against Nurse Toppan. But Captain Paul Gibbs was a "bluff, honest old sailor, who has learned from experience in all parts of the world that it is never wise to jump to conclusions." Even so, he had no doubt that "that woman, that Jennie Toppan whom we all treated as if she were one of our own, killed them all."

He had to do *something*.

Captain Paul reached out to two friends: Pocasset native Dr. Leonard Wood, the governor general of the Philippines, who was vacationing down the Cape, and his brother Edward S. Wood, professor of pathology at Harvard Medical, who'd testified at various trials as a government expert, including the sensationalized trial of Sarah Jane Robinson, another female serial killer of New England. (Her story is in Part IV of this book.)

The two doctors agreed that the deaths of Alden and Mattie Davis were not all that unusual because of their ages and health problems, but two healthy women in the prime of their lives dying within days of each other? The deaths of the Davis sisters, Minnie and Genevieve, made no sense. Very little doubt existed that someone needed to investigate these deaths. So, they urged Captain Paul to go to the authorities.

Captain Paul told his story to State Police Captain Rufus Wade, who assigned the case to General Jophanus Whitney of the same agency.

What motive could Jane Toppan have to murder the Davis family?

After Alden's funeral, Minnie had told Captain Paul that Jane had tried to persuade her to sign a document forgiving her debt to the Davis estate. Minnie refused. Had she done as Jane asked, Minnie probably would have lived to see her children grow into adults.

Money also went missing.

When Alden died, he had had roughly three hundred dollars in "his pocketbook," which disappeared. As his nurse, Jane had the perfect opportunity to steal the cash without being detected.

Mattie Davis and Genevieve Gordon had also had considerable sums of money in their pocketbooks when they fell ill. When the undertaker prepared the bodies for viewing, neither had any cash on them, except maybe a dollar or two. Before dealing with her parents' estate, Minnie had stashed $150 in her home, a short distance from Jachin House. Since she hadn't any money on her at the time of her sudden illness, Jane had no means to steal it. The exact figure each family member carried before their death Captain Paul could not state with any certainty, but he estimated the total must be upwards of several hundred dollars.

"She had every opportunity in the world to get the money the dead people had," Captain Paul told a reporter. "She was with them all the time they were ill, she washed and dressed their bodies when they died, and there wasn't a section of the house to which she did not have access and of which she did not have a perfect knowledge. I am positive that Mr. Davis had $500 a day or two before he died."

That fact alone pointed to motive.

Jane briefly closed her nursing business in 1900, but she owed several hundred dollars and was threatened with numerous civil suits. After Miss Sarah "Myra" Connors died at Nurse Toppan's home in Cambridge while under her care, Jane slid into Connors's cushy position of proprietress of the "mess" house at Woods Holl Summer School on the Cape. This new job had the potential of netting her a profit of about one thousand dollars per year in salary.

Captain Paul's daughter worked alongside Jane as the bookkeeper at Woods Holl. "One day," he told the reporter, "my daughter placed $100 aside for the cook, which was due her for wages, and shortly after it was missing. She thought the cook had received it, but [the cook] was able to prove that she hadn't, and my daughter gave her another $100. My daughter believes that the first $100 was taken by [Jane] Toppan, as she was the only one who was near the money my girl placed aside."

Even with this theory of Jane's greed, neither he nor anyone else could prove she was guilty of murder.

Minnie had also had her suspicions about Jane, and Captain Paul related this to the same reporter. "In her final 24 hours every time Nurse Toppan approached the bed, [Minnie] seemed to shrink away from her. Had she been well enough, perhaps she could have told something that [I] could now use as valuable evidence against her."

In the meantime, Jane left Cataumet and stopped off in Cambridge to visit Harry Gordon's seventy-one-year-old father, Henry Sr., to feel him out about the Davis murders. Jane asked how he accounted for the shocking sequence of deaths.

Henry Sr.'s shoulders half-shrugged in sadness. The most likely explanation, he opined, was that "as the family was an old one, it was dying out."

Murder hadn't even crossed the old man's mind. Rather, he blamed all the deaths on natural causes. Perfect.

After a few hours in Henry Sr.'s company, Jane left to board the train to Lowell—satisfied "that her guilt had escaped discovery," an alienist (as psychiatrists were referred to back then) would later report, "and that it would be safe for her to go on killing."

Ever since murdering her foster sister, Elizabeth, two summers before in 1899, Jane secretly har-

Oramel A. Brigham
Courtesy of Library of Congress

bored romantic fantasies about marrying her sixty-year-old brother-in-law, O. A. Brigham, whom she'd known since she was a child, when Jane first moved in with the Toppans as an indentured servant.

Soon after the death of Ann Toppan, Jane's foster mother who left her entire estate to her biological daughter, Elizabeth, O. A. moved into his new bride's home. Elizabeth then owned the spacious Toppan family residence at 182 Third Street in Lowell. But once Elizabeth died, Jane swore the totality of the Toppan estate should have gone to her rather than the measly two-hundred-dollar penance and a gold timepiece. Instead, the family fortune passed to Elizabeth's closest relative—her widower, O. A.

> Mr. Brigham came down to Cataumet to see me late that season and went in bathing with me and we went sailing together on the bay. It was then we became engaged to be married. He begged me

to come up to Lowell to see him in the early Fall and arrange for the wedding. When I got to Lowell in October, I was surprised at Mr. Brigham's coldness. He no longer wanted to talk of marriage.

When I pushed for a reason he said: 'Why, Jennie (they always called me Jennie at home), I'm going to marry another woman.'

'Who is it you're going to marry?' I said as calmly as I could, though it was a terrible blow to me.

'It is Miss C—'

I controlled the terrible passion that was rising up in me, so that he should not see it, and said, 'You could not marry a better woman,' but all the while I was thinking: 'Oh no, you shall not escape from me like that.'

Mr. Brigham then brought another woman into the house as housekeeper, Florence N. Calkins. I was jealous of her from the first. I knew she wanted to become Mr. Brigham's wife. He was my brother-in-law . . . but I was madly in love with him. So I poisoned Florence Calkins and she died January 15, 1900.

Over a year later, on August 26, 1901, one week after Jane returned to her childhood home in Lowell—as she'd done every year since she left home in 1885—General Whitney knocked on the door of 182 Third Street. Jane met him in the entryway.

He passed her his credentials. "My name is General Whitney of the Massachusetts District Police."

"Come in." She ushered him inside.

"I've been at Cataumet and vicinity investigating the death[s] of the Davis family," Whitney explained. "After the death of Mrs. [Minnie] Gibbs, in my investigation there was more and less talk in that vicinity in reference to the deaths. As you are the only one that I could ascertain who had attended each one of the family, I came to you. Can you tell me in narrative form of the sickness of the four people who died—Mrs. [Mattie] Davis,

Mrs. [Genevieve] Gordon, Mr. [Alden] Davis, and Mrs. [Minnie] Gibbs? I don't want to question you, but have you tell me the story as you know it."

"Certainly," Jane said. "Mattie Davis came to the Beedles' house in Cambridge and then took ill, probably due to heat prostration or the terrible fall she'd taken at the railroad station near her home in Cataumet."

Some details weren't as clear as others, like how two sisters in their thirties died within days of each other. Whitney pushed for information about Minnie's death, since it acted as the catalyst for the homicide investigation into the entire Davis family.

"After her father's death," said Jane, "Mr. [Harry] Gordon and Mrs. [Minnie] Gibbs stayed up late nights and were examining the papers in the two different deaths preparatory to having the matter brought before the Probate Court which met the following Tuesday, I think, after Mr. [Alden] Davis's death. On the evening prior to [Minnie's] death, Mr. [Harry] Gordon and Mrs. [Minnie] Gibbs were in the room examining papers when I retired. Before retiring I urged Minnie to retire, but Mr. [Harry] Gordon told me to leave her alone. Later, I went in and found them both asleep, one in one part of the room and another in another part of the room on the sofa. I endeavored to have them retire at that time, too. Then I retired to my room and went in again about half-past two but was unable to have them go to bed."

Scribbling her statement in his notebook, Whitney asked what she did next.

"I went to Miss [Beulah] Jacobs and asked her to get up and go downstairs to assist me. We tried to arouse Minnie and could not. She would moan and say, 'Oh, Harry' or 'Oh, somebody else' and lay her head on [Harry] Gordon's shoulder. Finally, [Harry] Gordon took Minnie in his arms and carried her to bed, and Miss [Beulah] Jacobs and I disrobed her and wrapped her up in a blanket. [Minnie's] lower limbs were quite cold."

Whitney urged Jane to continue. Suspects often spat out damning information if the investigator asked straightforward questions and allowed them to ramble, but with Nurse Toppan, the ploy didn't work. Throughout the interview Jane remained cool, calm, and professional. Pleasant, even. And all without a hint of anxiety, nervousness, or sweat beading on her forehead.

"Dr. Latter was sent for early the next morning," Jane continued. "Minnie was unconscious from that [point] on until her death in the afternoon of the following day."

Whitney asked if she knew what had caused her death.

"Dr. Latter claimed it was exhaustion."

"What about her heart?"

"Her heart was strong."

Deacon O. A. Brigham entered the room. A prominent figure, with a double chin, bald dome, and bushy, gray mutton-chop sideburns that morphed into a monstrous moustache, O. A. was a well-respected member of the community.

Not allowing the disruption to break his stride, Whitney kept questioning his prime suspect (his only suspect, really, as no other person had the means and opportunity to slaughter the entire Davis family). "Did you not think it would be a good thing to have an autopsy on the body?" He asked because the folks down the Cape were all worked up about it. "If these people died from natural causes, it would be better for all parties concerned. Don't you think it would be better?"

Notwithstanding the emotional tug, conducting an autopsy on a patient whose family employed one of the most successful and highly regarded private nurses in the state likened to spitting in Jane Toppan's face. Polite society simply did not work that way. But after Minnie's sudden death, it seemed an exhumation might be necessary after all.

Rather than answer, Jane rebuffed the question by turning toward O. A. "What do you think, Mr. Brigham?"

"I think it would be better to have the autopsy, and then it would settle the matter."

Jane did not agree. "I don't know . . . [that] it would."

Unbeknownst to General Whitney, another patient lay dying in the next room.

5

THE HUNTRESS BECOMES THE HUNTED

Not long after Jane arrived at the Brigham home, O. A.'s sister, Edna Bannister, stopped by the house on her way to the Pan-American Exposition in Buffalo, New York.

From May 1 through November 2, 1901, the World's Fair occupied 350 acres of land in Buffalo, on the western edge of what is today known as Delaware Park. The fair extended from Delaware Avenue to Elmwood Avenue and northward to Great Arrow Avenue and was also the location of the assassination of US President William McKinley. Thomas A. Edison, Inc., illuminated the fairgrounds, filming the festivities during the day and panning the exposition at night.

Not only did O. A. promise to cover his sister's travel expenses, he also invited her to stay for a night or two to help ease the heavy burden of a long trip. Edna had already made the long journey from her home in Turnbridge, Vermont, where she lived with her daughter (roughly 142 miles away), in blistering hot temperatures. Edna was not a well woman. She suffered with heart disease, though her condition was improving—until she strode through the door of O. A.'s Georgian-style home at 182 Third Street in Lowell.

Another woman in the house was the last thing Jane needed. How would O. A. learn to love her under the watchful eye of his sister? Not to mention her very existence meant another heir to the Brigham estate, which Jane might finally get her mitts on once O. A. married her.

> Mrs. [Edna] Bannister was a poor old woman, and she was better out of the way anyhow. I gave her the same stuff that I did to the others. She went by the same road as the others on August 27 [1901].

A few minutes after Whitney left the Brigham home, O. A. called Dr. William H. Lathrop, a general practitioner of over thirty-five years, to examine his sister. But he didn't arrive in time to see the patient before she expired. Rather than examine the body, the doctor took Nurse Toppan at her word.

"Edna died from a long-standing disease of the heart," Jane lied, "after a sudden and severe attack of characteristic breathing."

Dr. Lathrop had no reason to doubt her diagnosis. He'd known Jane for about ten years. Even though he had never personally employed her, her stellar reputation as a nurse proceeded her. Physicians could trust Nurse Toppan, and often recommended her to some of the most prominent families in Massachusetts.

While the doctor was still at the house, Jane posed a few hypothetical scenarios. "If a body had been poisoned and died and then was embalmed, would those poisonous drugs be found if they exhumed the body, that is, had an autopsy?"

"If they were a mineral poison," Lathrop explained, "they would be in the body, but if they were a vegetable [poison], they would be absorbed."

After listing numerous drugs, asking if each one was a mineral or vegetable, she thanked him for his time.

> Everything seemed favorable then for my marrying Mr. [O. A.] Brigham. I had put three women to death who stood in my way. Mr. Brigham suspected nothing—except he scolded me for my lack of sympathy and regret for the members of the family that had passed away. But he overlooked this in me, called me a frivolous child, and seemed fond of me. Then I was happy—happy as a girl in her first love.

If Jane relaxed after her conversation with Dr. Lathrop, this mindset was premature. The state police had ordered exhumations of the Davis family.

> "It's about the pleasure of the kill—the sense of power she gets—the buzz. Taking property is just a warm snack in the feast control—a little further satisfaction, a tingling in the killer's tummy."
>
> —Peter Vronsky, author of Female Serial Killers

On a cool autumn evening, flames licked the glass of lanterns held by Captain Paul, Captain Irving Gibbs, General Jophanus Whitney, Dr. Robert H. Faunce (the medical examiner of Sandwich), Professor Edward Stickney Wood (Harvard toxicologist), State Police Officer Simeon Letteney, and Reverend James Dicking of the Methodist church in Cataumet.

When the group trekked from the church grounds across the gravel road to the cemetery, the men headed toward a large monument topped by a Grecian urn—the Davises' eternal resting spot.

No one spoke on this solemn night. Echoes of spades chopping at the cold, hard earth pierced an eerie silence.

Playing lookout, Reverend Dicking ensured "this ghastly act would not be interrupted and the exhumation be conducted with fitting decorum" as—one by one—the men hoisted the coffins from their graves, carrying the dead to a nearby barn on the adjoining property, owned by Major Allen Swift who'd granted access. On a wooden shelf Dr. Faunce dissected the bodies of Alden and Mattie Davis, Genevieve Gordon, and Minnie Gibbs, removing all vital organs, including the stomachs, to test for poison. Professor Wood transported the samples back to his laboratory in Cambridge. Before proceeding toward an arrest, authorities would need to wait for the toxicology reports.

But the police also didn't want Jolly Jane to kill more patients. To keep her under constant surveillance, the state police assigned a crafty and sly detective named John S. Patterson to shadow her every move. He'd ridden the train with Jane from Cataumet to Cambridge for her brief chat with Henry Gordon Sr. and then stalked her to Lowell.

Under an assumed identity, Patterson rented a room in the Stevenses' household, not far from the Brigham residence. For the next few weeks, wherever Jane went—the post office, druggist, or out for an afternoon stroll—Patterson skulked in the nearby shadows, his gaze pinned on the prime suspect in a quadruple homicide case.

To the outside world, Jane looked like a plump, forty-five-year-old spinster with an honest face and short, dark hair dusted with subtle glints of silver. At all times she held a jolly, almost quizzical expression that bared no outward signs of a degenerate mind. Full and well-molded features, her eyes a deep, kind brown, her lips wore an inviting smile normally reserved for the most tender of mothers.

The facade didn't fool Patterson. This woman was a coldblooded murderess.

Inside the Brigham home Jane's lovelorn fixation for O. A. morphed into a full-blown obsession.

> The plan instantly came to me to give [O. A.] a little poison—a morphia tablet in his tea, just enough to make him sick, and then I could hover over him, nurse him, and win back his love. I was succeeding when a detective [Patterson] came to the house one day. After he left, a change came over Mr. Brigham. He struggled up from his bed, weak as he was from the morphia and the Hunyadi water I had been giving him.
>
> He ordered me away; saying: 'I want you to leave this house at once.'

I have since learned that the detective said to Mr. Brigham: 'Be careful of that woman or she will poison you.' Then it flashed upon him how three members of his home had died in my care within a year or two. I was frantic. Everything was lost, I thought—my lover, my future home I had counted on, fortune—and worst of all, I was discovered!

Later that afternoon, Saturday, September 29, Jane swallowed an overdose of poison—the same medicine she'd given numerous patients during her decades-long career. When O. A. poked his head in the doorway of her bedroom, Jane was unconscious. Frantic, he summoned Dr. Lathrop for help.

When the doctor arrived, he injected an emetic to induce vomiting.

Jane soon emerged from her stupor. "I want to die."

Dr. Lathrop said, "Did you take something?"

"Yes."

"What?"

Jane refused to answer. The doctor asked a great many more times, but Jane still wouldn't tell him what she'd taken. Instead, she repeated in a groggy voice, "I wish to die."

Rather than take any chances, Dr. Lathrop sent for a private nurse, Ann Tyler, to stay by her bedside. Before leaving the Brigham home, the doctor told O. A. it was obvious by Jane's condition—not fully unconscious but very sleepy and out of it—that she'd self-medicated with a narcotic. With a reassuring pat on the back, Dr. Lathrop said he'd return in the morning to check on his patient.

Ungrateful and bitter, Jane blamed O. A. "If you had left me alone, I would have been out of this world now."

The next morning her spirits had greatly improved. It seemed Jane was back to her jolly self again, so Nurse Tyler had no reservations about leaving her alone while she ate breakfast downstairs.

Upon Nurse Tyler's return, her mouth gaped open in disbelief—stunned by Jane's grave condition. Narcotized, she could no longer swallow, her lower jaw sagged, her nose pinched closed. Livid complexion, her breath ragged, heavy. After two suicide attempts in as many days, Jane might have succeeded this time if the doctor hadn't already arrived.

Dr. Lathrop rushed up the stairs and subcutaneously injected both of Jane's arms with apomorphine. (Apomorphine is a morphine derivative which primarily affects the hypothalamic region of the brain. It works by mimicking the action of dopamine, a natural substance. Given in high doses, it's also an effective emetic.)

Within minutes, Jane vomited into the chamber pot.

Afterward, the doctor asked Jane why she wanted to die.

"I'm tired of life," she said. "I know that people are talking about me. I just want to die."

If she was playing the sympathy card as a last-ditch effort to get O. A. to change his mind, the charade fell short. He insisted that she leave at once. With nowhere else to go, Jane admitted herself into Lowell General Hospital for "rest and treatment."

Detective Patterson feigned a hypochondriacal illness, complete with fictitious body ills, to get admitted in the adjoining ward.

After being discharged from the hospital, Jane took the train to Amherst, New Hampshire, to visit her longtime friend George Nichols, who lived with his sister, Sarah, a middle-aged spinster like Jane, in a gorgeous yellow farmhouse about a mile outside the village.

Patterson made the trip as well, but Jane mustn't have noticed him.

I had a fine time out there. I don't think I ever enjoyed myself as much as I did that Fall. There was a jolly lot of people there, and I had the kind of time I like to have.

The good times were about to end.

6

THE ARREST OF
JOLLY JANE

On October 27, Professor Wood sent word to the district attorney—testing showed Minnie's viscera contained traces of morphine and all four bodies had high levels of arsenic in the intestines.

District Attorney LeBaron Holmes marched straight to the Barnstable courthouse and obtained an arrest warrant. Concentrating on Minnie Gibbs's murder was the State's primary objective since they had the most evidence on her case. Secondary were the deaths of Alden and Mattie Davis and Genevieve Gordon, if they could gather enough evidence against Nurse Toppan.

Two days later, General Whitney arrived in Amherst, New Hampshire, by train, stopping briefly to pick up two Nashua police officers, Inspector Thomas Flood and Deputy Marshall Wheeler. After finding Detective Patterson at a boardinghouse in town, the four officers stormed the Nicholses' home.

Warrant in hand, Whitney informed Jane that she was under arrest for the murder of Minnie Gibbs.

Jane scoffed at the absurdity. "I wouldn't kill a chicken, and if there is any justice in Massachusetts, they will let me go." She then asked why she would be arrested before she'd had an opportunity to give her evidence.

Whitney explained that autopsies had been held on all members of the Davis family, and as she was absent from the state, he had secured a fugitive warrant from the New Hampshire authorities. Meaning, he had no choice but to take her into custody.

Whitney ordered her to pack her belongings. Jane didn't protest. In fact, she handled the situation with perfect composure.

One thing upset her, though.

I was annoyed because the detective insisted on remaining in my room while I was getting ready, and I did not think it was very gentlemanly.

Even though Jane wasn't surprised by the arrest, the Nicholses certainly were. They never knew how lucky they got that night.

I might have killed George Nichols and his sister at Amherst, New Hampshire, where I was arrested, if I had stayed long enough. [But] Detective Whitney came to the house in the night and took me away.

Jane never gave a reason for that statement. Perhaps after a relaxing four-week vacation, she was feeling "playful" again, and poisoning her longtime friends would be the proverbial cherry atop the red velvet cake. Or maybe, she sensed George's growing apprehension.

A *Boston Herald* reporter interviewed George at his home after Jane's arrest.

"We first formed the acquaintance of Miss Toppan in Cambridge, Massachusetts," George told the reporter. "She became acquainted with my sister, who lives with me. I knew Miss Toppan merely as a trained nurse of much ability. It was several years ago that she commenced to make visits to Amherst. She hardly ever stayed longer than a day or two."

In the front entranceway George rested his hand on the doorframe. "I always entertained a high regard for her, and it is hard for me to suspect her of any wrongdoing. She was always fond of talking about her business, and, according to her statements, enjoyed the work of nursing very much. She liked to be present when patients were being operated upon, and I am informed she was considered a valuable assistant on those occasions. I recall one time when Dr. Marcy and another Cambridge physician sent for her when about to perform an operation."

The reporter jotted down every word in his notebook. An inside scoop on the Toppan case would dominate the headlines. He urged George to continue.

"Very many times during her stay at my house Miss Toppan talked of surgical operations and autopsies," said George. "Her mind seemed to run entirely in that channel, but not for a moment did I suspect that something might be weighing on her mind. Whenever she talked of these subjects there was a distant look in her eyes. It was these actions that, toward the last of her stay, rather made me nervous. I was afraid her mind was unbalanced, and for that reason, kept a close watch over my sister, being fearful that something might happen."

The reporter asked, "Was there any sickness in your family during Miss Toppan's recent visit?"

"Well, no. Yes"—he corrected, hesitating—"there was a day or two that my sister was ill."

"Did Jane attend her?"

"I think she assisted her somewhat."

As if in deep thought, George's gaze drifted away from the reporter, and then returned when the reporter asked if Nurse Toppan had attended any sick people in Amherst at any time on her visits.

"No," he said, "I think not. Whenever she was here, she stopped at my house. She occasionally visited with the people of this place for a few hours at a time."

"Did she go about much on her last visit to your house?"

"Not very much. The fact of the matter is, when Jane came to Amherst, she was what I would call an invalid. Why she came to my place I do not know, other than it was the only one she had to go to. She was not a boarder but was making a friendly visit. I do not know how long she intended to remain. I had not thought of turning her out of doors as long as she behaved herself."

The reporter prodded, "What [about] Miss Toppan's finances?"

"As far as I know she was plentifully supplied with money. As a trained nurse she commanded good wages, and not being of extravagant tastes, I think $3 a day ought to keep any woman like her in good shape. If Jane Toppan is responsible for the alleged poisoning cases in Massachusetts, I don't believe it was money she was after. In my belief, if she committed the deeds charged to her, she must have been laboring under a hallucination of some kind.

"While Miss Toppan was at my house, I read about the autopsies being held over the bodies in Massachusetts. I believe I remarked to my sister that Jane Toppan had nursed the families at that time. Notwithstanding this, we had no suspicion [whatsoever] regarding Miss Toppan, and we were as much surprised as anyone else in this town when Detective Whitney and the Nashua officers made the arrest."

The day after Jane's arrest, L. W. Ferdinand of Cambridge—the same man who first brought Jane to Cataumet with his family—warned George "not to harbor Miss Toppan any longer." On this point George Nichols remained silent.

On the carriage ride from Amherst to Nashua, Jane asked General Whitney if she would need a lawyer.

"You certainly will," he said. "It is a very serious matter for you and the best lawyer you can get will be none too good for you."

Jane asked if the Commonwealth would furnish an attorney, and Whitney explained that if she had no means, in capital cases the court would furnish a lawyer for her defense.

Once they arrived at the jail in Nashua, Whitney arranged for the matron of the police station to stay with Jane all night in case she became suicidal. In the morning, at Jane's request, he purchased "a veil for her and some other little things." Before going into court Jane expressed her willingness to return to Massachusetts without extradition papers, which made his job much easier. Whitney shared her cooperation with the judge and urged the court not to process the extradition warrant.

On the train to Boston Jane mentioned how sorry she was to hear about Dr. Latter passing away. That gave Whitney the perfect opening. He told her, while questioning Dr. Latter prior to his death, the doctor had mentioned that he'd never prescribed morphine in any form to any of the Davises.

"No," Jane confirmed. "He, knowing the peculiarities and condition of the family, would not prescribe morphine."

"I ascertained where you did purchase morphine."

Jane's eyebrows arched in amazement. "Where?"

"You purchased morphine, I was told, by Mr. Robinson [the druggist] at Falmouth."

"Yes, I did."

"You bought one bottle of morphine tablets, either [a] combination of morphine tablets and atropine, or straight morphine tablets." Mr. Charles Robinson had told Whitney the bottle contained one hundred tablets.

Jane said yes, she had, and she also bought Hunyadi water and a number of other articles at the same time.

After showing the druggist a photograph, Robinson confirmed Jane's identity. "Mr. Robinson remembered of your coming there."

"Yes, I patronized that place the year before when I kept the [Woods Holl] summer school at Falmouth and I always used to trade with the proprietor himself."

Whitney said he'd figured out that she had purchased morphine tablets from a druggist at Wareham, as well. Jane explained Minnie had wanted her to purchase morphine and was particular to have her purchase the tablets from the proprietor himself, so Jane telephoned the druggist from Mr. Irving's or Erwin's grocery store at Cataumet. The first quantity he sent in a wooden box, and on account of the heat the tablets had melted and run together and were practically useless. Afterward she telephoned for the same quantity again and suggested the pills be packaged in glass instead of wood.

As for Minnie's death, Jane claimed innocence.

Whitney didn't push the issue. "One thing still puzzles me."

"What is that?"

He told Jane it seemed singular to him that after she had attempted to destroy her life that she would refuse to tell the attending physician what she had taken.

"I will tell you why." A slow smile curved the corners of Jane's thin lips. "If I was not successful, I wanted an opportunity to try it again."

Whitney asked if she had used the drugs that she purchased at Wareham or Falmouth, and Jane said yes.

"Straight morphine?"

"Yes."

The train stopped at North Station in Boston, where Whitney turned Jane over to Detective Simeon Letteney, a state police officer based on Cape Cod.

Letteney and Jane switched trains and promptly left South Station for Bourne. Haggard and careworn, Letteney buried his face in the afternoon paper while Jane gazed out the window at the crowd, "with an ever-changing smile, her half-shut eyes twinkling with amusement."

When Letteney brought up the Davises, Jane remained steadfast. "Those people all died of natural causes. Excepting old man Davis. He was crazy, and I think he poisoned himself."

Upbeat and relaxed, Jane "chatted pleasantly," according to Letteney. She even "laughed and joked about the stories of her arrest and alleged crimes which she read in the newspapers on the train."

That afternoon, the train stopped at Bourne. Jane bustled through the depot and into a flock of reporters all vying to capture a glimpse of "one of the most remarkable murderesses, a Lucretia Borgia without parallel in modern times."

Half the sleepy village of Cataumet had come to gawk at the woman at the center of "the most famous poisoning case Massachusetts has ever had." If the trial proceeded as planned, the case promised "to be one of the most remarkable cases the State [had] ever known."

Though the Commonwealth had only charged Jane with murdering Minnie Gibbs, she was the prime suspect in numerous other cases. But even this didn't seem to faze Jane as she smiled and waved to acquaintances and friends before Letteney whisked her off to the redbrick Barnstable jail.

For Captain Paul and his son, Irving, the arrest cut like a double-edged sword—relief that Jane could no longer do harm, but it also confirmed their worst fear that Minnie died at the hands of a heartless monster she had called a friend.

The full horror of "Jolly Jane" was yet to unfold.

7
HARSH BEGINNINGS

While confined at Barnstable jail, Jane insisted she had no relatives, living or deceased. But her cousin, Mrs. Jeannette E. Snow, shared a different story with the *Boston Herald*.

In a building on the corner of North and Blackstone Streets in Boston, Bridget Kelley gave birth to her youngest daughter, Honora "Nora" A. Kelley (Jane Toppan's birthname). Before Nora came three sisters: Mary, Nellie (common nickname of Ellen, her birth name), and Delia (nickname for her birth name, Bridget).

During Bridget Kelley's marriage to Jane's father, Peter Kelley, Bridget took in boarders to help pay the bills after her alcoholic husband foolishly spent the family's riches—an activity Jane repeated in her own adult life.

In 1857, the four sisters' sweet-tempered mother, Bridget, died of consumption (a wasting disease that we now call pulmonary tuberculosis). The death of his wife sent Peter Kelley straight off the edge of sanity. A blow of this type for a man who was barely functionable due to alcoholism was just too much to bear.

"It would not surprise me to know that Jane Toppan is insane," Mrs. Snow told the reporter. "And if she is, she inherited it from her father."

Nora's older sister Nellie had gone "violently insane" in her twenties. Authorities committed Nellie to Medfield Insane Asylum for life.

"When Nellie was a girl," Mrs. Snow recalled, her voice full of sorrow, "she was one of the sweetest and prettiest little things I ever saw. But even then, there was something peculiar about her. She had a strange love for little colored children, and every time she saw one on the street, she picked it up and kissed it. When the real insanity began to show in [Nellie], she had experienced a great change, and her condition soon became so serious that she could not be looked after at home."

Mrs. Snow swept the tears from her eyes. "I went to see [Nellie] once when she was in the mental asylum, and I never felt so badly in my life as I did then. I gave her some fruit, and while she muttered some senseless expressions, she lifted her clothing and began to push the fruit down her stockings. Poor Nellie! She did not know me, and it was terrible to watch her idiotic actions."

When the reporter asked about the latest allegations, Mrs. Snow regained control of her emotions. "If Jane Toppan committed the crimes of which she is accused, she has inherited insanity from the source [Peter Kelley] which was responsible for her sister's condition."

After his wife's death, Peter Kelley sent his eldest daughter, Mary, to live with family friends. Nellie had already been committed. Which left only his two youngest daughters, Nora and Delia. After a brief stint at their grandparents' house, Peter escorted his little girls to the Boston Female Asylum for children.

Anyone who placed a girl in the institution—parent, guardian, or next of kin—would be required to sign an official form of surrender, relinquishing "all right and claim to [the children] and their service[s] until they shall arrive to the age of Eighteen years." The asylum did this "on condition of [the children] being protected and provided for agreeably to the laws of that institution."

Anyone who forfeited their parental rights also promised "not to interfere with the management of [the girls] in any respect whatsoever nor to visit them except at the time appointed by the Managers without their consent."

In October of 1803, the board added this clarification:

Mrs. Green [presumably a manager at the asylum] then observed on the inconvenience and abuse, which the Managers had sustained and still remained liable to, from the unruly conduct of many disorderly mothers and relations of children on the Asylum from which place they were often unproperly taken and unreasonably detained. This being an error which was considered highly detrimental and undecent, it was immediately Voted, that no mother, or any person whomsoever be allowed on any occasion to take her or their child from the Asylum without having obtained from one of the Managers an order for so doing. And if any child be detained more than twenty minutes from the time specified for its restoration, such person shall be considered to have forfeited the like future indulgence . . . a copy of the same [shall] be posted in the Governess's Room.

Nearly one hundred girls between the ages of three and ten resided at the Boston Female Asylum when, on a brisk day in February 1863, Peter Kelley stumbled through the entrance with his two young daughters in tow.

On that day, the asylum noted in their records, "Their appearance indicated that they had been rescued from a very miserable home," with a father who reeked of alcohol. Kelley signed over eight-year-old Delia and six-year-old Nora, sidestepped out the door, and out of his daughters' lives forever.

Not much is known about Nora's early homelife, except that her father was a wildly eccentric drunk and prone to violent outbursts—earning the nickname "Kelley the Crack" (meaning "crackpot") for muttering to himself in public. Bizarre stories circulated about Kelley the Crack finally going completely mad and sewing his eyelids shut (he worked as a tailor). Whether this legend had any merit, we may never know. This juicy rumor, however, stirred an already explosive pot.

Two years later, Peter Kelley died from alcohol. In other words, he drank himself to death.

Imagine what this type of abandonment does to a young girl? Her mother was dead. Her drunken father signed her over to an asylum, with more rules and punishment than love and kindness. And now, the bane of her existence consisted of training to become a well-to-do New England mistress's slave.

For little Nora and Delia, the nightmare could only end badly.

The Boston Female Asylum relied on donors to keep their doors open. They served three squares a day, but the menu rarely, if ever, changed. Week after week, breakfast included hasty pudding, boiled rice with molasses, or milk porridge thickened with flour, depending on the season. Dinner consisted of soup on Monday and Wednesday, boiled meat on Tuesday, pork and beans on Thursday, lamb broth on Friday, fish on Saturday, and roasted meat and pudding on Sunday.

The asylum claimed to teach young girls "useful things suitable to their age, sex, and station." Though this wording sounded good in theory, the orphans lived a different reality. Yes, the asylum taught to them to read, spell, and cipher, but only "so far as necessary." Their main objective was to teach orphans domestic skills—sewing, knitting, cooking, and housekeeping—for greater appeal to prospective families. Once a girl reached the age of eleven, she "placed out" with a private family. Very few girls were lucky enough to get adopted. Most became indentured servants.

The Boston Female Asylum functioned as a source of cheap domestic labor for wealthy families. In exchange for room, board, and "the promise of kind treatment"—which no one ever bothered to check—the overburdened mistress could hire her own well-trained and contractually bound personal servant to perform any and all menial tasks in her home.

Of course, the official Boston Female Asylum records told a very different story. Founded in 1800 "to care for orphaned and destitute girls," the orphanage claimed to abide by biblical scripture.

When the Ear heard me, then it blessed me, and when the Eye saw me, then it gave witness to me. Because I delivered the Poor that cried, and the Fatherless, and Him who had none to help him. The blessing of him who was ready to perish came upon me.

—Job 29, 11.12.13

In the pamphlet the asylum included a plea to all women of means:

Those who are acquainted with the condition of the Poor, must know that many Female Orphans suffer for want of early patronage. . . . May the Ladies of Boston be stimulated to rescue some of the many from that wretchedness too common to the Poor. To them the appeal is made, and from them relief is wished.

Can Virtue, can Talents, can Wealth be employed in a more laudable way? Females will sympathize especially with the sufferings of their own Sex, when unprotected by Parents or Friends. Are there not many among the Children of prosperity, who work to lay the foundation of an Institution, which at some future period may prove extensive blessing to thousands of Unfortunate Females? To the Benevolent Heart how delightful the prospect!

Imagine all the ways this arrangement might downward spiral into verbal, emotional, and/or sexual abuse?

The contract expired when the girl reached eighteen years of age, at which time the mistress would be required to set the girl free, along with "two suits of clothes, one proper for Sunday, the other for domestic business," and fifty dollars.

At the Boston Female Asylum an orphaned or destitute girl could find a "permanent home, thorough instruction in domestic affairs, and moral guidance that youth requires." But sadly, most of the girls wound up taking the brunt of abuse from *Mommie Dearest*-type mistresses—a fact Delia and Nora learned the hard way.

In November 1864, widow Ann C. Toppan appeared before the board, desiring to adopt Nora Kelley. Since Ann "seemed like a very respectable woman [and] the home that she offered appeared to possess many advantages," the asylum wrote up the contract. But little Nora hadn't reached the minimum age of eleven. She was only seven. Nonetheless, the asylum made an exception and Nora became Ann Toppan's indentured servant.

As for Delia, she stayed at the asylum for another four years before being placed with the Waterman family in Athol, Massachusetts. No records exist

A photo of the Toppan family's home *Courtesy of Bourne Public Library*

of her time there, but it obviously wasn't a stable environment. Delia became an alcoholic prostitute who died destitute and in squalor.

Little Nora didn't have an easy life, either.

Contrary to Ann Toppan's statement before the board, she never formally adopted Nora. Rather, in an attempt to hide Nora's Irish heritage, Ann changed her name to Jane after a favorite aunt. With Jane's dark hair and eyes and light-olive complexion (known as Black Irish), she easily passed for Italian, which was a vast improvement over Irish. In fact, Ann even gave Jane a fake backstory, complete with its own tragedy. If anyone asked, Jane should say her birth parents died of ship fever on the family's journey from Italy to America.

At home, however, Ann made sure Jane never forgot her immigrant roots. "You can't help being Irish," she would often say, "but that doesn't mean you have to act like a Paddy."

Even under these circumstances, Jane grew into "a pretty, smart, and exceedingly clever child, but in no way precocious." Ann Toppan believed "the sparing of the rod was not allowed to spoil the child." Although accounts state "the rod was not used to excess," it bears the question, How many beatings constitute an acceptable amount?

Per the contract, Ann Toppan—whom Jane called "Auntie"—could return her to the orphanage at any time, for any reason, during an unspecified "trial period." Imagine growing up with *that* hanging over your head?

Dr. Charles Folsom, a prominent physician who treated Jane for "severe headaches" and knew her well, remarked on her childhood in his book, *Studies of Criminal Responsibility and Limited Responsibility*, published in 1842 and again in 1902.

> Everyday life had become a lie in [and] of itself in that [Jane] had not only concealed her race and origin, where they were not known, but talked against her people [Irish] and their religion [Catholicism], and in that her associates were people whom she constantly deceived as to her real character.

Dr. Folsom also treated Alden Davis, Charles Freeman, and Sarah Jane Robinson.

To survive, Jane morphed into the cleverest and most amusing storyteller. At picnics, "if Jane Toppan were there, it wasn't necessary to provide any other entertainment," according to a childhood friend.

In high school Jane became popular and active in the Congregational church in Lowell and in Sunday school. "She made lifelong friends there, and never once broke their confidence." But some students saw a different side of Jane. As a notorious gossip, Jane spread nasty rumors about classmates she envied or bore grudges against, for one reason or another.

By ingratiating herself with her teachers, and pinning her misdeeds on others, Jane transformed into the schoolroom snitch. And yet, she won the heart of her first lover, a sixteen-year-old boy who showered her with flowers. Once her childhood lover broke off their engagement, however, she viewed the world as a dark place filled with injustice. At home, Jane realized she was much more the servant than "a lady of the house," even though outside the doors of 182 Third Street, Ann and Elizabeth put on quite a show of treating Jane as one of their own.

At eighteen, Jane reported back to the asylum, per her contract, but told the managers that she liked her home with the Toppans. As prominent family in Lowell, they were upstanding members of the church, and well-respected within the community. Ann and her daughter, Elizabeth, also found Jane useful to the household. So, they allowed her to stay, as the servant, of course.

According to Dr. Folsom,

[Jane's] closest friends, very nice people who were proud of their New England ancestry, described Jane as amiable, sweet-tempered, deeply sympathetic, full of fun, always ready for a joke, rather impatient, generous to a fault, kind, devoted, loyal to friends, ever ready to do them a favor, audacious, unconventional in a way, but modest, virtuous, refined, though now and then showed a temper.

By her late twenties Jane seemed to settle into spinsterhood, allowing her youthful figure to balloon to nearly 170 pounds. At five foot three, USDA standards of the era listed 132 pounds for a woman of the same age and height.

[The weight] probably should not exceed these values by more than 5 pounds for shorter adults and 10 pounds for the taller ones.

Shortly after Ann Toppan's (natural) death in 1874, Elizabeth married O. A. Brigham. Even so, the family income suddenly reduced and the relations between the two foster sisters grew even more strained, while the differences between them became more apparent. Living there another eleven years, Jane now worked for Elizabeth—an arrangement that could only cause bitterness and hatred to fester. Jane eventually left the family home in 1885, at the age of twenty-eight.

No accounts exist as to whether Elizabeth had asked Jane to leave or if she'd left on her own, but Elizabeth and O. A. assured her that "she was welcome to visit her old home whenever she wished. There would always be a room waiting for her." And indeed, Jane returned every year, even after murdering Elizabeth.

Now on her own, Jane had no career, no skills other than domestic duties, and no husband. Mainly she bunked with friends, until 1887 when she decided to become a nurse.

For two years Jane trained at the nursing school attached to Cambridge Hospital, working seven days a week, fifty weeks per year, with no time off for Christmas, Easter, or Thanksgiving. She slept in a cramped, dimly lit, heated cubicle with three other students, and rose from her cot at 5:30 a.m. sharp, made her bed, changed into her uniform, and choked down the breakfast she'd prepared by 7 a.m., when she was expected on the ward. Between shifts that lasted twelve to fourteen hours per day, Jane got about seventy-five minutes per day to eat lunch and supper, both of which she had to fix for herself.

For the first month of nursing school her duties included scrubbing floors, emptying chamber pots, washing soiled bedclothes, and other grunt work. By the second month the school added a handful of patients for Jane to bathe, dress bedsores, treat wounds, administer enemas, and dispense medications.

Soon after I became a nurse, fifteen years ago, when I was thirty years old, it came into my head, I don't know how, that I could kill people just as easy as not with the very medicines that the doctors gave their patients, morphia and atropia.

Morphia and atropia weaken the heart's action and leave very little trace behind for a doctor or a chemist to detect. They are veg-etable poisons [which Jane learned from Dr. Lathrop] and are very unlike arsenic and other mineral poisons, which are easily detected. If I had used arsenic, my patients would have died hard deaths, gone into convulsions and struggled terribly. I could not bear to see them suffer, so I gave morphia mostly.

Regardless of what Jane alleged in her confession, she derived "the most exquisite pleasure" in watching people die. "Delirious enjoyment," "voluptuous delight," and the "greatest conceivable pleasure" as she stood by the bedside, or climbed into the sickbed with a patient, as she did with Amelia Phinney, while she watched the pupils dilate, felt the breath grow fainter and fainter, rejoiced in the pulse flickering lower and lower, and then stop. But what she most enjoyed was when, with a large enough dose of morphia, death would come with "violent convulsions," and she held them in her arms as they writhed, then yielded to "death throes."

After I had tried it in a few cases and it had worked so well, and they didn't suspect me, I thought how easily I could put people out of the way that I wanted to. My first victims were hospital patients. I experimented on them with what doctors would call a 'scientific interest.' I can't repeat the names of those cases—because I never knew them. They went by numbers in the hospital wards anyway. That was when I was at the Cambridge Hospital. Perhaps it was a dozen people I experimented on in this way.

Jane soon learned that death via atropine was by no means peaceful. Derived from both the belladonna and datura plants, atropine poisoning acts differently than an overdose of morphine. The mouth and throat become parched, as Amelia Phinney experienced, and the victim loses all sense of coordination—possessed by a strange giddiness that soon morphs into a wild delirium. They may burst into maniacal laughter, babble incoherently, or emit anguished groans, as Minnie did.

The worst symptoms of all include the incessant picking at real or imaginary objects; victims yanked on their finger and toenails or tried to grasp phantom objects floating above their heads. Even as they lapsed into a final stupor, they muttered feverishly, with full, uncontrollable body spasms.

55

Because the pupils widened with atropia and retracted with morphia, the combination of drugs dumbfounded attending physicians.

> My using morphia and atrophia on Minnie Gibbs was what so puzzled Professor Wood, the famous chemist of Harvard University. He could find some traces of morphia in the parts of the body he was examining, but there were some complications that he was utterly at a loss to explain. It was not until I confessed that I used atropia that Professor Wood was able to apply the test for that drug and make sure of his analysis.
>
> If my poisons could so fool a great physician and chemist like Dr. Wood you can see how much easier it was to deceive general practitioners. The physicians in Lowell, Cambridge, Boston, and at Cataumet were, however, skilled doctors. But the fact is that most physicians don't make any examination of a patient's body before writing out a death certificate. If a patient dies when they are away, they just fill out the certificate at their offices and put in for the cause of death the disease that they have previously diagnosed in the person.
>
> That is how it happens that physicians have given certificates for heart disease, diabetes, fatty degeneration of the heart, prostration, [anemia], etc., in the case of the people I have killed. Almost any person in middle life, when dosed with Hunyadi water and drugged with morphia and atropia will show symptoms of some of those diseases.
>
> But you mustn't think I killed all the patients under my care in the hospital. I nursed back to health some very bad cases of typhoid fever.

Indeed, she did. At Cambridge Hospital nursing school Jane excelled in her studies. Although, some classmates said "[she] liked operations and autopsies a little too much." To further her education, she transferred to the nursing program at Massachusetts General Hospital.

One of the physicians at the [Mass General] hospital suspected me. But he dared not accuse me of poisoning. So I was simply discharged.

That statement wasn't entirely truthful. What Jane failed to mention was that, before being discharged, she left the ward without permission, effectively quitting the program without her diploma, even though she had completed her studies and the diploma had already been signed.

But Jane didn't admit that in her confession. Instead, she wrote:

I didn't care for [being discharged], because I had made up my mind that I could make more money and have an easier time by going out by the day in families.

And she could. Private nursing paid better wages than hospitals, especially for someone with a stellar reputation like Jane's.

I took a room in Cambridge [at the Dunhams] and had cases in the wealthy families. I liked to nurse the men better than the women. In every case I gave the same poisons, only in varying quantities and in different ways, for it always worked well and no suspicion fell upon me.

Until October 23, 1901, when Jane was arrested and taken to Barnstable jail.

8

MURDERESS
CAPTURED!

The town of Bourne rebuilt the county courthouse and jail on the highest hill in Barnstable after the Spectacular Fire of 1827—high-reaching flames visible from the harbor, which left the former "old country house" in ashes. The "new court house vestibule," constructed in Greek Revival architecture of stone and wood, bared no outward markings of the evil who came before Jane—its first prisoner, Charles Freeman (1879), the religious fanatic who believed God ordered him to sacrifice his child, and Eleanor H. Jones, a Boston girl who spied for the South during the Civil War and who "so endeared herself to the Northern soldiers that they called her 'Major Jones,'" according to official records.

Overlooking the Barnstable Harbor, Sandy Hook, and Cape Cod Bay, Detective Letteney escorted Jane to the redbrick jail. A 6½-inch iron key clanged into the lock by Mrs. Cash's hand (the jailer's wife), signaling Jane to enter the cell.

Headlines splashed across every New England newspaper—*Boston Globe, Post, Boston Herald, Traveler, Daily Advertiser, Evening Transcript,* and *Morning Journal*—and wrote in lavish detail about the serial poisoner secured in Barnstable jail. Every vague rumor and alleged source(s) received front page attention. Some speculated that Jane bought the morphine for medicinal purposes; others claimed she "had the morphine habit."

"It makes me smile when I think of the stories that have been printed about the discoveries that have been made in connection with this morphia purchase," said one unnamed *Herald* informant, "and I will assure you that the defense is not in the least worried about them."

The court appointed Attorney James Stuart Murphy of Lowell—Jane's childhood friend—as guardian. Jane vehemently objected to her personal belongings being exhibited, as she felt they would "be used as curiosities." Her possessions totaled one hundred to two hundred dollars, and Jane said these items were "in the hands of people who have no right to it." The police also found a stack of pawn tickets, including one for Elizabeth's timepiece.

As for the defense, Murphy announced to the press,

> [I am] satisfied that the government cannot prove anything that will connect Miss Toppan with the deaths of the Davis family, and it ridicules the idea that it can show that she had exclusive opportunity to commit the crime with which she is charged. There were others in the house when Mrs. [Minnie] Gibbs passed away. They cannot testify that they saw Miss Toppan give her poison, or anything that they suspected contained poison until after the investigation was begun by the police.

"I wish Dr. Latter were alive," Attorney James Murphy told the *Herald* from his home in Lowell, "and he could perhaps clear up considerable of the mystery which now seems to exist."

The government also expressed regret over Dr. Latter's passing but "admits that he did not suspect that any of the Davis family had been poisoned."

Had the State not feared Jane Toppan might commit suicide, they wouldn't have arrested her so soon. District Attorney Holmes wasn't ready to prove the sole charge made against her—the murder of Minnie Gibbs—but, in the State's view, attempting to end one's life was a sure sign of guilt.

On this point, Attorney Murphy told the reporter, "From the time Miss Toppan left Cataumet until she was put under arrest at Amherst, [New Hampshire], the government knew her whereabouts. She did not attempt to hide, but all the time she was in Amherst she corresponded with friends. She worried considerably over the suspicions she realized the government had of her, after Officer Whitney talked with her about the Davis deaths, and it does not seem strange to me that a woman whose friends had turned against her should seek to destroy herself. [Jane] verbalized what a terrible position these suspicions had placed her in, and she did not care to remain in the world with them hanging over her. You must consider, how a knowledge that she was suspected of murder would affect any woman, and it does not seem strange, does it, that she should want to die?"

O. A. Brigham first told the *Herald*, "I had been warned by the government not to talk about the Toppan case," but later admitted, "I think now, although I did not when [Elizabeth] died, that there was something suspicious about my wife's death."

The reporter practically salivated over the juicy detail.

"When [Elizabeth] went to Cataumet to visit [Jane] Toppan she was in good health," O. A. recalled, "but in Cataumet she became suddenly ill, within 20 minutes she was unconscious, and within 48 hours she was dead."

The reporter prodded, "What was the cause of her death?"

"I don't know as I can say now what it was. [The doctor] said at the time that she died from apoplexy [stroke] and heart failure." O. A. opposed an exhumation. "No, I do not think that her body will be exhumed. I don't think there would be anything learned by taking her from the grave after she has been buried so long."

The reporter had previously interviewed Dr. Lathrop in connection with Elizabeth Brigham's death.

"She was not suffering from any illness when [Elizabeth] went [to Cataumet]," Dr. Lanthrop claimed, "but she was well advanced in years. [I had] no reason to believe that [Elizabeth] was poisoned." Of course, the doctor's reputation was on the line, so it wasn't all that surprising that he would try to save face.

Attorney James Murphy insisted, "[Jane Toppan] will be cleared of the charge against her. She is an innocent woman, who could have had absolutely no motive to kill people she considered among her best friends. When her story has been heard, I am sure the tide of public opinion will turn in her favor. She has made no statement since her arrest, by my orders. She has told the state officers everything that happened in the Davis house and she has told them the truth, but she will say no more until the proper time comes." Though a passionate defender, James Murphy missed the train to Barnstable on Jane's arraignment day.

Guided by Detective Letteney, all coloring drained from Jane's face as she tottered toward the courthouse dressed in a "black tailored skirt and jacket and white shirtwaist with a band of black about her throat."

Deep, dark circles clung beneath Jane's tired eyes, which some believed "proved she had suffered a restless sleep" during her first night in jail. According to an eyewitness,

> Upon her head her hastily combed hair was concealed by a black hat trimmed with black muslin. She carried her gloves and veil, but even these light objects were a burden as she dropped them while ascending the two steps to the courthouse.

Letteney escorted Jane into the courtroom, seating her on the bench in the prisoner's dock, a four-foot-high wooden box used to confine the accused during trial. When the clerk called Jane's name, she set her palms on the wood rail in front of her, rising to unsteady feet.

The clerk recited the capital charge of murdering Minnie Gibbs. "What do you say to this complaint?"

Voice quivering, Jane hushed, "Not guilty," then collapsed on the bench.

The court scheduled the trial for November 8 and remanded Jane to Barnstable jail. The entire proceeding took less than ten minutes. Once the judge left the courtroom Jane shuffled toward the doorway, grabbing the doorframe for a moment to steady her gait. Letteney escorted her down the long, narrow hallway, Jane's hand running the wall for support.

As Jane descended the courthouse steps, her veil and gloves slipped from her grasp. Letteney bent down to retrieve them, as any proper New England gentleman would, then guided her back to her cell on the second floor of the jail—the women's wing—where Jane stripped off her jacket, tossed her hat, and fell back on the cot.

Messages flooded into the jail.

"The newspapers would be very glad to publish anything you care to say in your defense," Letteney told Jane.

"Thank them very much, but I think I shall keep my own counsel until I have an opportunity to talk with my attorney." Feigning innocence, Jane swore to "know nothing about the deaths of the members of the Davis family, except that I suppose they all died from natural causes." Self-pity burrowed deep within her. "I am very sorry that I am obliged to endure this wide publicity, and the only wish I could offer would be that my name does not appear in the papers anymore."

Throughout Jane's life she adored children. While incarcerated she developed a genuine affection for the jailer's wife, Mrs. Cash, and her three-year-old granddaughter, Lucy. The *Barnstable Patriot* commented on Jane's attachment to little Lucy, calling her visits "the brightest moments of Miss Toppan's prison life." Nearly every afternoon Lucy would "toddle up to the cell door and, with her tiny fingers grasping the bars, stand for an hour at a time talking with the nurse."

When not chatting with the little one, her favorite pastime was reading, especially love stories, the more sentimental the better. During her time at the gloomy Barnstable jail, Mrs. Cash loaned Jane various novels. *Audrey* was her favorite.

"She talked to me frequently of the impression [*Audrey*] made on her," Mrs. Cash said, shedding an interesting and unexpected light on the murderess. In the parlor of her home in Barnstable, Mrs. Cash stored a library of books, all of which Jane had read during her incarceration, such as *Up from Slavery* by Booker T. Washington and *Mrs. Browning's Poems*.

[Jane] read all the series of the *Little Masterpieces* and six volumes of Kipling. She liked to read stories in which people were killed, but she preferred love stories, for she was very sentimental.

Mrs. Cash added a jarring remark. "The moment I laid eyes on that woman, I thought she was guilty. The evening she arrived . . . I took her up to her room and locked her in. Before the next morning I had made up my mind that she was a murderess, even before she confessed."

"Why?" Jane asked.

Mrs. Cash called it intuition.

Jane laughed. "I never said that I didn't do it, did I?"

A typical day at the Barnstable jail included rising early with the other female inmates. Jane sewed. She read. She performed simple household tasks as needed. In the evening, however, she was not allowed "to attend dances at the theatrical entertainments given almost nightly for less violent inmates."

The press acted as though no part of Jane's life was off-limits, including her sordid relationship with a young office worker named Charles May twenty years earlier. Shortly after their engagement, Charles accepted a position in Holyoke, Massachusetts. He'd been there a short while when Jane discovered he'd married one of his landlord's daughters. Since the promise ring he'd given to Jane had a bird engraved on the face, she quickly developed a hatred of birds, alive or dead, or any representation of them in print, photography, or on jewelry.

If a friend approached her with any bird depiction whatsoever, she'd scream, "Take it away!"

The newspapers also listed the contents of Jane's Dream Book, found in her belongings at O. A.'s house. Tucked neatly between the leaves was a strange list of "Good Days" and "Bad Days," as if Jane was trying to predict her own future.

19. This is a very good day. The vision of dreams will be realized within 8 days.

20. Good day. Dreams realized within 10 days.

21. Good day. Dreams prove delusive.

22. Good day. Dreams will be realized.

23. Inauspicious day. Dreams to be kept secret.

24. Good day. Dreams will be realized before close of day.

25. This is an inauspicious day.

26. Good day. Dreams realized within 10 days.

27. Excellent day. Dreams will be realized within 10 days.

28. Indifferent day. Dreams will soon be realized.

29. Good day.

30. Good day. Dreams soon realized.

Which month and year the numbers represented could not be determined, but if her writings were any indication, it seemed Jane Toppan was, at least in part, an optimistic psychopath.

9

A JAW-DROPPING
CONFESSION

On December 6, 1901, life moved at a slower pace, with visitors arriving to the courthouse via carriage or horseback. The grand jury filed indictments at 4:15 p.m. and 4:50 p.m. for the murders of Genevieve Gordon, Alden Davis, and Mattie Davis. Once again officers escorted Jane from the jail to the Barnstable courthouse for an arraignment before Chief Justice Mason of the Superior Court.

The clerk addressed the court. "Each is in four counts and charges death was caused by ten grains of morphine, by ten grains of atropine, by ten grains of morphine and atropine combined, and by poisons unknown to the jury."

When the clerk read enough of the first indictment to reveal the nature of the alleged poisons, James S. Murphy waived further reading of the indictments. Jane pleaded "not guilty" to killing Genevieve Gordon, Alden Davis, and Mattie Davis.

Because Jane had little to no money, Murphy asked if additional counsel could be assigned, as he'd taken the case *pro bono*. Judge Mason took the matter under advisement, the court adjourned, and Jane was remanded to jail.

District Attorney Holmes told the press that the trial wouldn't be scheduled until sometime after April, the next date reserved for trials. Any longer than that he could not say.

With the handing down of indictments, Jolly Jane's crimes faded from the newspapers until January 1902, when Chief Justice Mason granted

James Murphy's request for additional counsel. District Attorney Holmes said that not only did he believe Jane murdered the entire Davis family, she was also the prime suspect in seven other suspicious deaths.

Soon, the victim count rose to eleven: Elizabeth Brigham, Sarah "Myra" Connors, Mary McNear (who ran the theological school and whose job Jane had coveted), Israel and Lovey Dunham (Jane's former landlords), Edna Bannister (O. A.'s sister), and Florence Calkins (O. A.'s housekeeper), along with Minnie Gibbs, Genevieve Gordon, and Alden and Mattie Davis.

The court assigned Fred M. Bixby as lead counsel for the defense. As justice of the Brockton police court and a summer resident of Hyannis, Bixby had a "good working knowledge of the law . . . good abilities as a public speaker, and a remarkable capacity for seeing a point quickly and turning it promptly to his own advantage," according to the *Sentinel*. "He had the gift of humor, he [could] wound with ridicule, and be impressively eloquent when occasion demanded."

What more could Jane ask for?

With regard to the new victim list, Jane blamed all eleven deaths on everything from the weather to bad fruit. When a reporter visited Jane in jail, she said, "The fact that I am innocent will be established when the hearing is held next week. If there is any justice in Massachusetts, I shall be cleared. I cannot see how I can be convicted of a crime I never committed. I admit that the many deaths of which I am supposed to be the cause form strong circumstantial evidence, but they may have been due to many causes. All the deaths occurred in the summertime. The drinking water at Cataumet is bad. The land is low. The country is practically un-wooded, and conditions favor diseases that can be transmitted through drinking water. I myself was sick at Cataumet.

"Moreover, Mrs. [Elizabeth] Brigham, Mrs. [Edna] Bannister, and Miss [Florence] Calkins died in the intense heat of the summer, and Mr. [O. A.] Brigham's illness was also at this time of the year. All were of advanced age and ate freely of fruit that grew on the old place [182 Third Street]. Anyone who understands medicine or hygiene knows what this means. Each of the people who died I knew personally and was on friendly terms with."

Yet, the story Jane told Bixby ran opposite to this account.

On his first visit to the Barnstable jail, a bitterly cold January morn, Bixby intended to speak with his client about the eleven homicides for which the State was investigating. What he never expected was for Jane to admit she'd killed them all.

Managing to keep his composure, Bixby blinked, then blinked again. "Well, how did you kill them?"

"I gave them doses of morphine and atropine tablets in mineral water and sometimes in a dilution of whiskey," Jane said with the calmness of chatting about her beloved romance novels. "Then I also used injections, just as I did at Cataumet. I do not remember how I killed them all, but those that I [do] recall were poisoned by atropine and morphine. My memory is not good. I forget some things."

Jane used strychnine to murder Mary McNear but failed to mention that due to either memory lapses or an outright lie. More likely the latter.

"I know I am not a safe person to be at large," she said. "It would be better if I were locked up where I could do no one any harm. No one can tell when I am liable to have another paroxysm [a sudden attack or violent expression—in Jane's case an uncontrollable desire to murder]. I do not know myself, until it comes."

A visible shiver rippled across Bixby as he slid his chair away from his client. "Why, Jane Toppan, you must be insane."

"Insane, how can I be insane? When I killed those people, I knew I was doing wrong. I was perfectly conscious that I was not doing right. I never at any time failed to realize what I was doing. Now, how can a person be insane who knows what she is doing and is conscious of the fact that she isn't doing right? Insanity is a complete lack of mental responsibility, isn't it?"

"Yes, that is correct. But you have no remorse, have you?"

"No, I have absolutely no remorse." Jane used a matter-of-fact tone. "I have never felt sorry for what I have done. Even when I poisoned my dearest friends, as the Davises were, I did not feel any regret afterward. I do not feel any remorse now. I have thought it over and I cannot detect the slightest bit of sorrow for what I have done." She hesitated a moment. "There is one thing that makes me think my mind is not right. I have great difficulty in remembering things. My memory is good at times, but on other occasions I cannot recall what I have said or done."

Stunned by his client's cool demeanor, Bixby sat in horror as Jane recounted all eleven murders in lavish detail.

"Whatever else I have done I have never stolen a cent," she lied. "I did not care enough about money to steal it."

The sheer pleasure of killing gave Jane the "exultation" she experienced while she "kissed and caressed her helpless and insensible patients as they drew nearer and nearer to death."

It took the portly nurse one full hour to detail each of the eleven murders, a sly smirk revealing her callousness. By the time she'd finished, Bixby felt "satiated with homicidal details" and deeply relieved that his client had reached the end of her confession.

As Bixby stood to leave, Jane blindsided him with, "But that is not all."

"Why, what do you mean?"

The words that followed left Bixby speechless.

"Now I will tell how I killed the last member of the Davis family, Mrs. Irving Gibbs [Minnie], for which I was finally arrested. Minnie Gibbs was my best friend. But we always go back on our best friends. I wanted to marry her husband, Captain Irving Gibbs. Minnie was jealous of me. It made a fuss in the family, and I cut up and flayed Minnie before her husband [metaphorically].

"Still, they both thought a great deal of me, Minnie as well as Irving. This is just how I poisoned Minnie Gibbs. We all went driving to Woods Holl [Woods Hole, as it's known today, is a census-designated place within Falmouth] one day, and when we came back Minnie was not feeling well—I had given her a morphia tablet dissolved in hot whiskey before we started, to brace her up for the drive, I said to her."

Jane told Minnie, "You had better take some of Dr. Latter's medicine that he left you."

"I don't want any of his old medicine," Minnie replied.

"'But you must take it,' I said, and I gave her some, with morphia and atropia tablets dissolved in it, and she lay down on the lounge. The rest of the family ate their supper, and when it was bedtime Minnie was sleeping on the lounge. I told them she was tired out and was in a sleep of exhaustion. They tried to rouse Minnie but could not. She only made a groaning noise. So I got a blanket and covered her up. Most of the others went to bed and I offered to sit up with Minnie. But Harry Gordon [Genevieve's widower] said he would look out for her that night, and he lay down on a lounge near her.

"Harry Gordon said to me as he lay there: 'We are going to Barnstable in the morning to Probate Court, and when Minnie wakes in the morning she will be refreshed and we will look over some papers and talk business matters over.' That was just what I didn't want them to do, for I owed Minnie some money and had given her some notes. Several times during the night I stole in while Mr. Gordon was asleep to give more doses to Minnie, for I was afraid that she might come out of it. [Minnie] was too far gone to swallow, so I dissolved morphia and atropia tablets in water, filled my hypodermic syringe with it, and made injections of the poison in her arm. I had made up my mind that she must die that night."

Bixby's jaw slacked.

"Finally," Jane continued, "Harry Gordon awoke, got alarmed at Minnie's sinking condition, and in spite of my protests, at 3 o'clock in the morning, he called the others and they got Minnie upstairs to her room. They had to drag her up though, for she was beyond all feeling and consciousness. The family, that is, what was left of them, Beulah Jacobs, their cousin, and Harry Gordon, wanted to send for a doctor, but I told them it was only a fainting spell and that I could doctor her myself.

"Her husband, Captain Irving Gibbs, was away at the time, on his vessel, the *Golden Ball*.

"Finally, toward dawn, the family got thoroughly alarmed and sent for Dr. Latter at Monument Beach, five miles away. When [the doctor] arrived, Minnie Gibbs was almost dead. He said it was heart failure. After [Minnie] died, I did not go near her. I did not even bathe her and lay her out. When she died I felt as if I had got through with her and could not bear to go near her. I have a loathing of dead bodies [which contradicts her loving autopsies, but perhaps she felt a twinge of remorse over murdering her best friend]. But mind you I'm not afraid of any avenging spirits. I never saw any of the spirits of people I have killed."

That statement would come back to haunt her.

"I went to Minnie Gibbs' funeral though. After she died, he [presumably Harry] gave me Minnie's pocketbook with a $10 gold piece in it. And now, just think of it, he won't speak to me. No knowing what I would have done to him after he turned against me."

This "perfectly normal and natural woman" admitted to poisoning patients for almost twenty years, which began in nursing school and continued through her private nursing practice. Counting on her fingers, Jane said she'd murdered at least thirty-one men and women. Jane Toppan's outwardly placid life, it seemed, was torn apart by a secret and insatiable passion—the slow murder of those she loved most.

"I might say I feel hilarious, but perhaps that expresses it too strongly." Jane continued to psychoanalyze herself, attempting to grasp what made her different. "I do not know the feeling of fear and I do not know the feeling of remorse, although I understand perfectly what these words mean. But I cannot sense them at all. I do not seem to be able to realize the awfulness of the things I have done, though I realize very well what those awful things are."

Sharing her story helped to draw her stalwart counsel deeper into the dark crevices of her mind, her merciless deeds told in truths, adding more and more details to her narrative of crimes.

"I try to picture it by saying, 'I have poisoned [Minnie], my dear friend. I have poisoned Mrs. [Genevieve] Gordon. I have poisoned Mr. [Alden] Davis and Mrs. [Mattie] Davis,' but I seem incapable to realize the awfulness of it. Why don't I feel sorry and grieve over it? I don't know. I seem to have a sort of paralysis over thought and reason."

Dumbstruck by his client's confession, Bixby remained silent.

Sometime after the first of the year, Bixby met with District Attorney Holmes about Jane Toppan's case. Together they approached Attorney General Parker with a proposal. Rather than prepare for a lengthy and expensive trial, Bixby and Holmes planned to appoint an impartial panel of "insanity experts" to diagnose Jane's mental condition "with reference to her legal responsibility."

After considering the proposal for several weeks, Parker agreed. On March 20, 1902, Dr. Henry Rust Stedman, one of Harvard's most distinguished alienists, Dr. George F. Jelly of Boston, and Hosea M. Quinby, superintendent of the Worcester Hospital for the Insane, had all agreed that Jane Toppan suffered from "moral insanity."

What they failed to realize was that Jane had had a plan of her own, a surefire way for her "to avoid the gallows." She mustn't have known that she actually saved herself from being the first woman put to death in the newly installed electric chair.

I have poisoned thirty-one people as far as I can count them up and recall them. But there are more that I can't name, just hospital patients. I was advised to confess and plead guilty to the murder of the thirty-one persons whom I have sent out of the world by poisoning. But I thought of a better way than that.

When the famous insanity experts of Boston, Dr. Henry R. Stedman, Dr. George F. Jelly, and Dr. Hosea N. Quinby, came down to the Barnstable jail to see if I was insane, I knew how to fool them. I have been a trained nurse for fifteen years and know doctors and just how to manage them. I know that people who are really insane will always deny it.

So, I said to the alienists: 'I am not insane.'

I knew I could fool them all if I wanted to, and make myself out insane. Dr. Jelly and the others raked me hard with questions. They tried to play on my woman's sympathy and asked me if I didn't think it was a terrible thing to take those mothers, Mrs. [Minnie] Gibbs and Mrs. [Genevieve] Gordon, away from their young children. But I knew their game and said that I just up and killed them and didn't know why.

When I said that I killed four people in fifty-one days [actually, she killed them in forty-one days] and set three fires, they said: 'Why, Jane Toppan, you must have been insane to have done such

71

a thing.' But I still insisted that I was not insane, and did not want them to make me out insane. Then they went away and gave their verdict that I was insane, which was just what I wanted. I was too smart for the whole [lot] of them. I have the most spunk and grit of any person living.

The press lapped up the diagnosis of moral degenerative insanity, and the rumor mill once again churned with fury.

Meanwhile, in Barnstable, jail obviously agreed with Jane. During her eight-month stay, she'd gained fifty pounds. Mrs. Cash must've been one hell of a cook!

People say I have no heart, but I have. While I have been in jail, a friend in Lowell sent me some forget-me-nots, and I cried. They were the flowers that my first lover used to send me when I was a schoolgirl. And a forget-me-not was engraved on that precious engagement ring [not her engagement to Charles May; Jane's referencing an engagement at sixteen years old].

I will never tell my girlhood lover's name that is still sacred to me, even though he went back on me, and it seemed that my whole lighthearted nature changed after that. I still laughed and was jolly, but I learned how to hate, too. If I had been a married woman, I probably would not have killed all these people. I would have had my husband, my children, and my home to take up my mind.

That last statement was a little hard to believe, considering she also said the following:

I could have worked for years longer at poisoning if I hadn't killed four people in one family almost all at once. That was the greatest mistake of my life. I've made up my mind to being sent to an insane asylum. But I have hopes of getting out in ten or fifteen years—when doctors will say I am cured of insanity.

10
TRIAL OF JOLLY JANE

Even with the diagnosis of moral degenerative insanity, District Attorney Holmes moved forward with the trial on June 23, 1902, for the death of Minnie Gibbs. Chief Justice Mason appointed Judges Henry K. Braley of Fall River and Charles U. Bell of Lawrence to hear the case.

The following jurors were empaneled: Samuel Chapman, William F. Kidder, Samuel H. Drew, Edward E. R. McRay, Gilbert A. Dodge, Frederick O. Smith, Geo. H. Nickerson II, Ezra D. Perry, Sheldon H. Cowan, Joshua E. Holway, Henry R. Usher, and Aaron L. Crowell. The court appointed William F. Kidder as foreman of the jury.

At the request of Attorney General Parker, all witnesses except the witness on the stand and those expected to give expert testimony were asked to leave the courtroom.

Parker gave the State's opening address. "May it please, Your Honor, Mr. Foreman and gentlemen of the jury, you have heard read to you an indictment charging in the portentous and impressive phraseology of the law, perhaps the gravest crime of which humanity may be guilty."

The opening address continued for several minutes before Parker laid out the State's case against the accused. "It will appear as I anticipate, gentlemen, that on the twelfth day of August, 1901, Mrs. [Minnie] Gibbs was in her usual health; that she was out, and if I remember rightly, took a long drive, returning in the afternoon to her home. It will appear that the prisoner on the same day went to a neighboring town and there purchased a large quantity of morphine in the form of pills; that she also purchased

73

several bottles of Hunyadi water, familiar to you all, which doubtless you know possesses a very bitter flavor."

Parker glowered at Jane, then focused on the jurors. "The prisoner also procured a rubber sheet, which is a sheet as I am informed is used upon sick beds where patients are in such a condition that they cannot care for themselves, and which I am informed is a precautionary or sanitary measure taken where the patient is in a moribund condition, and death is anticipated.

"The prisoner returned from a visit to this neighboring town where she went in the company of a Mrs. [Caroline] Wood [family friend of the Davises], if I remember the name correctly. Upon her return she voluntarily, and as I remember without suggestion or inquiry or request from Mrs. [Minnie] Gibbs, advised her to take some Hunyadi water and informed her as reason for her taking it that she, the prisoner, had seen a physician in this neighboring town, Dr. Watson, if I remember the name correctly, who advised the administration of this Hunyadi water. As a matter of fact, it will appear to you that the prisoner had had no conversation with this doctor, and had received from him no advice or suggestion that this water should be administered to Mrs. [Minnie] Gibbs, and that the statement made by the prisoner in that regard was false."

Parker continued to list each and every infraction made by Jane Toppan. "There were certain statements made by the prisoner after the death of Mrs. Gibbs which were deemed to be of great significance, and which I believe you will consider of grave importance.

"After the death of Mrs. Gibbs, and the visit of the undertaker, to the undertaker the prisoner urged that great quantities of embalming fluid should be injected into the body. Embalming fluid, as you know, gentlemen, is made up in large part of arsenic, a deadly poison. [Jane Toppan] urged that much of this poison should be injected into the body so that the tissues might become permeated with it and the orifices and vessels of the body charged with it."

With his hands clasped behind his back, Parker's gaze ran across each juror's face, pausing briefly to make eye contact to ensure he held their attention. "It will appear also that the prisoner urged upon the residents of the household and the kindred of Mrs. [Minnie] Gibbs, or those who were there in charge, that no autopsy or post-mortem examination should be held, the prisoner asserting without truth that the family objected to any such process or procedure, and no autopsy was immediately had.

"Later, and I am going to briefly [go] over this, gentlemen, because I shall spare you so far as is possible in the discharge of my duties, details that can only give pain. You must charge yourselves with the duty of hearing, and we must charge ourselves with the duty of presenting to you all the essential facts, and we must shrink from nothing by reason of sympathy or emotion, yet I am not required to tell you at this time all of the harrowing incidents of this tragedy."

In closing his initial address to the jury, Parker hoped to clear up inconsistencies in the State's case. "I have said to you that some of the symptoms of Mrs. [Minnie] Gibbs while she lay ill were conflicting to the mind of the scientific investigator, difficult of diagnosis by the medical men, because it were as if the two causes were conflicting, the two conditions were conflicting with each other. The ordinary manifestations of poisoning by narcotic drug such as morphine existed in a measure, but again there would develop some symptom that was in conflict with the conclusions that would be drawn if morphine were the poison.

"But, gentlemen,"—Parker raised his voice for emphasis—"one who is skilled in the use of deadly drugs knows their counteracting effect, and often the history of medicine and the history of crime has revealed the fact that he or she who seeks the life of another, conceals her agency or his agency in it by using not one drug alone, the presence of which might be revealed by the symptoms and the sufferings of the tortured victim, but the poisoner uses in combination some re-agent drugs which cause either a mitigation of some symptoms or a combination of both, so that unless suspicion be already established, the diagnosis can never be perfect but must be in some respects inconclusive."

After several more minutes reviewing the facts of the case, Parker called his first witness, Beulah Jacobs, Minnie's cousin. He ran through the usual name, address, and relationship to the decedent, and then Mr. Swift, attorney for the prosecution, took over.

Swift approached the witness. "Tell us what took place so far as Mrs. [Minnie] Gibbs and you and the defendant were concerned after you arrived from the ride [to Woods Holl]."

"I went to bed," Beulah testified. "I went to sleep; and when I got up I asked where Miss [Jane] Toppan was, and she had gone to Falmouth, and Mrs. [Minnie] Gibbs and Mr. [Harry] Gordon were reading a magazine."

"Now, what time was that, Mrs. [Beulah] Jacobs?"

"It was somewheres around four o'clock. I don't know just the time."

Swift pressed for clarification. "When you woke up?"

"When I woke up," Beulah confirmed. "I think I slept something like two hours."

"Mr. Gordon and Mrs. Gibbs were where?"

"They were in what they called—well, it was in the front room, what they used for a sitting room, and little Genevieve [Genevieve Gordon's daughter] was there; just we three together."

"Now, in which house was this?"

"In the Jachin."

"The house called the Jachin?"

"Yes, sir."

"Which is the name—"

"Of the hotel."

"Of the cottage, the summer place?"

"Yes, sir."

"How many lived there at that time?"

"How many in the family, do you mean?"

"How many were staying [in] the house when you were there?"

"Do you want their names, or how many?"

"How many, I ask you first?"

"I can tell you the names, and you can count them," said Beulah. "There was Mr. Dunham [a relative of Israel and Lovey Dunham], and Mrs. McFarland [Davis family friend], Harry Gordon, and Paul and Jesse Gibbs, the two boys [Minnie's sons], and little Genevieve Gordon [Genevieve's daughter], and Miss Toppan and myself."

Swift asked the witness for clarification. "You say when you awoke, Mrs. Gibbs and Harry Gordon were reading somewhere?"

"They were not reading then when I first came out. Harry was writing a letter in his room."

"In which room was that?"

"[Harry] was in his own room, in the annex to the room when he was writing, but afterwards we were all together out in this little sitting room."

"And Miss Toppan wasn't there?"

"She had gone to Falmouth, Mrs. [Minnie] Gibbs said."

Attorney General Parker interrupted to correct the witness. "You mustn't tell what was said. You had been informed she had [gone to Falmouth]. The prisoner wasn't there?"

"No, sir."

Swift resumed the questioning. "When did you next see her?"

"When she returned from Falmouth."

"Did she herself say that she had returned from Falmouth?"

"Well," Beulah relented, "[Jane] had things she brought from Falmouth, so I supposed she came from there."

Bixby leaped to his feet. "Isn't that leading?"

Before a ruling could be made, Swift conceded. "Perhaps it is. I do not intend to lead." He refaced the witness. "Did [Jane Toppan] say anything?"

"I don't know whether she did or not. She came right from the train."

"Did you see what she had with her?"

"She had some bundles. She showed us some of the things she bought."

"What did she show you?"

"She showed us some Hunyadi water, a piece of rubber sheeting, and she gave Mrs. [Minnie] Gibbs a bundle which she said was borax."

Swift glanced over at the jury to emphasize the fact that Jane Toppan had purchased the mineral water that she later poisoned. "In what form was the Hunyadi water?"

"I think she bought half a dozen bottles for Mr. [Harry] Gordon."

"You saw the Hunyadi water?"

"I saw the bottles, yes, sir, the package."

"Was any one with her when she returned?"

77

"No, sir."

"And do you know whether anyone went with her to Falmouth?"

"I didn't know then," said Beulah, indicating she'd later learned more details about Jane's trip to Falmouth.

"You did not know it yourself. Did you hear [Jane Toppan] at that time, or shortly after she returned, say anything to Mrs. Gibbs?"

"Yes, sir."

"Will you tell us what you heard?"

In a hushed voice, Beulah mumbled, "She said that she met Dr. Watson at Falmouth and she was very glad that she saw him because—"

Swift cut her off. "I wish you would say that again, Mrs. Jacobs, and talk a little bit louder."

"She said she met Dr. Watson on the street in Falmouth, and she was very glad she saw him, because she wanted to ask him about Mrs. Gibbs, and she didn't like to go there [to the doctor's office] without Mrs. Gibbs . . . and so she said he suggested that when [Minnie] go to bed at night, as [Minnie] wasn't sleeping very well, that she take some whiskey, and [Jane] said that she told Dr. Watson, and he [had] suggested it would be much better if she would beat an egg up in it, and also suggested that [Minnie] had better take some Hunyadi water."

Swift must've smiled inside. "Do I understand you to say that [the defendant] said that Dr. Watson said this?"

"Yes, sir."

"To take the Hunyadi water?"

"Yes, sir."

"Anything further?"

"There was a douche pail that [Jane] wanted to cleanse, and she had gotten this borax to cleanse it with. I think she said that Dr. Watson said that would be as good as anything. [The doctor] said she could get some at the grocery store, but it would not be as pure as what was at the druggist's, and [Jane] got it at the druggist's."

Swift questioned the witness for several more minutes, and then asked a poignant question. "Did you see the defendant, Miss Toppan, give Mrs. [Minnie] Gibbs anything else that afternoon?"

"Not in the afternoon, in the evening."

"Well, at what time?"

"Oh, sometime after seven."

"And what was that, if you know?"

"Cocoa wine [a fruit wine made from cocoa pulp]."

"Was anything said that accounted for her giving that?"

"Yes, sir."

"What was it?"

Beulah shifted in the witness chair. "After supper Mrs. Gibbs was lying down upstairs and I went up there and [Minnie] said she felt perfectly awful ever since she drank the Hunyadi water, and she asked me if I would go downstairs and ask Mr. Dunham to go and get some water, because there was not any in the house."

Bixby jolted out of his chair. "Who was this talk with?"

Beulah said, "Mrs. Gibbs."

"Was the defendant there?"

"No, sir."

Bixby flung out his hands. "I object."

Swift interjected. "The defendant was not there."

After some back and forth between the prosecution and defense, Judge Braley issued his ruling. "I think for the present we will exclude it."

On the night Minnie's condition worsened, Beulah Jacobs stated she went to bed around 9 p.m., but Jane insisted for Beulah to sleep in the bedroom next to hers. When asked why, Beulah couldn't say. But she did state that Jane woke her about 12:30 a.m. to help her check on Minnie, who was still in the sitting room with Harry Gordon, though half asleep and out of it.

Swift asked, "Now, did you see Miss Toppan again that night?"

"Yes, sir, about two o'clock."

"What took place then?"

"[Jane] came and told me that [Harry Gordon and Minnie] had not gone to bed yet and [Jane] wanted me to get up and help her; that Minnie must go to bed; and [Jane] gave me a skirt and I got up and went into the sitting room and Minnie was sitting on the couch. Mr. Gordon was kind of holding her up, and she seemed to be what I called asleep then."

"And Mr. Gordon was there you say?"

"Yes, sir."

"Was he dressed in his day clothes, or night clothes?"

"They had not been to bed at all, neither of them."

"Tell us what took place after that."

"[Jane and Harry] tried to arouse [Minnie] and she did not seem to arouse. She would say, 'Oh, Harry! Oh, yes . . .' and they would ask her if she could get up, and she would say yes, but did not seem to have any power to get up. . . . Miss Toppan said [Minnie] would have to go to bed, and Mr. [Harry] Gordon took her up in his arms and carried her into the next room and put her on the bed."

"What took place after that?"

"We did not get her undressed, but her feet were just like ice. [Jane and I] got her shoes and stockings off, and rolled her feet up in a blanket, and Miss Toppan gave her some whiskey."

"Did Miss Toppan say anything during any of this time?"

"She spoke about [Minnie] not going to bed; thought she should have gone before she got chilled."

"Anything else?"

"Not that I recall at that time, no, sir."

"Tell us, after that what took place?"

"A little while afterwards [Jane] said if [Minnie] did not get any better she was going to have Mr. Gordon call Dr. Latter, so [Jane] sent Mr. Gordon to call Dr. Latter, and he came. I do not know just what time it was, but it was just about the break of day. It was getting light enough to see when he got there."

Swift asked for clarification. "That was Dr. Latter?"

"Yes. [The doctor] said that all [Minnie] needed was rest and she would be all right."

"Did you hear any talk between Miss Toppan and Dr. Latter?"

"[Jane] went off in another room and talked with him."

Later in the testimony, Swift uncovered an intriguing detail.

Beulah Jacobs told the court that Dr. Latter had left Jachin House, and Beulah went back to bed, as did Harry Gordon. Jane and Minnie were then left alone.

"What was the next you knew about the matter?" asked Swift.

"[Jane] called me in the room just a moment before I went down to breakfast, and [Minnie] seemed to be sleeping then all right."

"What time was this?"

"I think about half past seven, and then I went down to breakfast, and [Jane] went upstairs before we did. I was sitting down talking to Mr. Gordon."

"Did Miss Toppan go to breakfast with you?"

"Yes."

"When you say she went upstairs before you did, you mean Miss Toppan?"

"Yes." Beulah leaned forward, her hand braced on the wooden rail around the witness stand. "The dining room was in the basement, and she went back up into the bedroom. I stayed in the dining room talking to Mr. Gordon, and [Jane] called me and asked me to come into the room quick, and I went in there, and [Jane] said that she was afraid that Minnie was going just like the rest, and asked me if I would stay until she got some whiskey . . . [Jane] said that she must send Harry for Dr. Latter, and told him to go as quick as he could and to tell [the doctor] that Minnie was in utter collapse, and that [Dr. Latter] would know what that meant, and to ask what she should do for her. I stayed [in the bedroom] until [Jane] went and got some whiskey for [Minnie]. . . . [Jane] gave her a rectum injection."

"That was all?"

"Then Mr. Gordon came back and we asked him if he got the doctor, and he said [Dr. Latter] was coming up on the train and [Jane] asked him if [the doctor] said anything for us to do, and [Harry] said no, that [Dr. Latter] did not tell him anything to do. I said that [Dr. Latter] could come quicker than to wait for the train because that would not come for an hour, and then [Harry] went back to the telephone. [After he made the call] he said the doctor was coming in a carriage, and while we were waiting for the doctor Miss Toppan looked at Mrs. [Minnie] Gibbs's eyes and shook her head. I asked her what the trouble was and she said [Minnie's pupils] were set."

Swift tried to drive home Beulah's final statement for the jury. "How many times in all did you see the prisoner examine the eyes?"

"Two or three different times."

"By examining the eyes what do you mean?"

"Raising the lids and looking at them."

"Coming back a little bit so as to keep events in their order, when you were summoned from the breakfast table, did the prisoner say anything else at that time?"

"She said [Minnie] was all right when [Jane] came into the room, and [Jane] walked around the other side to tuck her in, and she noticed this sudden change come over [Minnie]."

"Tell us [Minnie's] appearance at that time?"

"She looked just as though she was dead; looked as though she would die before Miss Toppan got back into the room."

"Do you recollect the prisoner saying something like this, 'How can she blame me?'"

"Not at that time I don't, but [Jane] said that they would blame her; she seemed to blame herself for not making Mrs. Gibbs go to bed; that [Minnie] got chilled staying up."

Swift arched his eyebrows. "When was that?"

"Several different times."

"You did hear her say something like that?"

"At several different times, yes."

"Do you recall exactly what she said?"

"'How can they blame me?'" Beulah repeated. "'I could not make anybody go to bed in their house if they wouldn't.'"

After the prosecution finished with Beulah Jacobs, Bixby made a statement. "May it please, Your Honor. I think that in view of the nature of the defense which will be offered later, which perhaps, has been outlined somewhat by the learned Attorney General, that there will be no necessity of cross-examining this witness, or, perhaps, any of the witnesses offered by the Commonwealth."

The State continued to call witnesses to the stand, even though the panel of alienists had issued its ruling of moral insanity, as though the attorney general put on a trial for the mere purpose of satisfying the public. This theory became more apparent when the three alienists each testified,

"[Jane Toppan] was insane and irresponsible for the crimes for which she is charged; that she was suffering from a form of degenerative insanity characterized by the absence of moral sense, by defective control and by an irresistible impulse to the commission of extreme crimes."

Attorney James Murphy urged Dr. Henry R. Stedman to emphasize the point that the defendant, Jane Toppan, was insane at the time of the murders. "What in your opinion was her condition in August of 1901?"

Dr. Stedman testified, "I consider that she was laboring under insanity."

"Under the same conditions you found when you visited her [in jail]?"

"Under the same conditions excepting that then the opportunities were present which allowed the insanity to manifest itself in its full form."

"What form of insanity would you term this form with which she is afflicted?"

Dr. Stedman had a look of bewilderment. "I have just endeavored to give a definition."

"As to its technical classification?"

"[The insanity] belongs to the degenerative type. It is constitutional, probably hereditary, confirmed, and renders such a person always dangerous and a menace to society if at large."

Attorney General Parker approached the defense witness. "And are you of the opinion that the prisoner is incurably insane?"

"I am."

"And the opportunity offering for insanity to manifest itself might again be manifested in homicide if [Jane Toppan] was at large?"

"Unmistakably."

After the State and defense had rested, Judge Braley cautioned the jurors before they left the courtroom to deliberate. "In this case, gentlemen, the evidence has been so presented that it seems to me that it requires on your part, although you are the final judges of all questions of fact, it seems to me it requires these findings on your part: First, that the death of Mrs. [Minnie] Gibbs was caused by poison; that it was caused by poison deliberately and maliciously administered by this defendant with intent to cause her death; and, last, that at the time of the administration of that poison, the defendant was not in a condition of mind which made her criminally responsible for

Newspaper illustration from Dr. Stedman's scrapbook
Courtesy of the Francis A. Countway Library of Medicine at Harvard University

what she was doing; and the result of those three propositions is that the legitimate verdict, is, Not guilty by reason of insanity."

The jury only deliberated for twenty-seven minutes. When they returned to the courtroom, the clerk asked Jane to stand and face the jury. "Prisoner, look upon the Foreman. Foreman, look upon the prisoner. What say you, Mr. Foreman, is Jane Toppan, the prisoner at the bar, guilty or not guilty?"

"The verdict we have written."

"You can answer guilty or not guilty."

"Not guilty."

Judge Braley said, "By reason of insanity?"

The foreman concurred. "By reason of insanity."

The judge then polled the jurors, and all the men agreed to the verdict of not guilty by reason of insanity, and Judge Braley sentenced Jane to life at the State Lunatic Hospital in the city of Taunton, Massachusetts.

Bixby remarked, "I think, Your Honor, the defense would be perfectly content with that disposition of her at that institution."

Judge Braley asked Jane if she had anything to say on her behalf.

A faux demeanor concealed her satisfied grin. "I have nothing to say."

And so, the court arranged for Jane's transfer to the asylum to take place on June 27, the day following the one-day trial. Before she left the jail, Jane couldn't resist hinting that her insanity would go away because her violent impulses were merely caused by a hormonal imbalance that would subside once she hit menopause.

Jane never predicted she would soon face a fate worse than death. Or had karma finally bitten back?

11

A FATE WORSE
THAN DEATH

When the sheriff escorted Jane to the asylum, the brick neoclassical-designed building boasted cast iron capitals, cornices, and numerous ornate cupolas along the roof line. The hospital perched on a tranquil 154-acre farm north of town, the location meant to help soothe troubled minds.

Although the State Lunatic Hospital of Taunton (known today as Taunton State) sat close to the center of town, the Mill River created a natural boundary line to prevent the encroachment of bustling city life. East and west wings branched out from the central administration hub, with tiered wards to segregate residents by sex and symptom severity.

Even though little could persuade the negativity from surfing the air inside the asylum, the cast iron framed window in Jane's room allowed natural sunlight to cascade over her perpetual smile.

Soon the mania became uncontrollable passion. No voice has as much melody in it as the one crying for life, no eyes as bright as those about to become fixed and glassy, no face so beautiful as the one pulseless and cold.

Over time, the asylum grew into a city within a city, with its own golf course, amenities, and floral gardens skipping across the landscape. Only the second of its kind in Massachusetts, the government built the facility to help

Taunton Insane Hospital *Courtesy of Library of Congress*

house mentally disturbed patients when Worcester State Hospital became dangerously overcrowded.

A seventy-foot-tall dome climbed the center of the building and offered panoramic views of the town and the blue hills of Norfolk County's scenic countryside, but Jane would only experience its tranquility for a short while. Off the main building, curved enclosed breezeways grasped the tips of nursing wings—a far cry from the gloomy Barnstable jail cell where Jane had spent the last eight months.

Even so, Jane much preferred her former living quarters. The prison guards never conducted psychotherapy water or shock experiments in the basement like the asylum doctors. Keeper Cash and his wife treated her with kindness and respect, and so did the other inmates. Looking back, she could not recall one unhappy moment while incarcerated in Barnstable.

Now, her only form of entertainment was to razz the attendants with, "Hey, dearie, grab some morphine and we'll go out in the ward. You and I will have a lot of fun watching them die." Jane cackled with delight.

On the other side of the riverbank the city sat at the center of an important iron-making industry. By utilizing impure iron deposits taken from surrounding bogs and swamps, numerous factories created goods, such as stoves, tacks, and machinery. Mason Machine Works, Taunton Locomotive Works, several textile mills, and brick-making factories employed hardworking New Englanders from miles around.

On its coast, Taunton became a major shipping point for grain, from the inland rural farms of Massachusetts to the rest of the nation via Weir Village and the Taunton River. But that made little difference to Jane.

Peering through the double-barred door of her room in the west wing, an outsider could never tell her greatest ambition in life was "to have killed more people—helpless people—than any other man or woman who ever lived." And that was by design. At five foot three in her soft, heelless nurse's slippers, her facade masked a morbid imagination on par with New Hampshire native Herman Webster Mudgett, better known to the world as H. H. Holmes.

From the hospital's lofty hilltop, the sultry July air breezed through the opened windows in the hopes of adding therapeutic value for the patients. But even sunlight and warmth had no bearing on Jolly Jane's cold-bloodedness.

When the jury found her not guilty by reason of insanity, many folks believed "the electric chair had been cheated of its rightful victim. No form of execution known to law could be torturesome enough for this inhuman woman."

Some even went as far as calling the verdict "a travesty of justice to allow such a tigress in human form to escape legal execution."

What the public could not know was that "Nature, through God, in its own way, [was] working a punishment more terrible than mediaeval torture could have devised upon this woman, who dared to violate one of the great Ten Commandments: Thou shalt not kill."

As casually as Jane shrugged off her confinement, saying, "Anyway, in a few years I'll be right. Then they will let me out," she had no idea what was coming.

Back on the Cape, Captain Irving Gibbs married Minnie's cousin, Beulah Jacobs. Amelia Phinney finally put the puzzle pieces together of that strange night in Cambridge Hospital, fourteen years ago. Even though Jane might've remembered her as "the one who got away," Amelia credited God for sparing her life.

As for Captain Paul, he died of natural causes in 1904. Years later, Paul Gibbs (Minnie's eldest son) founded the Gibbs Oil Company. And O. A.? Deacon Brigham regained his quiet, respectable life at 182 Third Street in Lowell.

"During Jane Toppan's decades-long nursing career, she had enjoyed the confidence of the best families in Boston, Cambridge, Lowell, and all the other large towns of Eastern Massachusetts," the *Evening Star* reported. "In the very moment of the passing of the spirit she found her greatest joy, demonic though it may be, and left the stiffening bodies in order to lie down to [a] refreshing, dreamless sleep."

But Jane had one last surprise for the public.

I have given the alienists and [Attorney General] Herbert Parker the names of 31 persons I killed, but as a matter of fact I killed many more whose names I cannot recall. I think it would be safe to say that I killed at least 100 from the time I became a nurse at a Boston Hospital, where I killed the first one, until I ended the lives of the Davis family.

Jane rejoiced in holding "to her bosom a patient racked with the death struggles brought on by her poison, gloating in the convulsive quivers and twitches of the muscles, the moans of pain, the sweat of death."

About two years into her confinement at the State Lunatic Hospital at Taunton, in 1904, Jane's mind fractured and she imagined avenging spirits setting fire to her bed, just as she had done on at least four separate occasions. On some evenings Jane's whole wing would be aroused at night by piercing shrieks and the cry of "Fire, fire!"

Dr. J. P. Brown, the superintendent of the State Lunatic Hospital of Taunton, described Jane's mental and physical breakdown.

She seems to me to be wholly devoid of moral sense, or a clear apprehension of what is right or wrong as to her relations to other people or to society. Lack of pity and sorrow for others in trouble or distress has been evident whenever any difficulty has occurred in the ward between patients, or between a nurse and patients. At such times [Jane] has manifested a good deal of glee, and laughed like a silly child, but never has expressed any sympathy or pity for the patient or person in distress or trouble. Trouble or pain for others seems to excite in her merriment and joy instead of sorrow.

In speaking of the homicides, she says that at the time she committed [the murders] she was not conscious of committing any crime or doing any wrong for which she should justly be punished; that the thought of doing wrong did not enter her mind, and gave her no concern [whatsoever]. . . . At the present time she apparently has no comprehension that the decree of the court in committing her to the hospital was right and just, and must be obeyed; and she asks for her freedom as though it could be granted on the same basis as that of any other patient.

In her early interviews with Dr. Brown, Jane exhibited self-awareness of her condition but also an innate curiosity. "I don't appear like these other patients," she said. "I can read a book intelligently. I don't have bad thoughts, so I don't see where moral degeneracy comes in."

But nothing Jane said could sway Dr. Brown's steadfast opinion of her.

Recently, during the past three or four months, Jane Toppan has seemed more moody and emotional, either depressed or exhilarated at short intervals, and has exhibited less self-control and with it she gives one the impression that her mind is weakening, and that she has less mental grasp of past and present events, and of her relation to her surroundings. Of this she seems to be painfully conscious . . .

She has been observed to be laughing immoderately to herself, and when it is noticed by others she blushes as though she would conceal it, and seems confused.

This weakening of her mind as time goes on is what is to be expected, and will probably continue. In every case of more or less impairment of what are called the intellectual faculties in distinction from the moral, especially reason and judgment to decide ethical questions presented to the mind, otherwise the moral obliquity and perversion would be controlled, and the criminal act averted.

From my examination and observation of [Jane Toppan] since she has been under my care, and my knowledge of her previous history as made known to the court before her sentence, I am of the opinion that she is insane and irresponsible, and that her mental disease, resulting as it probably does from ancestral vice and degeneracy, which her family history so far as known clearly indicates, is incurable.

Dr. Stedman also continued to take an interest in Jane, and often visited to study her. Even he told of Jane's "physical collapse this year [1904] by starving herself and becoming reduced almost to a skeleton, through fear of being poisoned through her food. [Jane became] very abusive toward the nurses, defying their authority and inciting patients to do the same, going so far as to shout to a melancholic, whom the nurse was trying to feed, not to eat the food as it was poison."

By February 1904, Jane had whittled down to a skeletal sixty pounds, and was so weak the staff had to force feed her via tube. During one of Dr. Stedman's visits Jane went on a tirade, insisting, "everything was rotten" and "the meat was embalmed beef."

As Jane's mind fractured more and more, she came to believe "not only that every article of food, every cup of tea or coffee, and every glass of water, had been poisoned, but she could see the spectres of her victims hovering over her and dropping the poison into these things just as she used to do to them."

TERROR-STRICKEN POISONER
AFRAID OF DEATH BY POISON

Jane Toppan Chooses Slow Starvation to the
Food at the Asylum—Iron-Nerved Nurse
a Prey to Her Own Fancies

JANE TOPPAN FED
IN STRAIT-JACKET

Four of the Biggest Female Nurses
at Taunton Hospital Watch Her
Constantly—She Re-enacts Incidents of Her Victims' Deaths.

Articles from Dr. Stedman's scrapbook
Courtesy of the Francis A. Countway Library of Medicine at Harvard University

When Jane was first admitted, the staff permitted her to mingle with the other mildly insane patients. But as her delusions became more frequent and "she broke forth into violent tirades against the other patients and the hospital attendants," they sent her to the infirmary. It soon became apparent that they needed to move her to a secluded cell in the north wing, because "the windows had gratings and it [was] in reality a prison."

When one of the nurses, carrying a tray of crust, coffee, and bread, ambled into Jane's room one morning, Jane said, "I saw them all last night."

"What do you mean, Jane?" At that moment, the nurse did a double take at an "unnatural brightness" illuminated in Jane's hollow, sunken eyes.

"Why, all the people I have killed. They all came and gathered round my bed in the night. There were the Davises, and Mr. and Mrs. Dunham, and Myra Connors, and Mrs. [Elizabeth] Brigham, and Mrs. [Edna] Bannister, Mrs. [Minnie] Gibbs, and Mrs. Harry Gordon [Genevieve]—oh, I'm sorry I killed her, she is so pretty." The hardened murderess broke into an uncontrollable sob.

Once she'd regained composure, she said, "But they're all after me now—thirty-one of them—some want to poison me, and some come at me with their skeleton hands as if they would choke me. See, they're coming for me now—help, murder!" Jane fell back on her cot, trembling in fear.

The press leveraged Jane's suffering to make a point.

Jane Toppan is paying the penalty of her crimes by Nature's or God's own law in a way that is an appalling moral object lesson—that no one can take human life, even if he [or she] escapes the punishment of human law, without suffering the most awful tortures to the end of his or her own wretched existence.

"In recent years," the *Washington Herald* reported in 1938, "hospital authorities find it hard to reconcile the quiet patient they knew with the woman described in published accounts of poisonings. In her last years she was just another patient and caused no trouble."

Jane Toppan died on August 17, 1938, at eighty-one years old. Hospital records show she had never received any visitors outside of Dr. Stedman and, for a brief period after the verdict, her childhood friend James Murphy.

Taken from Dr. Stedman's scrapbook
Courtesy of the Francis A. Countway Library of Medicine at Harvard University

When no one came to claim Jane's remains, the asylum laid her to rest in an unnamed grave in Potter's Field at the Mayflower Cemetery in Taunton, one mile from Taunton State, her eternal resting spot marked only by the number 984, which someone later stole.

If Jane wasn't exaggerating when she claimed to have killed one hundred victims—a body count which could never be substantiated without names and dates—Jolly Jane easily "outdistanced the unsexed and ferocious murderers of the past."

"Don't blame me, blame my nature. I can't change what was meant to be, can I?"

—Jane Toppan

PART II: LYDIA SHERMAN

1

THE DAY BEFORE
THE TRIAL

The murder trial of any human being was sure to excite the minds of the public in 1872, but when the accused was a female charged with multiple grisly crimes, much more interest befell the bustling city of New Haven, Connecticut. This same curiosity showed in the case of Mrs. Wharton of Baltimore who was accused, and later acquitted, of murdering General W. S. Ketchum, and in the case of Laura Fair from San Francisco, an attractive thirty-three-year-old blonde, her face and body obscured by a veil and cloak as she hustled across the deck of a San Francisco-bound ferry in November 1870.

When Laura Fair was within a yard from her target, she "pulled a four-shooter out of her cloak," took aim at her adulteress lover (standing with his wife and fourteen-year-old son) and shot him through the heart, dropped the pistol, and walked away.

But now, in April 1872, New Haven, Connecticut, had a new murderess, a woman whose crimes gained far more excitement than both these cases. Police suspected Lydia Sherman of committing a series of murders, including "the death of innocent little ones, whose prattling tongues she had so often listened to, and for whose welfare she had shown a mother's solicitude," a hotshot *New York Herald* journalist noted.

That same reporter scored an interview with the accused as she sat in her cell the day before the trial. He wrote:

No wonder, then that the arrest of Lydia Sherman in July last for murder caused a commotion in the aristocratic circles of Birmingham, [Connecticut], where several of the alleged murders were committed, and that the people of this county should again revive their interest in the case on the eve of her trial by a jury for the murder of her husband, Nelson ["Horatio"] Sherman, of Birmingham, in May last [1871], by means of arsenical poison.

Proceeding out Broadway a distance of a mile and a half, a fine brick structure surrounded by a beautiful lawn and dotted with stately firs . . . presented the appearance of a gentleman's country house . . . [the] temporary abiding place of the accused murderess, Lydia Sherman. On stating my business the janitress retired, and soon ushered into my presence this remarkable woman—remarkable is she [if] innocent of the high crimes against humanity that are charged to her, as a victim of suspicious circumstances, and if she be guilty still remarkable as one who, under a serene exterior, has the faculty of hiding her guilty secrets from the observer.

She presented the same calm appearance that astonished the spectators of the preliminary examination, but her prison confinement had changed her appearance slightly and given her a careworn look that plainly told of the anxious hours she had watched and waited for the end.

Failing to recognize the reporter he remarked, "You will remember me, Mrs. Sherman, as the reporter of the *New York Herald* who attended your trial at Birmingham [grand jury hearing]."

With her rich chestnut hair and porcelain complexion, Lydia's languid blue eyes brightened, and she responded by extending her delicate hand. "Oh, yes. I remember."

Waiting for the reporter to ask a question, Lydia clasped her hands in her lap.

"I have called to see you and converse with you regarding your case. Do they treat you well here?"

"Oh, yes, sir. I have the same privileges given me as are accorded to other prisoners. I have the freedom of the halls, and receive every attention compatible with the rules."

"I have seen your counsel to-day, and he seems to be quite hopeful of your acquittal on the present charge; but are you not disappointed at the postponement of the case, Mrs. Sherman?"

"Not at all," said Lydia. "I am in the hands of my counsel, and all he does [is] for the best, I think." (Lydia's counsel, Mr. Waterous, had requested a postponement to better prepare a defense.)

The reporter prodded for answers. "Can you tell me why he desired the case to go over?"

"I cannot. [Attorney Waterous] has not informed me on the point. But I presume he has good reasons."

"I have heard that his motion has taken everybody by surprise, as it was believed that the defense sought an early trial."

"I am anxious to be tried. My counsel may have reasons for delay that make an adjournment necessary." (What those reasons were became obvious at trial.)

"I may say, Madame, that after listening to all the testimony given by the people at Birmingham [grand jury hearing] I have grave reasons to think that on the present charge, bad as it appears now, you can scarcely be convicted. The facts show that you were a devoted wife to [Horatio] Sherman and as [an] affectionate mother to his children . . . there was no motive for you to make away with them."

"Yes"—Lydia's eyes tilted downward—"that is true. Mr. [Horatio] Sherman, when sober, was a good man, but when under the influence of liquor was not himself by any means. When intoxicated he was kind but funny, and more pleasant and kind to his family than when sober."

"Was he subject to periods of melancholy?"

"Yes, sometimes he appeared quite strange and unnatural."

"It is said that you received $10,000 from Hurlburt [Lydia's second husband, whom authorities believed she also murdered, but weren't prepared to charge her yet]. To-day I have been informed that the amount was much less."

Lydia nodded. "It was much less than $10,000."

"How much of it did you expend upon [Horatio] Sherman?"

"That is a question I have never considered. It may come someday, however. Yet I spent money upon him. The people say I poisoned [Horatio Sherman] to prevent him [from] squandering my fortune, when the truth is, I held the money in my own right and he could not obtain a cent except by my free consent."

"There is another strong point in your favor."

Hope cascaded across Lydia's alabaster skin. "What is that?"

"That you endeavored to reform [Horatio] Sherman."

"Yes," she said, her navy blue eyes shining more brilliantly still. "I did endeavor to reform him. I first joined a temperance society and then requested his brother [George] to do likewise. He objected on the ground that he was already a teetotaler [one who never drinks alcohol], but I urged him to do it as an example for Horatio, and be initiated with him to give him confidence, as [Horatio] had so often fallen away from his good resolutions. His brother consented, and I got them both into the lodge."

"And you gave a free consent to the holding of a post-mortem on the body of [Horatio] Sherman?"

"Yes. Dr. [Beardsley] came to me and suggested it, and I told him to hold it by all means. If guilty, I would hardly have consented."

"And your affection for Ada [Horatio's daughter from a previous marriage] was unbounded?"

"I could not have treated her more affectionately had she been my own child. Between us there was ever the greatest affection, and the neighbors say that she used to tell them that I was as kind to her as her own mother, although she knew I wasn't [because there's no stronger love than that of a mother and child—a sentiment Lydia recognized]."

"Mrs. Sherman, while, were I a juror, I could scarcely convict you of [Horatio] Sherman's death on the evidence, unless more is in possession of the people than came out at [the grand jury hearing at] Birmingham, I must say, in all candor, that the death of Dennis Hurlburt [Lydia's second husband] points very strongly to you as the guilty party. You were the only one in the house with him during his illness, and Professor Barker's [the chemist] evidence shows that there was poison both in the stomach and liver. This is the most suspicious case of all, but I sincerely hope you may be able to establish your innocence."

"That does look bad," admitted Lydia, who betrayed an unusual calmness under such a severe comment, "but I have given Mr. Gardner, one of my counsel, an explanation of matters attending Mr. Hurlburt's death that may materially affect this case."

"Dr. Shelton, who attended [Hurlburt], gives very singular testimony."

"Yes, he did. He treated Mr. Hurlburt, and said to me that the disease was—" Her words trailed off. "Some months later, while passing the house, [Dr. Shelton] called and presented his bill, and I then said, 'Doctor, what did my husband die of? The people are asking me, and I cannot tell them.' He then made the same [non]answer."

"But on the examination, he swore that the symptoms were suspicious." The reporter paused for a deep breath before continuing. "Mrs. [Lydia] Sherman, I wish now to speak of the Struck family, of New York. I had an interview some months ago with the Presbyterian minister who was present at the death of Lydia Struck [Lydia Sherman's biological daughter from her first marriage], in Manhattanville. It appears that your first husband, Edward Struck, and four children died. Were these your children?"

Lydia frowned, her eyes misty. "They were."

"The minister spoke of you as a devoted Christian and a woman who betrayed great maternal affection."

Visibly affected by the statement, her gaze fell to her lap. "Did he?" Lydia asked, her voice full of hope. "Mr. Payton [the minister] could say nothing less. He knew me well."

"But"—the reporter stopped a moment to "weigh well" his words, "lest they should wound the feelings of one already bowed down by grief"—"he says there is one circumstance he could never understand."

"What is it?"

Again, he hesitated, fearing that he was "trespassing too much upon the confidence of the unfortunate lady." The reporter said, "[Reverend Payton] states that some time before [your daughter] Lydia's death, while in the company of a young lady friend, she suddenly stopped in her *tête-à-tête*, and remarked: 'Dear [Miss Wildley], I will soon be stricken down and will not recover. I have a request to make. When I am dead have me laid out in this way,' and that [young Lydia] immediately lay down upon the carpet of the floor, in front of the glass, and assuming the posture of a corpse, indicated in what way and in what material she should be clothed for the grave."

The answer came quickly from Lydia Sherman's lips. "That is true. It occurred in my house. I came into the room, found [my daughter] Lydia in this position, and asked her what she was doing? She responded, 'Showing how I wish to be buried.'"

"But [Reverend] Payton says he understands that you refused to allow her to be buried in the clothes she named; that you buried [your daughter] without any other clothing than sufficient to cover such portions of the body as were exposed in the coffin, and that, worse than all, you refused the corpse a pair of stockings."

"That is not so." Lydia's tone revealed determination, yet her composure never wavered. "[My daughter] said to me, 'Mama, bury me in my black dress; don't use my best dress.' I was present at the laying out of the corpse, but I know [my daughter] was fully clothed as she requested. The young lady of whom she made the request is Miss Wildley, and the present wife of Reverend Payton. . . . Another lady, who is still living, assisted in preparing her for the grave. I can't see how Mr. Payton could say this."

"He merely said he had heard this."

"Well, [the rumor] is untrue. Mr. Payton would not say so of his own knowledge."

"I saw Cornelius Struck [Edward Struck's son from a previous marriage] a few weeks ago. He is still a conductor on the Third Avenue Railroad. He does not seem to think that you poisoned his family."

"The doctors gave certificates in each case of death in Mr. [Cornelius] Struck's family. They all died of natural diseases. Dr. Rosenstein would hardly have recommended me as a nurse to his patients had he suspected anything wrong. He gave the certificates of death in two of the cases."

"That is in your favor." The reporter jotted down notes. "Mr. Payton made the same remark to me. Then all these four children of Struck were yours?"

"Yes. All his children [from a previous marriage] are still living. But another of mine by him is dead."

"The record in the New York Bureau of Vital Statistics does not show another."

"Still another, a child, died of measles years before. It ought to be on record."

At this point in the interview the reporter withdrew, even more perplexed over the guilt or innocence of Lydia Sherman, the accused, after cordially assuring her that "[he] would endeavor not to misrepresent her language, unlike others in reported interviews that had never even taken place."

The reporter summed up his interview in the *New York Herald.*

In all of the nine murders [suspected in at least eleven] charged upon this unfortunate, but somewhat polished prisoner, the absence of a motive for life-taking is apparent, with the exception of the case of Hurlburt, and even the prosecution [was] befogged on some points. Judge Foster, however, in drawing the indictment has betrayed much legal acumen, and in it, it will be difficult for the distinguished counsel for the accused to find a technical flaw. Taken as a whole, the case of Lydia Sherman is destined to be one of the most remarkable trials of the period.

2

IN HER OWN WORDS

D r. Ambrose Beardsley, Birmingham (Derby) Town Health Officer and Sherman family physician, had "carefully woven the web of circumstantial evidence around the accused." He and an associate, Dr. Kinney, relayed this information to the local grand juror, A. H. Gilbert, who secured an arrest warrant for Lydia Sherman and "placed [it] in the hands of Sheriff Henry R. Blackman," who arrested Lydia at the train station, escorting her to jail at New Haven.

While awaiting trial, Lydia told her story to Jailer Webster, who "indulged in the common Yankee weakness of making an honest dollar out of it."

"I was born near the town of Burlington, New Jersey, on the 24th of December 1824," Lydia told the jailer, "and am now forty-eight years old. When I was about nine months old my mother died, and I was taken to live with my uncle, Mr. John Claygay. He was a farmer and the father of three children. In his family I was treated with the same kindness as the other members of it. We all worked hard, and I was able to go to school only about three months during the year. I never attended school much when a girl."

Jailer Webster raised a finger for her to wait as he scrawled her words on a notepad, then nodded for her to proceed.

Lydia Sherman
Courtesy of Library of Congress

"When I became sixteen years old my two brothers came to visit me, and when they returned to their home in New Brunswick I went with them, and after a stay of three weeks I returned to my uncle's, accompanied by my younger brother Ellsworth, who remained there for about five months. We both then went back to New Brunswick and I went out to service in the family of Reverend Mr. Van Amburg, who resided in the town of Jacksonville, twenty-five miles distant from New Brunswick. I lived in his family for three years, at the end of which time my brother [Ellsworth] came again to see me, and I went back with him to New Brunswick."

The jailer could hardly believe his good fortune in scoring a firsthand account from "The Poison Fiend," as he would later dub Lydia Sherman, who to many was one of Connecticut's most notorious murderesses.

"Soon after, I began to learn the trade of a tailoress," Lydia continued, "with the sister of my brother's wife, and boarded at the same time with my brother Ellsworth. For three months I worked, making pants and vests, without pay, and then was employed by a Mr. Owen, for whom I did sewing a part of the time at his shop and a portion of the time at my home. I continued to work in this way until trade became dull, and then I went to work in Mr. Owen's family. He was a class leader in the Methodist church there. He was a very fine man and his wife was an excellent lady, and both are now [in 1872] living. I remained in this family about four months and then went back to work in Mr. Owen's shop and boarded with my brother Ellsworth at the time. I continued thus employed for a year. During all this time I was a member of the Methodist church."

But soon, Lydia's life would nosedive into an endless pit of suffering.

"While with Mr. Owen I became acquainted with Mr. Edward Struck through my class leader, Mr. Jacob Edmonds. Mr. Struck was then a member of the same church with which I was united. He was a very devoted Christian and remained such until a few months before his death. Until then [Edward] had family prayers during most of the time. I was his wife for eighteen years, and he died about eight years [ago]. I do not remember dates."

Edward Struck died May 26, 1864 at fifty-nine years old, after a sudden and mysterious illness.

"We were married at the residence of my brother Ellsworth in New Brunswick, and then my husband went to Yorkville, where he worked at his trade, that of a carriage blacksmith. He worked for six weeks, coming home only on Saturday nights and returning on Monday mornings. We then went to Yorkville to live, and [Edward] Struck worked for Mr. Brewer for one year. Our first child, a girl, was born during this time, and we named her Lydia [after me]."

A weak smile barely arched Lydia's thin lips as she spoke of her namesake, her face full of sympathy and concern.

"Then we moved down to New York City and my husband [Edward] worked for Mr. John Butler, at the corner of Prince and Crosby Streets. We resided two doors from the corner of Elizabeth and Houston Streets. We lived there three years, and during that time two boys were born, whom we called John Wesley and George Whitfield. At the end of three years Mr. Butler moved his business up to Carmansville [a lost city in New York], and [Edward] Struck went with him and remained in his employ for ten or eleven years. While we lived in Carmansville we had four children born. Their names were Ann Eliza, Josephine, Martha, and Edward."

In total, the couple raised thirteen children—seven by Lydia and six by Edward's former wife.

"At the end of the time stated, [Edward] Struck left Mr. Butler's employment and obtained an appointment on the police force. This was at the time of the organization of the metropolitan police force of New York. After he had served on the force about six months one of the children, Josephine, was taken sick with measles. She caught cold and this caused inflammation of the bowels, which, after an illness of two weeks, occasioned her death, at the age of twenty-two months. This occurred in the Spring, but I do not recollect the date. Dr. Mitchell attended her. Soon after, my husband was transferred to Manhattanville. He then moved his family there, and we went to live in 125th Street. Then occurred our first trouble."

Captivated by Lydia's story, Jailer Webster urged her not to exclude details. The more she included the greater the chance of selling the confession to a publisher.

"It came about in this way—a man came up to Stratton's Hotel, on the Bloomingdale Road, and made a disturbance in the barroom. He attacked the barkeeper with a knife, and immediately the cry of murder was raised. He [an unnamed detective who happened to trot by the hotel on horseback when someone yelled, 'Murder!'] rushed at once into the hotel; but, finding he was powerless to accomplish anything, he asked for the assistance of a policeman. There was none near and [the detective] endeavored to quiet the man by talking to him; but he could not succeed. The [crazed, knife-wielding] man appeared deranged. The detective struck him with a cane, but the man would not desist from his conduct, and after he was struck, [the crazed man] attacked the officer with a knife and the latter drew a pistol and shot the [the perpetrator] dead."

How Lydia Sherman's crimes stemmed from this one incident, Jailer Webster could never have predicted.

"The stage [coach] drove on and soon met [Edward] Struck, and as he was a policeman the driver told him the circumstances about the killing of the [deranged] man at the hotel. Mr. [Edward] Struck started immediately for the hotel, and when he reached there, he found that the [perpetrator] was dead. Word was sent to the Manhattanville police station and doctors were called in to examine the dead man. A jury of inquest was called, and the doctors gave it as their opinion that the man was deranged. My husband afterwards reported the affair at the headquarters, and soon after a rumor prevailed that [Edward] would not arrest the man in the first place because he had a pistol to defend himself with. This was incorrect."

At the time, corruption ran rampant through the Manhattanville precinct. Edward was an honest gentleman—too honest for his superiors.

Whether Edward knew something he shouldn't, or they feared he'd expose the corruption, we may never know, but they used this incident at the hotel to destroy him, which in turn, obliterated his entire family.

"Before the jury of inquest," Lydia continued, "the employees of the hotel testified that Mr. [Edward] Struck was at the place and was afraid to go in. The result was that [Edward] was discharged from the police force upon their testimony, as he had no witnesses to call in his favor except the stage driver. Then [Edward] had nothing to do and he became downhearted and discouraged. Captain Hart told him that he was trying to get [Edward] on the force again. Matters stood in this way for about three months, when Captain Hart sent for [Edward] and told him that he [Captain Hart] had done his best [but] that he could not get him on [the force] again."

Marital discourse soon erupted in Lydia's household.

"Then [Edward] gave up and acted as if he did not care to get any work. He said he could not get work to do, and I went to see Mr. Butler [Edward's previous employer], and he said [that] he would take him back and pay him, even though [Mr. Butler] did not do more than half a day's work, as [Edward] had always been a good workman. I returned home and told my husband what Mr. Butler had said, and advised him to do the best he could. [Edward] refused to go, [but] finally went with me to Mr. Butler's shop, when Mr. Butler said, 'Mr. Struck, I am glad you have come back to work. You do the best you can and I will pay you well.'

"[Edward] worked for a few days and then stopped and stayed at home. He was sent for several times, and finally Mr. Butler came down to see him, and Mr. [Edward] Struck told him he would not go back again to work. Then my husband did nothing but fretted all the time. Mr. Butler came again and coaxed [Edward] until he consented to go to work again."

Jailer Webster inquired about what she did to help the situation, if anything.

"Then I used to go up to the shop with him and keep him company for hours at his work. One day he came home and said he would not work anymore, because he was ashamed to be seen in the streets, as everybody was looking at him as if he was a coward. The next morning I could not get him out of bed, and he told me that he should never go out of the house again. He would allow me to bring no one in to see him and would allow none of the children in his room. I used to try to get the neighbors to come in and see [Edward], but he would not notice any of them."

Though Lydia found it difficult to deal with a husband who had suffered a mental breakdown, she persevered. After all, she'd been married to the man for eighteen years and wasn't ready to throw away the many milestones they had achieved as a couple. But that mindset would change as Edward's depression worsened.

"A gentleman by the name of Olmstead, who he thought a great deal of, called to see him, but he would not look at him or have anything to say to him. [Edward] would lay in bed seven or eight weeks at a time. I wanted him to have a doctor, but he would not see one. He said he wanted to see one of his first wife's children, a daughter named Gertrude, who was married to a Mr. William Thompson, and I went down to New York and brought her up to see him. When [Gertrude] came he would say very little to her. One of the neighbors was sick, and Gertrude, seeing the doctor leaving their house, called him in to see her father.

"The doctor asked him what was the matter, and if he was sick, and [Edward] said, 'No, I am not sick.'

"The doctor got [Edward] to take some medicine and left some for me to give him, but he would not take it. He acted as though he was out of his mind, and finally [Edward] began to lose the use of his limbs. He could hardly use his hands and feet. One day he got to the bureau and took out a pistol and put it to his mouth and said, 'Mammy,' (this is the name he always called me), 'if I should fire this off it would blow my head off.'"

Jailer Webster asked how Lydia handled the volatile situation.

"I was frightened and took [the gun] away from him and put it back in the drawer. Then he wanted a razor, and I took [the razor] and the pistol and locked them up, so that [Edward] could not find them. I got [Edward] back to his room, and then he got it in his head that he was going to be arrested. One day I sent for Captain Hart to come and see [Edward] and try and quiet him."

Did that work? The answer would knock the jailer back in his chair.

"When the Captain came Mr. [Edward] Struck would neither look at him or speak to him nor have anything to do with him. The Captain told [Edward] that he was out of his mind. [Captain Hart] advised me to have him sent to the lunatic asylum. Many others told me the same thing, and said if I did not do it he would do some of us injury. One night [Edward] got up and told me to bring him his clothes and shoes and said [the police] were going to take him away in the morning. I quieted [my husband] by telling him that no one would harm him, for he had done nothing [wrong]."

But no amount of reassurance could soothe Edward.

"He kept getting worse," Lydia said, a sadness to her tone. "He got so he could not dress or undress, and he caused me at this time a great deal of trouble. He wanted me to get places for the children [to live] because I could not take care of them. I told him I could take care of [our children] and that he need not worry about them. One night he was acting very badly and I called in the Police Sergeant Mc—" She refused to name the officer. "Sergeant Mc— lived in the lower part of the house with us. He came in and talked with my husband for a while, and then he told me that Mr. [Edward] Struck was out of his mind, and that he would never be any better. I sent for Dr. Jackson, of Carmansville, and he came in the evening. He asked Mr. Struck how he felt, but [Edward] did not speak to him.

"I said, 'Doctor, he is very sick.'

"The doctor stayed a short time, and left with me two white powders, and told me to give them to [Edward] during the night. When the doctor went away I went with him to the door, and asked [Dr. Jackson] if he thought [Edward] was very dangerous, and he said that [Edward] was a very sick man, and that he thought he had softening of the brain and that he would never get well again. That night [my husband] was very bad, and I was up with him all the time. Towards morning he began to fail very fast, and about eight o'clock in the morning he died."

By this time, Edward's six children from his previous marriage had grown up and left the house, but Lydia and Edward's children all died over the course of about two years—doctors misdiagnosing the deaths as typhoid fever (also known as gastric fever or infantile remittent fever), bronchitis, and painter's colic—except John, who was about fourteen years old when he went to work in the city as a butcher.

[John] used to help me all he could until the children died, and then I told him to keep his wages and support himself, as I was alone in the world and could take care of myself. I remained house-keeping and the doctors recommended me as an excellent [unlicensed] nurse. I continued to be employed as a nurse until the following April, when a family named Maxom, who were going out to Pennsylvania, wanted me to go with them, and my son John also; they wanted that he should work on the farm and they were going to take [John] and myself to live in their family. They said they were going to a place called Sailorsville, [Pennsylvania], and that if I would go they would pay us both well.

This move turned disastrous for Lydia.

Finally, we went out with them; but upon arriving we did not like the place, and Mr. Maxom did not do as he promised. We remained, however, from the 18th of April until the 9th of September and worked very hard. We then determined to stay no longer, and at length I got Mr. Maxom to give us money enough to get back to New York; but I was obliged to leave all the furniture, which Mr. Maxom promised to send to me when I wanted it.

I wrote frequently for [the furniture], and he always replied that he would buy it, and then I wrote for the money and he sent back one feather bed. I wrote again asking him to send the pay little by little, and he wrote back that I need[n't] send no more [letters], as he would pay me when he came to New York. I have never heard from him since.

Now in New York, Lydia and John were on their own. So, her step-daughter, Gertrude Thomas, allowed them to board with her.

John went to work again for Mr. Hall, the butcher, who keeps a market, or did then, at the corner of Thirty-fourth Street and Third Avenue. I finally got a situation in a sewing machine establishment in Canal Street, I do not remember the number. It was kept by a Mr. Cochran. It was my business to show goods to customers, run a machine, and explain how it worked to those who called to examine it. When anyone purchased [a sewing machine] I had to teach them how to work it. Mr. Cochran was absent from the store frequently, and then I had the full management of the business. I was, in fact, helper and clerk. While working at this place I felt good and enjoyed my occupation. I had nothing to fret or trouble me.

Which was safer for everyone involved. When something "troubled" Lydia Sherman or she felt "downhearted," family members tended to drop dead after a sudden, painful, mysterious illness.

"While I was at this store," she told Jailer Webster, "I became acquainted with Mr. James Curtiss. He was there one day and asked me what I was going to do when [Mr. Cochran closed his store]. I told him I thought I should go back to New Brunswick, [New Jersey], to my friends. [Mr. Curtiss] asked me if I would not like to go to Stratford, [Connecticut], to live. I told him I thought I should like [that] very much. He told me that he had an aged mother living there who was very helpless, and that he wanted someone to take care of her and keep house, and that he thought I would be just the one for the place. I asked him how much of a family there was, and he said no one but [his mother]. I consented to go . . . [for] eight dollars per month."

According to the Department of Economics, single women in the US dominated the female labor force from 1870–1920.

Single working women at the turn of this century were historically unique in the terms of their home lives and occupations. They worked at a time when there were primarily two positions available to urban women—manual factory work and service employment—and their occupations, unlike those in the then nascent clerical sector, did not particularly prepare them to reenter the workforce after marriage.

Lydia explained, "Mr. Curtiss gave me directions where to go, as he could not go up with me at that time, and I . . . arrived in Stratford in the evening and a hackman [the driver of a hackney, a horse-drawn carriage] took me to the house. I had a letter to give to Mrs. Curtiss [as proof of employment], and she was very much pleased to see me. I stayed with her eight months, and [we] got along nicely. Mr. Curtiss came up every Saturday evening and returned Monday morning. His family lived in New York; but he spent the Sabbath with his mother."

Once Jailer Webster convinced Lydia to talk, she spilled her life story. This woman had a remarkable memory at times, but couldn't recall the dates her husband and children died?

"After living there eight months, one day, when I went to Mr. John Fairchild's grocery store to get groceries, [Mr. Fairchild] asked me how I would like to keep house for a man who had just lost his wife. I told him that I did not know—that I had not thought of leaving . . . that I did not like to leave Mrs. Curtiss. Then I asked him who the man was, and he told me that he was an old man who lived up in Coram, in Huntington. [Mr. Fairchild] said that he thought it would be the best thing I could do to go and hire with [this old man], as he was well off and would make me a good home. I told him I would think of it. Mr. Hurlbut [the man referred to] came down to Stratford in a few days to see Mr. Fairchild."

Old man Hurlburt (as he was called) had said, "John, I think I shall sell my place."

Mr. Fairchild urged him not to. "No, Hurlburt, get some woman to keep house for you."

"Yes, but where can I get a good woman?" [To a modern woman this idle chitchat sounds more like the men are discussing where to find a good horse, but this type of language is indicative of the period, when women were considered second class citizens.]

Fairchild said, "I think I know of one. I will see."

A few days later, old man Hurlburt returned to the store and Mr. Fairchild gave him Lydia's name, along with a glowing character reference. Fairchild had no way of knowing that he'd just signed Hurlburt's death warrant.

"[Hurlburt] called at the house," Lydia told Jailer Webster, "and asked if I was the woman Mr. Fairchild spoke to him about. I told him I was, and he said that he would be down in a few days and see me again. During this time I went to see Mr. Fairchild, and have a talk with him. He told me that it would be a good place for me, and that I had better go. [The question, "Or what?" springs to mind.] I told him I would not go till I had seen the place, as he was a stranger to me."

Was Lydia ensuring her safety or casing the joint to see if seventy-three-year-old Hurlburt would be worth her time?

"When Mr. Hurlburt came down he took me up to see the place, and then we made a bargain that I should keep house for him. I did not name the price."

Knowing Hurlburt was well off, Lydia probably didn't want to underbid her services.

"Mr. Hurlburt told me he thought he had enough [money] to keep us, and if I did well by him, he would do well by me. I stayed two [more] weeks with Mrs. Curtiss, and during that time Mr. Hurlburt was down three times. Mrs. Curtiss did not like to give me up, and she told me if I did not like the place to come back to her. Mr. Hurlburt came for me and took me home with him."

Lydia was only there a few days when Hurlburt proposed marriage.

Later, she admitted, "[Hurlburt] told me that if I would marry him all that he was worth should be mine."

That's all Lydia needed to hear. The couple married on November 22, 1868.

"Everything went along happily for fourteen months. One Sunday morning we got up and were going to church. I commenced to shave [my husband], as I always shaved him two or three times a week."

Because of Hurlburt's advanced age, his hands trembled too much to use a straight razor. Halfway through the shave, Hurlburt felt off, dizzy, unsteady. Perhaps fresh air would help. While outside he could also feed the horse.

Upon his return, "I commenced to shave him again, when I saw that he felt bad, and I thought we would not go to church. [Hurlburt] had three of those dizzy times during the forenoon. I thought he was going to have a sick turn. He had two or three turns when we had been married about three months. When [my husband] had one of these bad spells he made his will, er, rather Mr. William Bennett made [out the will] for him. This happened some time before Mr. Hurlburt was taken sick the last time."

The jailer had to think: Gee, I wonder why?

"[Hurlburt] continued quite feeble but he split a little wood and said he thought he would try and work it off. He was quite anxious to do what he had to do. Monday evening [January 17, 1870] one of the neighbors gave him some clams and I cooked some [in a chowder] for supper, and after supper [Hurlburt] said he wanted a glass of cider. I told him that he had better not drink [cider] after he had been eating clams. But [Hurlburt] took a pitcher and went down the cellar and drew some [cider], and he wanted me to have some, but I told him no, and did not drink it."

There's only one reason why Lydia would be hesitant of the cider.

"[Hurlburt] said he would take some [cider] with saleratus in it [saleratus (potassium bicarbonate) is a chemical leavening agent similar to baking soda (sodium bicarbonate)], and he went into the pantry and fixed [his drink]."

Poor Hurlburt probably thought the bicarbonate would settle his stomach, but he would be oh, so, wrong. Unbeknownst to old man Hurlburt, he'd been sharing a bed with a female serial killer—one hellbent on dusting off her mourning attire.

"That night he was in great distress all night. On Tuesday morning he got up and went into the pantry, but I do not know what he took. He was in the habit of taking his bitters in the morning."

Bitters, a medicinal infusion of vegetable matter in alcohol, was a nineteenth century remedy to stave off disease. Today it's used as a digestif and/or an aromatic flavoring in some cocktails.

"He was sick all of that day," Lydia explained, "and he did not do anything."

From past behavior, we already know how Lydia felt about laziness, no matter how ill her husband might be.

> I asked him in the afternoon if he did not think he ought to have a doctor.
>
> "No," he said, he'd be better soon.
>
> That night he took another glass of cider. Whether he put anything in it or not I do not know. To my knowledge he never took anything [nefarious].

In order to cover her tracks, Lydia claimed her husband had purchased arsenic in the past from the druggist, Henry Northrop, "as he had some rats about the house." She even created a backstory for this lie, saying that Northrop's wife objected to her husband selling arsenic to Hurlburt. Thus, Lydia didn't know if any arsenic had entered the house. But if it did, perhaps the deadly poison found its way into the cider by accident.

> Mr. Hurlburt used saleratus in his cider, and I remember of having two papers that I supposed to be saleratus, but they both may not have contained it. I think so for this reason, and I should say that this happened some time before Mr. Hurlburt was taken sick—My son, John Struck, was up on a visit to my house. Mr. Hurlburt and John and myself were going out to spend an evening at Mr. Charles Tomlinson's; but before we went Mr. Hurlburt and John took a drink of liquor.

Hurlburt had offered Lydia an alcoholic beverage.

"No," she said, "I don't want any."

Rather than drink liquor, Lydia agreed to sip cider. What she failed to consider was Hurlburt's habit of adding saleratus.

"Then we started for Mr. Tomlinson's to spend the evening," she explained to Jailer Webster. "We had not got far from our house when I began to be dizzy, and I had to stand still until I got over [the spell]. We went in to Mr. Tomlinson's [where] I was taken sick with vomiting, and I became so sick that [Hurlburt and John] took me home. I was very sick for about three hours, vomiting all the time. I finally got easy and went to sleep and in the morning I felt better."

Did she drink the cider to prove it wasn't poisonous? Or was this a fictitious story for the jailer?

"On this Tuesday night [January 18] Mr. Hurlburt was very bad, and I was up with him all night. Wednesday morning, he wanted to have a doctor. Mr. Edwin Wakelee and Mr. Sidney Blakeman [Hurlburt's neighbors] came down with a team . . . they were going into the woods to get wood. I went out and asked them if they would come in, as Mr. Hurlburt wanted to see them."

One of the men, Mr. Thomas, had asked Hurlburt what was wrong.

"I am very sick."

"Would you like a doctor?"

"I would."

Thomas told Hurlburt that he (along with other friends) would take a load of wood to Birmingham (also known as Derby, Connecticut), and would send a doctor to see him.

"They went away," Lydia said, "and Mr. Thomas went to Derby and saw Dr. Phinney, but [the doctor] could not come. He said that if Mr. Hurlburt was down again, he would never get up, as he was an old man. [Thomas and the group] went to see Dr. Beardsley [the town physician], and he was not at home," nor did anyone know when to expect him back. "Then they went and got Dr. Shelton, of Huntington. He was not at home when they called, and they left word for him to come as soon as he got back."

Unfortunately for Hurlburt, Dr. Shelton had gotten tied up and didn't make it to the house till midnight.

"I told him that Mr. Hurlburt was very sick and had been looking for him all day. [Dr. Shelton] said he was very sorry, and asked Mr. Hurlburt what was the matter, and my husband said he was very sick. [Hurlburt] said he had not taken anything [other than] cider and clams. The doctor stayed with him until two o'clock that night and gave him medicine and left some with·me to give him. He said he would stay longer, but that he was up the night before and he had some patients waiting for him. I asked [the doctor] if he would come down in the morning, and he said he would before he went anywhere else."

But Hurlburt was running out of time, with wracking abdominal pains, constant vomiting, and an insatiable thirst.

"The doctor came down the next morning about ten and found Mr. Hurlburt much worse. I asked him if he thought [my husband was] dangerous, and he said he was a very sick man, and that if he had any friends, I had better send for them. The doctor said that he had done all he could for [Hurlburt], and that if I wanted another doctor, I had better send for one. I told him I did not know who to send for as I had sent for two [doctors] already and they did not come. I asked [Dr. Shelton] if he would come again, and he said [that] he would, if I wished to have him. I told him by all means to come again as soon as he could."

Hour by hour, Hurlburt inched closer to death, "and along about two o'clock he was taken with a sinking turn. Then some of the neighbors came in and [Dr. Beardsley and Dr. Kinney, the two doctors Thomas had left word for] came about five o'clock. Mr. Hurlburt died shortly after the doctor[s] came."

But why he died, Lydia claimed she had no idea. Rather than admit guilt, she feigned innocence.

"Now I wish to say that I never gave Mr. Hurlburt anything to my knowledge that would cause any sickness [whatsoever]," she told Jailer Webster. "There may have been arsenic in one of the papers that I put together, but if there was, I did not know it."

As the farm now belonged to Lydia, she remained in the house after Hurlburt's funeral.

"Shortly after, my brother and sister sent for me to come down to New Brunswick to live. They thought it would be better for me to come there with them, but I could not go, for I had my business to settle and I wanted to sell the place. About two months after my husband's death, Mr. William Thomas used to bring me my letters from Birmingham, he being one of our neighbors and I living so far from the village."

One day he asked Lydia if she could take "a little baby to board." A friend of his from Derby, Horatio N. Sherman, had just lost his wife and strapped him with a sick child. Thomas had told Lydia that Horatio asked if he knew of anyone who might be able to take care of the baby.

"When I got home," Thomas explained, "I was speaking to my wife about it, and she said that Mrs. Hurlburt [Lydia Sherman], she thought, would like it, as [the baby] would be company for her, and she wished you would take [the child]."

"I [do] not know where I could get milk from one cow, as it was necessary for the child to have it."

"Mr. Wakelee [one of Lydia's neighbors] had plenty of cows," he said. "I could get him to furnish [you] with [milk for the baby]."

"I would rather see Mr. [Horatio] Sherman myself and then I could make a bargain with him."

"[I] should be in Birmingham in a few days," said Thomas, and would send his friend down to see her.

On Sunday morning Horatio Sherman visited Lydia's farmhouse, and asked if she was old man Hurlburt's wife.

"Yes, sir."

"I am Mr. [Horatio] Sherman."

"I suppose you are the man Mr. Thomas spoke to me about."

"Yes."

"Come in, Mr. Sherman." Lydia held open the door for Horatio. "Mr. Thomas told me you wanted someone to take your babe to board."

"Yes, I got someone who expected to do it, but I have another object in view. I want to get a housekeeper, as my mother-in-law is at my house, and my daughter Ada cannot get along with her on account of the old lady being queer and finding a great deal of fault with Ada."

Horatio pressured Lydia to keep house for him, but Lydia said she wasn't sure, as she had her own house to look after and the farm to care for. But Horatio persisted, even going so far as saying he would store her belongings and pay the fee. Once again, Lydia mulled over this new proposition.

Two weeks later, Horatio showed up on her doorstep again. Lydia explained that she hadn't made up her mind yet, but Horatio said he'd be willing to marry her if she would move into his home.

Lydia told Jailer Webster, "Before I went, I thought we ought to become better acquainted, as we were both strangers to each other."

This sounded all too familiar. But unlike her previous relationships, Lydia was about to meet her match—a certified "bad boy" disguised as a proper New England gentleman.

According to Lydia, Horatio insisted, "He must have someone, as he could not have the old woman in the house, on account of her making a disturbance all the time."

For three or four weeks, Lydia didn't see hide nor hair of Horatio.

"Then he called and again asked me if I would marry him. I did not then fully give my consent."

After all, she hadn't checked out his worth.

"He told me that if I wanted to sell my place he knew a man who would buy it, and that he would bring him down. In about two weeks he came with two brothers, George and Henry Taylor. They looked at the place and liked it very much. George Taylor said he would like to have it, and I told him I would rent it to him. After this occasion Mr. [Horatio] Sherman came down quite often."

On July 1, 1870, George Taylor rented the farm and moved his family into the house. Lydia boarded with the Taylor family till July 7, when Horatio came down and asked her out for an afternoon stroll.

"[During the walk, Horatio] said he had an interest in the business where he worked," said Lydia, "of about six hundred dollars, and that he could earn from $175 to $200 a month. He also stated that he was in debt about four hundred dollars and that he had had a great deal of sickness in his family. He had lost a brother a short time before, and that it cost him over one hundred dollars a year to help his mother who had to live alone and had no one to help her but her boys. His daughter, he said, was taking lessons on the piano, so that his expenses were very heavy. He said that if he could get money to pay his debts, he thought he could get along."

Lydia admitted to the jailer that she'd fallen for his sob story. "He thanked me and said he could be a gentleman if he could get squared up once more."

The next day she went to Bridgeport, Connecticut, and withdrew the funds from the savings bank. Come nightfall, Horatio was at her door. "Up to this time he had never been to see me in the evening. He had always come in the afternoon and left before night."

The following evening Horatio traveled to the farm, only this time, he brought his daughter, Ada, and son, Nattie (Nathaniel). Lydia handed over the three hundred dollars and told him "to make good use of it and pay his debts." He said he would.

"After that when he came down, he brought one of the children with him and sometimes both. On one visit he left his daughter Ada with me, and she stayed a week. [Ada] said she would not go home again until I went with her; that the baby, Franky, was very sick, and she wanted me to go home with her, because she was afraid the baby was going to die."

But Lydia wasn't ready to make the move. Instead, she persuaded Ada to return home. A few days later, however, "Ada ran away and walked over to my place—three miles—and when her father came home at night and did not find her, he came over to my house and found her there."

The next time Horatio appeared on Lydia's doorstep she told him she was headed to New Brunswick to visit friends.

"He said he would like to go [with me] and take Ada." Lydia smoothed out the creases in her lap. "I told him I would be pleased to have him go. In a few days we all went, and Mr. [Horatio] Sherman stayed a couple of days at my brother's. Then he returned to his home and left Ada and me in New Brunswick. We stayed a few days and then we came back, and Mr. [Horatio] Sherman met us, with a hack [horse-drawn carriage], at the depot and took us to his house. The old lady [Horatio's mother-in-law, Mrs. Jones] treated me very kindly. I remained there overnight, and Mr. Sherman took me home [in the morning]."

Several days later Horatio returned, begging Lydia to return to his house to care for little Franky, as the child was very sick, and Mrs. Jones couldn't nurse him properly. Playing on her "womanly sympathies" worked. Lydia agreed.

Later that July, Horatio asked Lydia for more money. Once again, she traveled to the savings bank and withdrew another three hundred dollars.

"I remained at his house for two weeks." She eyed Jailer Webster for any reaction, but he remained stone-faced. "Then he said that as soon as Franky got a little better, he would take Ada and we would go to his sister's, in [Bridgewater,] Massachusetts, and get married."

As promised, Horatio Sherman married Lydia on September 2, 1870, even though Franky's condition never really improved.

"We stayed [in Bridgewater] about two weeks. Ada was with us, and when we left to go home . . . [Ada stayed behind] to go to school."

Ten weeks rolled by, with Lydia footing the bill for Ada's education. The young girl had only been home about a week when an argument broke out between her father and grandmother. Mrs. Jones had loaned Horatio seventy-eight dollars for a piano, which he failed to pay back.

"One day Mr. Sherman [told me] he wished Franky would die," claimed Lydia, "and that if he was dead the old woman [Mrs. Jones] would not stay another day in the house."

If one considers the lengths Horatio was willing to go to care for little Franky, including his marriage to a virtual stranger, Lydia's story didn't ring true. Soon, a throng of experts would take the stand in the hopes of lassoing the noose around the Derby Poisoner's neck, tightening the rope for each of her eleven victims, including the death of little Franky on November 15, 1870, at the tender age of about one year. But Lydia was nowhere near done with the Sherman family. Within six months, fifteen-year-old Ada and her father, Horatio, forty-seven, would follow Franky to the grave. And that detail Lydia failed to share with Jailer Webster.

3

TRIAL OF THE DERBY POISONER

After Horatio Sherman's sudden death on May 12, 1871, two of his attending physicians, Dr. Beardsley and Dr. Kinney, brought their suspicions to the district attorney. Along with disinterring Horatio from his final resting spot, the State ordered the exhumations of Ada, Franky, and old man Hurlburt. Professor Barker, the chemist who tested the organs, found toxic levels of arsenic in all four corpses.

But could the Commonwealth of Connecticut prove Lydia Sherman had administered the poison? On this point the evidence was wholly circumstantial. The defense argued the arsenic was in the house because the property was overrun with rats. The State claimed she had intentionally fed poison to Horatio, Ada, baby Franky, and old man Hurlburt.

The motive for killing old man Hurlburt wasn't difficult to reconcile. He'd bequeathed his entire estate to Lydia. But what could be the motive for murdering the Shermans? Horatio had no estate. If anything, he was drowning in debt. Folks who knew the couple said Lydia adored her new family and doted on each and every member like the perfect wife and mother.

When the police arrested Lydia, she remained "cheerful and collected," and continued this front while incarcerated, awaiting trial.

A source close to the investigation said:

It is difficult to say what the termination of the case will be. Mrs. [Lydia] Sherman will unquestionably be held to await the action of the grand jury, but whether she can be convicted on a regular trial is another question. It is the opinion of lawyers here [in New Haven] that she cannot be. It is true it has been proved beyond question that the four victims whose stomachs were examined died of poison, but there is not the slightest proof that Mrs. Sherman administered it. There is no doubt in the minds of the people that she did, but there is no legal proof of it.

In the case of Hurlburt the evidence is stronger against her than in any of the others, for the reason that she lived alone with him and was his sole attendant . . . but the lawyers say even then it will be 'an even chance' if a jury will convict on mere circumstantial evidence, and [there's] not much of that indeed. Altogether the case is a mysterious one.

Even so, the grand jury indicted Lydia Sherman on September 21, 1871, for first-degree murder.

A correspondent from the *New York World* interviewed Lydia in prison and wrote:

Mrs. Sherman had expressed entire confidence in her acquittal if she could get fair play.

One incident struck the journalist as odd, though.

She would laugh very heartily at any remark that amused her, but in the next instant a cold gloom came over her face which made one's blood turn cold. It would only last for a moment, until the conversation was resumed, when her features would assume a more agreeable expression.

The preliminary examination of Lydia Sherman brought to light some facts that dumbfounded the medical community. Even with the classic symptoms of arsenical poisoning, Dr. Shelton, who attended Hurlburt during his decline, confessed that he had suspected foul play "but held his tongue."

Then the question became: Was it conceivable to think that eleven alleged murders, seven within in a single family, were the result of a poison with such marked effects as arsenic, and that these sudden deaths continued through the years without criminal negligence on the part of the attending physician? What explanation could Dr. Shelton offer for not insisting on a postmortem when he suspected Hurlburt died of poisoning?

Newspaper reporters also seemed puzzled.

Physicians are properly sensitive about the secrets of their patients, and we are not sure but an exaggerated estimate of the sacredness of professional confidence may have induced the attendant of Hurlburt to smother his half-formed suspicions, and resolve to let the crime, if there was a crime, go unpunished. It is unnecessary to show how grossly [Dr. Shelton] was mistaken, if this really was the case. Between [the doctor] and [Hurlburt's wife, Lydia] there was no confidence. His professional honor was pledged not to her but to Hurlburt, and it required, if his patient died by unnatural means, that the crime should be exposed and punished.

Questions about how far a doctor was morally bound became a constant point of contention among the medical community, especially if the doctor was only mildly suspicious.

New England newspapers cried out for change.

[The attending physician] must consider the danger of inflicting irreparable injury upon the innocent as well as of suffering the guilty to go unwhipped.

In the case of old man Hurlburt, Dr. Shelton's hesitance to file an inquiry with the authorities might have prevented the tribulations of future victims.

What could justify his unfortunate reticence?

If nothing else, the case of Lydia Sherman pointed to a moral compass for doctors "who might be tempted to neglect their duty to the dead out of mistaken tenderness to the living." If Dr. Shelton had taken the proper steps to inquire about the death of Hurlburt, Horatio and his two children might have lived years longer. That is, if Lydia Sherman was guilty of the charges against her.

Hailed as "the most hated woman in the country," the public had already convicted Lydia Sherman by April 16, 1872, the first day of trial when the State of Connecticut had one chance to prove her guilt. Or could a hot-shot defense attorney sway the jury enough to find her innocent on the sole charge of murdering Horatio N. Sherman?

Flocks of good wholesome New Englanders poured into a New Haven courtroom to catch a glimpse of the "Derby Poisoner," the "Connecticut Borgia," the "Modern Lucretia Borgia," or "The Poison Fiend."

Dressed in a neat black alpaca dress, trimmed in silk velvet, Lydia paired her outfit with a black-and-white woolen shawl and white straw hat, accented with black velvet and a brown feathery plume. She bustled from the prisoner's box to sit beside her counsel, Mr. Waterous of New Haven and S. M. Gardener of Derby.

Draped over Lydia's face, a thin lace veil obscured her features from the wide-eyed stares of the audience, all gawking at the latest American Borgia. The accused murderess folded her black kid-gloved hands in her lap and waited for either E. K. Foster or Colonel William B. Wooster, attorneys for the State, to call their first witness. The law required two judges—one district court, one superior—to preside over homicide cases, so Superior Court Justice Park joined Judge Sanford at the bench.

At 11 a.m. State Attorney Foster rose to his feet. "The grand jury have indicted Lydia Sherman for the murder of [Horatio] Sherman, and I move the Court that she be put on trial."

Colonel Wooster asked, "Has the prisoner been put to plea?"

"She has not, I think," the state attorney admitted.

Lydia rose while the clerk read the indictment, but Waterous inter-rupted. "Is it necessary that she should stand? The indictment is rather long."

The court agreed to let the defendant rest during the reading, "but she smilingly declined," and chose to remain standing.

After the clerk read the indictment, he asked Lydia, "To this indictment what is your plea, guilty or not guilty?"

"Not guilty, sir."

Judge Sanford said, "Call the jury, Mr. Sheriff."

Right then, Lydia's sister and her husband, Mr. and Mrs. Nafey, hurried over to the dock. With a halfhearted smile, tears rolling down her face, Lydia kissed her sister's cheek and shook hands with her brother-in-law. She also gave her biological brother, Joseph Danbury, a quick peck before her family slid into the wooden bench behind the prisoner's dock.

Twelve men made up the jury: Horace Thompson, Almon P. Rowe, Dwight W. Tuttle, Eli Parmele, Ira A. Doolittle, Leonard Doolittle, Hiram Wooding, Edward N. Potter, Philo Bradley, Chauncey Williard, John Williard, and Walter Hough.

The State called Dr. Beardsley, who testified that he was the Sherman family physician and called to the house on Tuesday, May 9, 1871. "[Horatio] Sherman told me that he thought he had one of his old turns." For years, Horatio had suffered with bouts of pain. "I found his symptoms to be nausea, vomiting, parched mouth and throat, great thirst, sharp pain in stomach, racking pain in bowels, hot, dry skin, quick pulse, and some faintness. [I] was told that he had been off on a [drunken] spree of a week and came home sick."

It wasn't unusual for Horatio to flee at a moment's notice with his drinking buddies, and sometimes not return for days.

Dr. Beardsley continued. "In reply to my question why Mrs. [Lydia] Sherman gave her husband money, she said that she had some trouble with him, that he had spent $1,200 or $1,500 of her money, and that she had tried to control [Horatio] in vain. I gave [my patient] one-eighth grain morphine and one grain blue pill to be taken every two hours."

Finely dispersed mercury was the main ingredient in the blue pill also known as "blue mass." Commonly prescribed in the eighteenth and nineteenth centuries for melancholy (depression), doctors had diagnosed President Abraham Lincoln with hypochondriasis (technical term for hypochondria) and prescribed this same medication.

In the form of the blue pill, mercury acted as a potential neurotoxin, and Lincoln suffered with the neurobehavioral consequences of mercury intoxication. To his credit, and perhaps benefitting American history as a whole, Lincoln recognized the effects of mercury intoxication and stopped the medication soon after his inauguration.

"[Horatio] said he had eaten a light supper," Beardsley testified, "and had eaten nothing unusual. I gave with [the] prescriptions named some directions in regard to treatment during the night and departed."

Without prodding from the prosecution, Dr. Beardsley laid out the timeline of events as best as he remembered them. "I [next] saw him at 11 p.m., and found him no better, with symptoms same as before. I took precautions in regard to [the darkness of] night and left. On Wednesday morning [May 10, 1871], there appeared a lull in the degree of severity in symptoms; vomiting, thirst, etc., etc., were less severe. This was Wednesday, May 10th, when I prescribed cooling drinks [beverages kept in the ice box, used to help lower a fever], [a] means to obtain an evacuation [bowel movement,] and measures to relieve pain. That evening all of the symptoms were aggravated. The [bile] thrown from the stomach was dark and offensive, breath heavy, retained hardly anything on his stomach, mouth and throat very red, respiration quick, complained of faintness, constantly hawking and choking, loss of voice so that he could not speak above a whisper. I gave [Horatio] brandy and water."

Dr. Beardsley leafed through his notes. "Thursday [May 11], [Horatio] Sherman was decidedly worse, and symptoms pointed to fatal termination. Pulse imperceptible, extremities cold, cold all over, complained of being faint, burning pain in pit of stomach . . . these symptoms were not from a debauch or ordinary disease. Both Mr. and Mrs. Sherman said that nothing had been administered, save what was ordered—that is, the [brandy] sling and soothing drinks."

Since ancient times physicians trusted that alcoholic beverages had medicinal value. By the early nineteenth century, the widespread use of alcohol in medical treatments was not unusual. The rise of scientific medicine after 1850 led to changing views, and by the end of the century, the therapeutic value of alcohol became widely disputed and discredited among advanced practitioners. But it wasn't till 1916 that whiskey and brandy were removed from the list of scientifically approved medicines in *The Pharmacopeia of the United States of America.*

Even though alcohol as a prescribed medication wasn't used as much by the end of the nineteenth century, it still held an important position among the scientific community. The problem for doctors was reconciling how brandy (the most common form of medicinal alcohol) seemed to have both a stimulant and sedative effect.

Diluted alcohol had inconsistent effects on the heart rate, according to the US National Library of Medicine, but the concentrated form wasn't much better.

> When concentrated alcohol, 20 to 50 percent, is taken by the mouth the pulse during the space of a minute or two always accelerates. This is not an action peculiar to alcohol and it can be observed after the administration of any irritant such as mustard and water, or even after water alone if it is sufficiently hot.

A 50 percent alcohol solution worked as a more efficient stimulant. A brandy sling, like Dr. Beardsley had prescribed, contained brandy diluted with sugar and bitters—most likely used to sedate Horatio Sherman, thereby offsetting his more agonizing symptoms.

"Thursday morning," Dr. Beardsley testified, "in reply to a question from the deceased, I told [Horatio] that I feared he had his last sickness. He thought himself that he was going to die. I said I did not understand this intolerable thirst, vomiting, and other symptoms, and asked [Horatio] if he had taken anything [other than prescribed medications]. He said nothing except that which was ordered, and that his wife had been particular to do as directed.

"Dr. Kinney was called in consultation, and in my absence gave a recipe of [a] compound mostly of sub-nitrate of bismuth [a chemical element in the nitrogen family with properties similar to its lighter homologs, arsenic and antimony]. This was administered to [Horatio] that night, but I then expressed the opinion that nothing would save Mr. Sherman. . . . He died about eight o'clock [Friday, May 12, 1871]. There was a livid appearance of [the deceased's] skin, especially under the eyes—all leading symptoms which correspond to those originating from poisoning by arsenic."

After Horatio's death, Dr. Beardsley confirmed that he'd consulted with Dr. Kinney and they both came to the conclusion that their patient had died of arsenical poisoning. Beardsley asked Lydia for permission to conduct an autopsy on the body, and without hesitation, she agreed.

Although most female serial killers murder for money or other profit, some do it for the attention and sympathy they receive following the death of someone they cared for.

—Psychology Today

On the second day of trail, Colonel Wooster, attorney for the Commonwealth, recalled Dr. Beardsley.

"In my testimony yesterday, where I spoke of the constriction of the throat, I meant to say it produced a whisper, or, in other words, [Horatio had] lost his voice. This was on Wednesday evening—he constantly complained of it and appeared to be choking."

"Did he take anything other than [a brandy] sling by way of nourishment?"

"He took tea, bread, water, and thin gruel," explained Dr. Beardsley. "The effect on the stomach was very bland."

Colonel Wooster helped to steer the witness toward the State's theory. "In any of these, if arsenic were mixed [in], would it be perceived by the patient?"

"It would not, in an ordinary poisonous dose."

"Was [Horatio] Sherman able to sit up at any time after you [arrived at the house]?"

"He was not. [Horatio] was prostrated from the first. I did not see him out of a recumbent position. He may have had attempted to sit up."

Colonel Wooster prodded, "What was he physically?"

"[Horatio Sherman was a] man of fine physique and enduring constitution, very little impaired by his [alcohol] habits, and [I] should say a strong muscular man."

"How old?"

"About forty-five or forty-six," Beardsley guessed [Horatio was forty-seven]. "I cannot tell exactly."

"What was the condition of his mind during his illness?"

"During the whole of it, [his mind was] remarkably clear and collected. I could not see that it wandered at any time, not even in a state of dissolution."

Since the defense would undoubtedly raise the question of alcoholism, Colonel Wooster jumped in front of the argument. "What were his habits?"

"He used to have spells of drinking to excess in the last few years. Except his drinking, I know of nothing to effect his constitution."

"How frequent were the [drunken] spells?"

"Not often, to my knowledge. He would go for months without [alcohol]."

"What were his spirits—desponding?" [In other words, what was his frame of mind?]

"Rather jovial. I saw him despondent [only] when under the influence of liquor."

Which was the exact opposite of what Lydia told Jailer Webster. She preferred Horatio a little tipsy, because then he treated her with kindness. When Horatio got sober, Lydia inferred that he was verbally and emotionally abusive; in fact, by the time he became ill, the couple weren't even sharing a bed anymore.

"How did despondency manifest itself?"

"By being embarrassed and in financial matters, I believe."

Donning a horsehair periwig, with curls at the sides and tied in the back, a stiff winged collar with two white linen bands hanging down from the neck, a black waistcoat with tapered sleeves—known as a bar jacket or court waistcoat—and black trousers, Attorney Waterous, counsel for the defense, cross-examined the State's witness. "[What do you mean] by his embarrassed condition?"

"Yes, he talked about it a great deal."

Even though Dr. Beardsley never quite answered the question, Waterous moved on. "You were sent to go there on Tuesday [May 9]—by whom?"

"I think his son came after me [Horatio's eldest boy, Nelson]. The order was on the slate. I was told that [Horatio] Sherman's son was looking for me, as his father was very sick."

"[At the house] you were met by Mrs. [Lydia] Sherman?"

"Yes."

In an attempt to change the public's opinion of Lydia as the heartless monster, the image perpetuated by the newspapers, Waterous focused on his client's doting wife and mother side. "She appeared gratified at your coming?"

"Yes, we had a talk together," Dr. Beardsley agreed. "Don't recollect whether Hubbard [the landlord who lived on the other side of the duplex-type home] was there or not. My impression is, he was not. It was at the time of the first visit [Tuesday, May 9] I saw the contents of the stomach in a bowl . . . on a chair between the bed and the wall. Think my attention was not called to the contents. Mrs. [Lydia] Sherman said he had been vomiting nearly all night."

"Did [the accused] say she had saved [the bile] to let you see the horrible stuff that came off his stomach?"

"She may have said so," Dr. Beardsley flimflammed, "but I do not recollect it. [The stomach contents] was not horrible stuff. It was healthy bile more than vitiated bile. She may have said she had saved the bile. I think she did, but I will not be positive."

"How long had [the bile] been off his stomach?"

"He had just finished vomiting as I entered, I was told."

"Was there another time when your attention was called to the character of the vomiting by Mrs. [Lydia] Sherman or someone else?"

"I don't recollect."

Waterous pointed out, "[Then] Mrs. [Lydia] Sherman may have done so?"

"She may have done so."

"You testified in this case before the magistrate in Birmingham [the grand jury]?"

"I did."

"Did you there attempt to give a history of [Horatio Sherman's] sickness and what passed during it?"

"I did."

"When, after your first visit to the bedside, you had an interview with [Lydia Sherman] and asked why she gave [her husband] money to go on the [drunken] sprees, what did she say?"

Beardsley spat out Lydia's words as best as he remembered them. "I have already had trouble. He has spent from $1,200 to $1,500 of my money. I have tried but can't control him."

"Did you state that before the magistrate?"

"I did not."

A satisfied smirk hid behind Waterous's cool facade. "How long after [Horatio Sherman's] death did you testify before the magistrate? Was it a little less than two months?"

"Yes."

"How long is it now since his death?"

"Nearly a year," Beardsley admitted. "He died May 12 of last year."

"Did you tell Mrs. [Lydia] Sherman that you were going to tell [her husband] he could not have many more [drunken spells] without being taken off [the patient list]?"

"I have some faint recollection of something of the kind. I intimated to her that I would speak to [Horatio] Sherman before he recovered. We very often tell people that they will be taken off [the patient list] when we do not mean it; his habits were bad. I do not recollect that I made her a promise to talk with him on the subject."

"Did [Lydia Sherman] not say at that interview that [Horatio] had not been on that [drunken] spree with her money?"

"No," Beardsley said, indignant. "I do not recollect that such [a] declaration was made by her."

"You were there daily during his illness?"

"Yes, sometimes twice a day. I promised [Mrs. Sherman] Tuesday at two o'clock p.m. [that] I would return early in the evening of that day, but did not get around early, although somebody came for me."

Waterous's next question showed Lydia had no real motive to kill her husband, because Horatio owned no property, and she wasn't financially dependent on him. "Mrs. Sherman was attentive and devoted to [Horatio's] welfare, was she not?"

"As far as I could see, she was."

"Did you prescribe tea, bread, water and gruel?"

"She asked me if a little tea would hurt him," Beardsley clarified. "I ordered bread, water and gruel, and either prescribed or concurred in the use of tea."

A true professional in the courtroom, Waterous ignored the splitting of hairs. "You first prescribed morphine and blue pill?"

"Yes."

"What else [did you prescribe] during his illness?"

"A weak solution of ipecac with an aromatic to allay purging. The purgative pill was mostly aloes and rhubarb and one grain of the extract of mandrake. The blue pill is mostly mercury, it is a mild form of mercury; don't recollect the exact ingredients."

Then Waterous hinted at theories that stabbed at the heart of his defense. "What quantity of arsenic is sufficient to produce death?"

"From three to five grains. There are instances where two and [a] half grains caused death."

"What was the composition of the morphine?"

"It is the essence of opium," Beardsley explained. "I gave him also blue mass."

"What is blue mass?"

"It is blue pill."

Waterous reviewed the testimony for the jury. "These are all you prescribed—morphine, blue pill, ipecacuanha, slings, bread, water and tea?"

"Yes, sir."

"Arsenic is not a cumulative poison, is it?"

"In some cases it is."

"If a person took a quantity [of arsenic] one week, insufficient to produce death," Waterous hypothesized, "another dose a week later, do you say it would produce death?"

"I'd not. Arsenic, if rubbed upon the surface of the body, will find its way to the liver and stomach. It will also find its way there if inhaled in the air."

Exactly. Waterous must've smiled inside. "Are there not cases of poisoning caused by persons sleeping in rooms papered with green [wall]paper?"

"There are cases where they have been affected, but not killed."

Arsenic was everywhere in the Victorian period, according to the Smithsonian, "from food coloring to baby carriages. But the vivid floral wallpapers were at the center of a consumer controversy about what made something safe" to have in one's home. The root of the problem stemmed from the color green, which Swedish chemist Carl Scheele invented by mixing in copper arsenate. The result was a bright green called "Scheele's green" which became the in-color. Copper arsenate, however, contained arsenic, and many people died from inhaling toxic fumes.

Waterous set out to disprove the doctor's last statement. "Have persons not been poisoned from eating colored confectionery?"

"I am not aware of cases."

"Does arsenic enter into the coloring of confectionery and toys?"

"Yes."

"What did you mean when you asked [Horatio] Sherman if he had not been taking something?"

"I wanted to get at the cause. Thursday morning [May 11] I had my suspicions that he might have swallowed something deleterious and destructive to life."

Lydia tugged on Waterous's robe, and he bent down to confer with his client. Straightening, he asked the witness, "You say there was a lull on Thursday morning in the symptoms. Did you attribute it to the medicine?"

"I did—at least I hoped it had."

"Is it not common in cases of arsenical poison that the symptoms fluctuate—that they are more severe at one time than another?"

"Yes."

"So that it is not necessary to repeat the doses to cause these fluctuations?"

"It is not necessary to repeat them."

Waterous hinted at another possible reason for the chemist finding arsenic. "Where was the body from death until Saturday when the postmortem was held?"

"It was in the front room where he died. After that I do not know where it was or in whose charge. I took no part in making the incisions; but I assisted in tying [up the stomach] and packing it."

"Did you examine the cloth wrapper around the stomach to see if there was anything on it?"

"I did not. But had there been I would have observed it. I first saw the wrapper in the room. Dr. Kinney brought the cloth there, I understood."

Waterous continued to hint at different theories but focused on contamination. "Did you examine the jar in which the stomach was put, with a view to see if it was clean?"

"I did."

"With a view of seeing if it was clean?"

"Yes."

"Was there a tinge of green in the jar?"

"I don't recollect. I think it was not."

"Did you see the jar washed?"

"No."

"And you never had the custody of it?"

"No, sir."

At length, Waterous cross-examined Dr. Beardsley as to how he packed the liver after its removal from the body. "Had you the custody of the box [with the liver] at any time?"

"No, sir, not after I left the room. What became of [the box that held the liver] after Dr. Kinney took it away, I know not."

Waterous told Justice Park and Judge Sanford that he had no further questions for this witness. The court excused Dr. Beardsley from the stand. Even though it looked like the top-notch defense attorney had won this round, his not-so-subtle insinuations would soon work against him.

4

FORENSICS OF
YESTERYEAR

The fact that no modern forensic equipment existed in the nineteenth century made no difference to chemists. Thus, determining the precise poison(s) from human tissue became a tedious, arduous task that required dozens of hours, intense concentration, and a hefty dose of patience. Many of the following toxicological tests are still valid today.

The esteemed George Frederick Barker obtained the liver and stomach of Horatio Sherman and old man Hurlburt. As a professor of physiological chemistry and toxicology at Yale University, with past employment as a chemistry assistant at Harvard Medical, and professor of chemistry and geology at Wheaton College, Professor Barker was more than qualified to test for toxins.

With Horatio's stomach and liver, Barker "finely divided" the organ and placed the pieces in an evaporating dish (laboratory glassware used for the evaporation of solutions and sometimes—as was the case here—to their melting point). Adding twice its bulk of distilled water, strongly acidulated with pure hydrochloric acid and a few grams of potassium chloride, Professor Barker "gently heated" the mixture.

Three to eight hours later, the organic matter was destroyed, leaving behind a clear yellow liquid. The professor filtered the clear yellow liquid with heat until a chlorine odor rose from the dish.

With a slow stream of washed hydrogen sulfide gas, Barker let the liquid stand for twelve to sixteen hours. He then washed out the chlorine with a water bath, "thoroughly oxidized with pure nitric acid, then heated with pure sulfuric acid until completely charred."

Fumes of acid encircled the chemist's head.

After cooling, Professor Barker treated the material with various chemicals to obtain a fused mass. The increase of weight represented the amount of arsenious sulfide, from which the quantity of white arsenic could be measured.

Arsenic is an element that naturally occurs in rocks and soil, water, air, plants, and animals (fish and shellfish contain the highest concentrations of arsenic, but the proportion of inorganic arsenic is very low, below 1 percent). Volcanic activity and forest fires are both natural sources that release arsenic into the environment. This elemental compound can be classified into three major groups: inorganic, organic, and arsine gas. Inorganic arsenic is generally more toxic than organic arsenic, so there's no need to pass up a juicy Maine lobster, New Englanders!

Forms of arsenic more rapidly absorbed by the body are more toxic, while those most rapidly eliminated tend to be less toxic. Nineteenth century women applied arsenic powder to whiten their faces and to their hair and scalp to destroy vermin. It was also believed that arsenic consumption gave a woman's complexion a "beauty and freshness." What they failed to recognize was that arsenic damaged the capillaries of their skin. Hence the rosy cheeks.

Cosmetics continued to include arsenic well into the early twentieth century, resulting in a common source of accidental poisoning.

Professor Barker tested a second portion of the residue with cupric sulfate, ammoniated. The sulfate gave a green precipitate of copper arsenate.

The residue in the capsule was then divided into two portions, one of which was treated with pure sodium carbonate in excess, carefully and thoroughly dried and mixed with ten times its weight of a well-dried mixture composed of one-part potassium cyanide and three-parts pure sodium carbonate. [Portions of this mixture were] heated in bulbs blown on the ends of tubes of hard glass.

From this, Barker obtained brilliant mirrors of metallic arsenic, with a strong garlic odor.

On sealing one of these tubes and heating the deposit within, the chemist found it "to be readily volatile, condensing, if sufficient air be present, in brilliant transparent crystals easily identified as octahedrons of arsenious oxide." Professor Barker also tested other portions of the mixture by the "method of Fresenius and Babo, i.e., placed in tubes of hard glass drawn out at the end, through which a slow stream of carbonic gas was passing, and heated to redness."

Brilliant black mirrors of metallic arsenic glimmered in the burning glow of an oil lamp, which afforded, on oxidation, brilliant octahedral crystals of arsenious oxide. The second part of the above solution was divided into two equal parts—one of which was tested by the method of Reinsch.

Named for Hugo Reinsch in 1809, the Reinsch test detected the presence of arsenic, antimony, and mercury by heating a strip of pure copper foil with the testing material in a test tube to produce sublimate deposited in the upper part of the tube.

Another test practiced by Professor Barker was the Marsh test. Developed by an English chemist named James Marsh and first published in 1836, this forensic toxicology test was so sensitive that it could detect minute amounts of arsenic in foods or stomach contents.

In case the question arose in court, Barker tested the purity of his chemicals and equipment by "submitting a piece of beef's liver about the same size as the piece of human liver . . . using the same materials and the same vessels. No trace of arsenic could be found by this means. The materials must therefore have been pure, and vessels employed [were] clean."

The quantity of white arsenic obtained from six to two-thirds ounces of Horatio Sherman's liver equaled 0.485 grain, corresponding to nearly five grains for the whole liver. From eight ounces of the liver of old man Hurlburt, Professor Barker obtained 0.929 grain, which meant the whole liver contained seven to eight grains of arsenic—more than enough to produce death. Two-thirds of Hurlburt's stomach contained 4.75 grains of white arsenic which equaled 6.33 grains for the entire stomach. A lethal dose for an average-size adult is 0.145 grain, or less than one-eighth of a teaspoon.

These tests became the basis for Lydia Sherman's arrest and subsequent trial.

5

THE PROSECUTION'S CASE

Horatio's son Nelson "Nellie" Sherman was the first family member called to the witness stand. The prosecution asked him to tell the jury how he was related to the victim, to describe the living arrangements within the home, and what he witnessed in the days leading up to his father's death. "I am twenty-one years old and live in Boonton, New Jersey," Nellie testified. "[I] have lived there since the 25th of last May [1871], and previously . . . resided with my father in Birmingham up to the time of his death. My father, brother, sister, myself and prisoner, and the servant girl were the occupants of the house. [My] father was taken sick on Monday evening [May 8] before his death. He left home on Wednesday, the second week previous, and did not return until Friday of the week before he died, so he was absent one week and two days. While Father was in New Haven I did not know where he was. On the day he returned I told the prisoner I thought I had better look for Father. She said it was useless, as I might not find him when I got to New Haven."

State Attorney Foster continued to allow Horatio's brokenhearted son to tell his story. The court transcript showed the following narrative:

I had to urge [Lydia] several times before she would give me the money to come to New Haven. She finally gave me the money, and I came down on the 9:15 train. [I] came to the Park House to find [my father, but he wasn't there, so I] proceeded to the depot. Stood there some time, as it was raining, walked toward the west end of the depot, and while looking out of the door [my father] and another gentleman came along. I took [my father aside] and asked where he had been. I walked around with him till half-past four or five p.m. [We] went to the Park House, leaving the horse and carriage at the depot. He had a horse and wagon . . . all the time he was in the city.

We went home in the evening, arriving at the Union House, Derby, about ten minutes after seven. He got out of the wagon and entered the hotel [but] he refused to go home with me right away. [So,] I left him and started for home. [My father] took dinner with me on the day of his return, in this city [New Haven]. He was perfectly sober on that day. When I arrived home, I asked the prisoner if he had been home, and [Lydia] said he came about nine o'clock that night, or an hour before I arrived. I had been home to supper after leaving father and had gone out and remained downtown until about ten.

When I returned home the prisoner told me he was in bed. Father remained in the house on Saturday [May 6], and did not go to his work during the day. I think I saw him at his meals on that day but am not positive. [Father] seemed to have as good an appetite as usual on Friday [May 5]. On Sunday [May 7] he remained home until after three p.m., when we dined. I saw nothing unusual in his manner that day. On Monday [May 8] he was at work. His business was a tack-maker (tending machines and keeping the machines in repair) . . . in the employ of E. L. Shelton, where he had been for twenty years.

On Monday morning before he got up, [I] went to the factory about eleven o'clock. He asked me to go up and tell Lydia (the prisoner) to send down his dinner. I ate my dinner, and [Lydia] prepared [Father's] dinner. I took up the shad [a type of fish] and handed it to her, and [Lydia] prepared the rest of the meal, which was put in a small basket. I took the dinner to the factory [and] left it with [my father]. On returning [Father] said he had eaten all but two or three crullers, that he would eat [the rest] by and by.

I remained about the village till supper time, partook of supper and went out without seeing [my father], as he was not yet home. At that time, [the] prisoner, my brother [Nattie], and the [servant] girl were present. Don't know who proposed the supper. [The] next time [I] saw [my father was] about half-past seven that evening [Monday, May 8] at the drug store on the corner, where there was an outdoor auction. He was reclining against the box of a tree. He turned around and left, and I saw nothing of him until I got home about nine o'clock in the evening.

I inquired of [the] prisoner if he was in, and she told me he was sick, that he had been vomiting. I went to the door and spoke to [Father], and he also told me he had been vomiting. I said no more, [then] went to bed. [The] next morning (Tuesday) he requested me to go for the doctor. This was between seven and eight [a.m.]. I went for Dr. Beardsley, who was absent, but I found him at the drug store, and told him my father wanted him to come to the house. I did not return until dinner time. I then inquired how [Father] felt, and he replied, 'very bad.' I then returned down street, and did not go home until supper time.

On Thursday [May 11] I was at home and remained in the sitting room with [my father's] mother (Mrs. Sherman), and the prisoner (Lydia) told me he had had a spasm. They both requested me to go after Dr. Beardsley; he was not in. I returned and told both women that he had left. Old Mrs. Sherman requested me to call Dr. Kinney as soon as possible. I found [Kinney] absent and returned and reported to them that I had left orders for him (Kinney) to come the moment he came back.

"Dr. Kinney came about dusk to the house," Nellie said on the stand, "think Beardsley had been there before. The prisoner and servant were there in the kitchen. Old Mrs. Sherman asked Dr. Kinney the cause of [my father's] sickness, and he replied that he was a very sick man, but I do not remember that he stated the cause of the illness. Friday morning [May 12], he died."

Colonel Wooster asked Nellie, "Who had the care of him?"

"The prisoner had sole care of him in that sickness until Thursday noon, when Mrs. Sherman, his mother, arrived."

"And after that, who?"

"They both assisted in his care."

"Did your grandmother prepare anything for him?"

"Not to my knowledge."

Waterous stood to cross-examine the witness, but it backfired on him. When questioned, Nellie said his father's spasms were very unusual, that he had never known his father to experience any type of convulsions. Nellie then explained how his father and Lydia didn't share a bed anymore, "owing to some trouble."

Next, the State called Dr. Kinney to the stand. As a practicing physician for nineteen years, Dr. Kinney lived a half-mile from the Shermans' residence and had known Horatio for eighteen or nineteen years.

"I saw [Horatio] Sherman first on the 11th of May, the night before he died," Dr. Kinney testified. "He was suffering from intense thirst, constant nausea, pain in the region of the stomach, with occasionally a tendency to go to stool. The vital parts appeared very much depressed, the extremities cold. He had difficult and peculiar respiration, and [I] could detect no pulse at the wrist. [I] asked [Horatio] how long he had been sick, and he told me since the previous Monday. [I also] learned from him that he had worked as usual, and that after supper he was taken with pains in the head and vomiting."

Colonel Wooster asked the doctor to go into more detail about Horatio's symptoms during the final days of his life.

"I understood that those symptoms had continued up to the time I saw him, except the headache. The vomiting, nausea and purging had continued; the purging had been slight. There had been no copious discharges, it was more of a disposition to go to stool. [I] inquired particularly of [Horatio] Sherman if he had enjoyed his usual health up to the time he came home to supper, and he said he had. I was unable to account for his symptoms, except on the supposition that he had received some irritable poison. He had the symptoms of no disease with which I was familiar. The friends asked me what his disease was. Mrs. [Lydia] Sherman and Mrs. Hubbard [the landlord's wife] asked me . . . [but] I declined to give an opinion, saying that I wished to consult with Dr. Beardsley before giving an opinion, [and then] went 'round to the doctor's house. Think I went twice and did not find him [but I] was anxious to find [Dr. Beardsley] to consult with regard to the fact of poisoning."

After about an hour of looking for Dr. Beardsley to no avail, Dr. Kinney returned to Horatio's bedside. And it was there that he accepted the fact that he could not save his life. The doctor left a prescription to alleviate pain, then returned home and "saw nothing more of the case." But he did get a chance to question Horatio. He asked if he'd been drinking heavily in recent days.

"He said he had drunk some but not excessively," Dr. Kinney confirmed. "[I] asked him if his appetite was good, and he said it was. [I] asked if his stomach had been deranged, and he said it had not. [I] asked if he had bilious trouble, and he said he had not. [Therefore, I concluded] he had been in perfect health up to the time of the attack."

Dr. Kinney had also asked Lydia about Horatio's health and she told him Horatio "had been on a debauch [drunken spree] and that she expected it would kill him."

The doctor testified that Horatio's voice was husky, and he could hardly speak above a whisper. "It was a peculiar voice, and I hardly know how to describe it. [The patient] complained of sore throat and intense burning in the throat. The respiration was irregular, accompanied by constant sighing. . . . [Lydia] told me Dr. Beardsley gave him medicine, but did not state what it was. She said she had given him brandy and water and some tea. My opinion at the time was that [Horatio] was dying from arsenic [because] I could not explain his symptoms by any known disease."

When the prosecution asked about the postmortem examination, he said, "I found Dr. Beardsley the next morning, and it was agreed to hold a postmortem. The result was I went over and saw Dr. Shelton. After we arrived at the house, Dr. Shelton, Dr. Beardsley, and I found the body laid out in the parlor. We exposed it. There was nothing peculiar about [the corpse's] appearance. I made an application to the prisoner to make a postmortem and said the case was peculiar. She made no objection. [Even Lydia] said it was peculiar and she would like to have it done."

The three doctors removed the stomach and liver and wrapped the organs in cloth. The stomach contents went into a jar and the liver into a wooden box.

"The prisoner was not aware that we took away a part of the body," Dr. Kinney admitted. "The cloth was new and clean. The jar was a new glass jar that never had been used. The box was a wooden one about sixteen inches long, twelve inches wide, and eight high, and furnished with a lock and key. [I] think it was clean. After taking out the parts of the body I drove directly to New Haven and gave [the organs] to Professor Barker, who removed them from the box while I was there."

During the cross-examination, Attorney Waterous asked Dr. Kinney if he'd told Lydia the cause of her husband's death.

"Not much but inflammation of the stomach," Kinney admitted. "She asked me if it was the result of drink [alcohol], and I said perhaps so. I intended to evade the question. Don't recollect that I said the inflammation might have been caused by a cold."

Waterous acted "pettishly" when he inquired about the postmortem details, narrowing in on the box used to transport the liver.

"The box had not had medicine in it for four years." Dr. Kinney seemed appalled by insinuation that he would use an unclean vessel to house an organ. "It had been standing in my garret."

No amount of outrage could rattle the hot-shot defense attorney. "What symptoms did you observe in [Horatio] Sherman on Thursday that you never had seen in a sick person before?"

"The respiration—it was peculiar. Had never seen such before. It had a tendency to syncope. [I] had seen irregular respiration before, and sinking [dying] before, but not such peculiar irregularity. [I] cannot describe it. It was the difference and the combination of symptoms."

Waterous objected to the phrase "combined symptoms," and "desired to speak of each symptom by itself." He first asked the doctor to describe the sighing.

"There was no difference in cases seen before [except] there was more sighing . . . it was very variable; cannot describe the peculiarity of the sighing."

"What other symptoms did you observe that you had not seen in other cases?"

"It was not one symptom but the combination of symptoms."

Rather than re-object, Waterous grimaced. "I don't want you to argue the case. I don't inquire about the combination of symptoms."

"Excuse me, sir. I did not know I was arguing the case." Dr. Kinney took a minute to regroup. "Purging is one of the symptoms of poisoning, also vomiting. Never had a case of arsenical poisoning in my practice before. As I understood the case from the attendant [Dr. Beardsley] there had been a disposition to go to stool and little evacuation. He told this, [and so did Lydia] Sherman. If there was no purging, then there would have been one of the symptoms absent upon which is based the opinion that the case was one of poisoning."

Moving on, Waterous asked what prescriptions the doctor prescribed.

"I gave subnitrate of bismuth, hydrocyanic acid, and mucilage."

Waterous cocked an eyebrow. "Doesn't bismuth contain arsenic?"

"Some English bismuth has arsenic in it [but I] did not see the prescription myself."

The court adjourned till 9:10 a.m. on Thursday.

Waterous's defense was nothing short of genius. Bismuth poisoning occurred when ingested as a nitrate. As little as one ounce could be fatal. Symptoms included gastrointestinal upset, vomiting and diarrhea, headache, body and bone aches, confusion, disorientation, irritability, black stools, stupor, coma, convulsions, psychosis, and death.

Conversely, bismuth subsalicylate—the main ingredient in Pepto-Bismol—is relatively safe because this form of bismuth is insoluble in water. Although, bismuth poisoning and allergic reactions can still occur, especially in people who are allergic to aspirin due to their similar structural properties.

Like other heavy metals, elemental bismuth occurs naturally, though its effect on the environment remains unknown and is still being researched today.

A simple and reliable way to test for bismuth poisoning is a modified Reinsch test, but the chemist would never test for a medicine that a doctor prescribed.

"While for many serial killers death is only a conclusion to their fantasy or a function of it, females kill to kill. It is their mode of expression."
—Peter Vronsky,
author of Female Serial Killers

On Thursday, April 18, 1872, Horatio's mother, Mrs. Sherman, took the stand. As one journalist noted, "This bright-looking old lady was ready to tell her story faster than lawyers or judges could take it down."

Anxious to express her opinions, Mrs. Sherman broke up the monotony of the court proceeding by not taking any bull from the prosecution or the defense.

"I was only at the house of the prisoner at the funeral of my granddaughter Addie [her pet name for Ada Sherman], in January 1871, and at the sickness of my son [Horatio]," she testified. "I first saw the prisoner at the funeral [for Ada]. She told me that if things did not go differently she should leave my son, as she had money and friends. She made this remark without provocation on my part. I did not see the accused or my son until about 11:30 a.m. [on Thursday, May 11] the day before he died. [Horatio] was very glad to see me, and the relations between himself and wife appeared friendly. He was much distressed in [the] stomach and his throat smarted badly. His voice was very husky."

Without prompting from the prosecution, Mrs. Sherman added, "The prisoner gave him all of the medicines."

Colonel Wooster asked, "What were the medicines?"

"I knew nothing about them, and was not told. I knew the doctor ordered some brandy for him . . . but I did not give it to him. [I] thought there was a very peculiar effect upon [Horatio] after drinking a cup of tea."

"What was the peculiar effect of the tea?"

"[My son] put his hand on his stomach and said, 'Oh my God, my stomach,' and fainted away. [Then] he said, 'Fanny.'"

Colonel Wooster urged Mrs. Sherman to clarify. "You speak of fainting. Did he faint entirely away?"

"He did, and when he came to, he said, 'I never expected to see you, my dear,' and I said the same, and then I made the remark—"

Waterous jolted to his feet. "Was Mrs. [Lydia] Sherman there?"

"Yes, she was there. I made the remark that it was strange that the tea should make his stomach smart so after taking brandy. I thought it was a very strange sensation."

"Was there any reply made to that, ma'am?"

"I don't remember that there was. Had not seen him take brandy before he took [the] tea, that I remember."

The slick defense attorney wasn't finished with his follow-up. "How did you know that brandy did not have such an effect?"

"Because [Lydia] said she had given him brandy, and there was no such spells."

Not allowing the defense to muddy the testimony with innuendos, Colonel Wooster regained control of the State's witness. "What time did your son die?"

"I think it was a little before eight o'clock, Friday morning."

"Who took care of him that night?"

"The prisoner did."

The State fished for a motive behind the murder. "If anything occurred after your arrival about money between yourself, the prisoner and Nellie, will you please state it?"

"I was in the room with my son alone, standing by his bedside. He said to me, 'Mother, hand me my wallet in my pants' pocket,' and I did so. I had some trouble in getting it, because the pants were so high, and just as I got it, I heard the prisoner's step on the stairs in the basement, and I knew by the way [Horatio] asked for [his wallet] that he did not want her to know of it."

In case the jury missed the point, Colonel Wooster urged the witness to slow down. "State what first took place."

"He looked around the room and said, 'Where is my wife?' I said, 'She is in the basement.'"

"That is the first he said?"

"That is the first."

"What then?"

"He said, 'Hand me my pocketbook, Mother, in my pants' pocket.'"

"What did you do?"

"I threw [the wallet on the] bed, and he put it under his pillow."

"Well, you skipped a portion."

"Well," Mrs. Sherman said, indignant, "I am telling the truth, ain't I?"

Cringing, Colonel Wooster cleared his throat. "Now then, what was the next step you took?"

"I took [the wallet] and threw it to him, and he put it under his pillow."

"How did you get it?"

"I had to go to the foot of the bed, and pull away a portable sink, which made a considerable noise and trouble, and I succeeded in getting the pocketbook, and threw it to him."

"Why did you throw it?"

"Because I heard the prisoner on the stairs, and I knew by the way he asked for it he did not want her to know. The pants were at the foot of the bed where my son lay—on a hook on the wall. [I] had to remove the sink because there was not room."

"Did the prisoner immediately come into the room?"

"She did."

"What did your son do with the pocketbook while she was there, or before she came in?"

"He put it under the pillow before she came in."

"How near was she in?"

"Pretty near. He had just time to get back to his pillow before she got in [the bedroom]."

"Was there anything said after she came in?"

"My son asked for a knife."

"What did the prisoner say?"

"Don't recollect that she said anything," replied Mrs. Sherman. "The knife was not there. I was standing at the foot of the bed, near where the pantaloons were. I examined the pantaloons for the knife. Nothing further was said about the knife. [I] told him there was a key there, and he said, 'Hand me my keys.' [Lydia] did not remain [in the bedroom] a great while—not half an hour."

"What followed after she left the room?"

"As soon as he discovered she was gone, he said, 'Mother, take this money and give it to Nellie . . . and tell him to take it and make good use of it.' I said, 'I will.'"

The implication that Lydia could also be a thief added to the State's case. Colonel Wooster probably had to hide his excitement. We know he enjoyed Mrs. Sherman testimony by his desire to compel her to continue. "If he said more, state it."

"A short time after, I had an opportunity to give it to the boy [Nellie], and I said to him, 'Tell your father that you have received this package of money, and it will be all right.' I was in the room with my son a while afterward, and I told him I had given Nellie the money, and he said, 'Very well.'"

"What followed in reference to that money after death?"

"The next day after death, on Saturday [May 13], the prisoner was in the sitting room and she said, 'Mother, you have that money of [Horatio's]?' I replied, 'No, I have not.' She asked me about it, and I told her I gave it to the boy, and she said it was very strange, for [Horatio] had told her she should have it. She said that [Horatio had given] it to me to give to her. I told her I might be mistaken, but I did not think [so]. . . . [Lydia] seemed rather surly toward me for some reason or other."

Colonel Wooster pushed for more details. "What else took place in reference to the money?"

"Nothing more took place between her and me, except that [Lydia] called for the money [from] the boy, and I advised [Nellie] to give it to her rather than have trouble. . . . [Nellie] did not say much of anything. [Lydia] said she needed [the money] very much indeed to pay her bills, and that she had no money short of Bridgeport [Lydia kept her inheritance from Hurlburt in a Bridgeport bank]. . . . [My grandson] told her that he needed [the money] very much indeed."

Lydia looked over the wad of cash and handed Nellie five dollars.

"Don't know how much money there was," Mrs. Sherman admitted, "but my grandson told me there was $105. [Nellie] gave her the pocketbook with the money. [I] was sitting on the day of my son's death in the sitting room with the prisoner when—"

Waterous rose again. "The testimony from the ruling up to this point came in under the exception taken. I object to all of it."

"Overruled."

"The prisoner said to me, 'I had about made up my mind to leave [Horatio], but as things have turned out I am very glad I did not.' I remarked to her that I was very glad she did not. There was no conversation to me when the subject of divorce was alluded to. There was no other conversation, except one before he died. I made the remark, 'The room was very damp. I would not have thought you would have slept here,' and she said, 'Oh, I haven't slept here for several weeks. [Horatio] and Nattie [Horatio's younger son, Nathanial] slept here.'"

Waterous bombarded her with questions until Mrs. Sherman admitted she'd arrived in Birmingham on Thursday [May 11] after receiving a telegram from her grandson.

"When you arrived, you met the prisoner first?"

Mrs. Sherman snarled. "Of course, I met her first."

"Do you remember, after the greetings were over, of telling [Lydia about] a remark you made to your [other] son in Brooklyn [New York] before you left [the city]?"

"I do not. Please repeat it."

"This is in substance." Waterous thumbed through his notes. "'I said to my son on receiving the dispatch, I know that [Horatio] will not get well, for he has had several of these spells, and one of them will take him off.' I think that is nearly it."

"I think I did [say that]. I was present when something was said about who should have the future care of Nattie. [That] could not have been more

151

than a half an hour before my son died. Mr. Hubbard was present . . . the second time it was repeated."

To prove Horatio trusted Lydia, Waterous asked, "To whose custody did [Horatio] commit the care of the boy Nattie in your presence?"

"To the care of the prisoner."

"Do you remember what he said?"

"I do. He said, 'I want you to promise before God and man that you will protect this dear boy of mine,' and she said, 'I will.' He repeated it twice over, at my request, the second time Mr. Hubbard [the neighbor/landlord] was present. I called him in from an adjoining room to hear it repeated."

"Had your son any property at that time, except the $105?"

"I could not tell you. I don't know anything about it."

"Why did you request [Horatio] to repeat the injunction to his wife?"

"Because I wanted another witness."

Waterous pointed out, "That was about the last act of his life, was it [not]?"

"Yes, sir."

"Was his mind clear then?"

"Very."

"Do you know what Mrs. [Lydia] Sherman was doing in the kitchen when you got the pocketbook?"

"No, sir. She made no inquiry about the noise I made."

"Had [Nellie] the money on his person [when Lydia inquired about it]?"

"Yes, sir, I think he had."

"Did he not say, 'It is upstairs, I will go up and get it'?"

"I cannot say," Mrs. Sherman admitted. "It had been in a box upstairs, and he had showed it to me. I do not know whether [Nellie] had it on his person or not, or whether he went upstairs after it. [I] don't remember. It was in the pocketbook when he showed it to me."

"Did he not go upstairs and get the bills and bring them down, and lay them on the table?"

"There were only two bills."

"Did he not bring them down and lay them on the table?"

"I think he did."

"Did you then inquire of [your grandson] what he had done with the other seven bills?"

"I don't think I did. He said he had counted the bills, and said he thought his father must have been mistaken as there was but $105."

Moving on, Waterous attacked other statements made by Mrs. Sherman. "I understand that [your son] drank some tea and immediately fainted?"

"Yes, sir, he did."

"What was done with the tea left in the cup?"

"I do not know anything about it."

"Do you not know that the cup was placed on a chair?"

"No, sir, I do not. Nothing was said about its being hot."

"Did not this occur?" Waterous leafed through his file. "When [your son] took a swallow and began to be faint, did not his wife put the tea down on a chair, and after he came to, did not Mrs. [Lydia] Sherman say, 'What is the matter, [Horatio], is it too hot?' and then taste it and say, 'No, it is not'?"

"[I] do not recollect any such remarks."

"You will not swear that she did not taste it at that time?"

"No, sir, I will not. I was in the room when he took the tea, standing near him. [I] was not as near to him as his wife was [and I] did not see the tea administered to him at any other time. [I] saw medicine given to him, but did not know what it was."

"When was it you saw him faint after taking tea?"

"It was at that time when I saw him take the tea, and he said, 'Oh my God, my stomach! How it smarts!'"

Not allowing the mother's drama to overshadow his defense, Waterous droned, "I suppose you will go on till you find a place to stop." It became obvious to Waterous that Mrs. Sherman did not like being put in her place. "Now, then, when was [this]?"

"It was Friday morning, between seven and eight o'clock. He died about eight. [I] did not sit up with him [Thursday] night. Mr. Hubbard was there at the request of my son. I arose [on Friday] between six and seven [a.m.]."

"Did you hear [your son] when he said that morning—in the presence of his wife and Mr. Hubbard, and perhaps Mrs. Hubbard— 'Why don't I die? I ought to'?"

"No, sir, [I] never heard any such expression."

Waterous thanked the old woman for her time and told the court he had no further questions.

George Peck, a druggist in Birmingham for eight years, testified that Lydia had come into the store to buy arsenic, saying her house was overrun with rats. But Peck remained vague on the details.

"I cannot fix the time definitely," he said, "but it was in the warm spring days of 1871, perhaps several weeks before the sickness. I do not generally weigh [arsenic] as I dislike it in the scales. I poured out three-quarters or one ounce, tied it up and gave it to [the prisoner]. I remember the time, not exactly, but it was after the warm days had come, and the store doors were open. When [Horatio] Sherman's death occurred, I remembered that but a little."

In fact, it was Lydia who reminded Mr. Peck that she'd been in the store.

Peck admitted, "I think Nattie, the little boy, a bright child, was with her, when she purchased [the arsenic]. [Lydia Sherman] remarked that they were overrun with rats, and she inquired, what was [the] best way to kill them? I mentioned exterminators and may have suggested that arsenic was as good and cheaper. I think she may have said that she did not like to have [poison] around. I do not remember whether I gave her any instructions, but often do."

Professor George Barker was the State's last expert witness. He testified to the tests he'd performed on the liver and stomach.

Colonel Wooster asked, "Is metallic arsenic poisonous?"

"There is yet a question to be settled whether metallic arsenic is poisonous. The general principle is, that no metal in itself is poisonous." The professor seemed to contradict his own testimony by adding, "Yellow and white arsenic are both poisonous, the white arsenic more poisonous than the yellow." But arsenic falls in the category of a metalloid or semi-metal.

"Have you the means of telling the quantity of arsenic in the stomach you analyzed?"

"The tissue of the stomach contained no arsenic. The contents contained an amount which, though I did not weigh it, I estimated—"

From his table, Waterous objected to a guess.

Professor George Barker, who discovered the poison used by Lydia Sherman
Courtesy of University of Pennsylvania Libraries

"Objection overruled."

Professor Barker continued. "Judging from the bulk obtained from the stomach, the quantity present must have been about a tenth of a grain."

"Will you tell how long it takes arsenic to find its way to the liver?"

"White arsenic taken into the stomach is removed therefrom by absorption, and as it has not been detected in either the lymph or the chyle [a milky substance that drains from the small intestine into the lymphatic system during digestion], therefore this absorption must take place by the blood. [Arsenic] has been detected in the urine within one hour after it had been taken. The liver acquires its maximum quantity, in the opinion of several authorities, from fifteen to eighteen hours after administration."

"Does it pass off from the liver, or does it remain once [it's] there?"

"It is eliminated from the liver and may entirely disappear from eight to fifteen days after being taken, depending on the quantity and other circumstances."

"What is the maximum quantity [of arsenic] the liver will contain in an adult?"

"I have no opinion on that subject. I think the maximum quantity . . . is the quantity I found in this present case."

Colonel Wooster asked the chemist for an approximate timeline. "From the quantity found in the liver, how long must it have been taken before death?"

"I believe at least fifteen hours. How much longer I cannot say."

"From your examination do you think that more was given than you found, supposing the arsenic to have been administered five days before death?"

"If there was vomiting or purging, portions of arsenic taken Monday night would have been removed before death on Friday. Of the quantity absorbed a considerable portion might have been eliminated during the five days by the kidneys. However, arsenic is distributed through the entire body, and the analysis of a single organ or two does not discover the arsenic elsewhere contained. For both of these reasons the amount obtained cannot have been the whole amount taken. It must be less."

Professor Barker faced the jury and explained how arsenic worked in layman's terms. "When arsenic is taken more rapidly than it is absorbed or eliminated, then it may be considered accumulation in the same sense as apple pie if taken faster than it is secreted. If by cumulative is meant a substance which enters into a combination with other tissues, so far as to form a compound less readily removed than the original substance, then arsenic is not a cumulative poison. The arsenic found in the stomach may have been, in my opinion, either the last traces of a very large quantity taken on Monday night, or the residue of a smaller quantity taken subsequently, which I cannot tell, but the latter appears to me the more probable."

The audience remained silent while some of the men on the jury leaned in as though riveted by the chemist's testimony.

"The first effect of arsenic is local." The esteemed Professor Barker exuded respect, his posture erect, his gaze never leaving the jurors. "It is classified as an irritant and not a corrosive poison; that is, it inflames the parts without destroying them or perforating them. The local effects first produced cause local symptoms. These appear generally within an hour after the poison has been swallowed. They are burning pains in the stomach which, as the poison passes down, extends along the intestinal tract it increases in severity and is accompanied by a great thirst, dryness and constriction of the throat, vomiting and purging. By this time, more or less of the poison has become absorbed. It enters the blood and produces a second class of symptoms called remote, the action being apparent upon the blood corpuscles and blood vessels.

"These symptoms are characterized by great prostration of strength, anxiety and depression of mind, a peculiar lividity of the face, the blue line under the eye, the intellect being as yet unaffected and the mind clear. Death may ensue at this stage on the action due to prostration, usually taking place under these circumstances from one to eight days. If life be continued, the effect of arsenic will be apparent upon the nervous system and brain, stupor passing into profound coma will develop itself, in case the action is primarily upon the brain or delirium and convulsions, passing into chronic spasms, in case the spinal cord is also involved, may precede death. All of these symptoms may not be present. The patient may recover from all these symptoms, which may be called primary, and may die from the secondary effects of the poison years afterwards."

No one in the courtroom could've wondered why the Commonwealth had saved Professor Barker for their final expert.

To wrap up their case, State Attorney Foster said, "Will you state how arsenic passes from the stomach to the liver?"

"White arsenic, when taken in the stomach, is dissolved in the stomach and intestines by gastric and intestinal juices," explained Barker. "Spread out upon the posterior surface of these intestines is a set of blood vessels which compose what is known as the portal system. The arsenic passes into these blood vessels through their walls. These vessels unite them to form the large trunk, as the portal vein which empties itself directly into the liver, so that this organ is not more fully supplied with blood than any other, but it is supplied with blood charged with arsenic from the intestines. Hence the liver is more likely to contain poison than any other organ. It passes from the liver into the general circulation, thus producing its remote effects. It does its fatal work most probably upon the blood itself, disintegrating the blood corpuscle, thus rendering the blood unfit to perform its functions."

Sometimes the simplest of questions could result in the greatest impact. State Attorney Foster obviously agreed. "What quantity of arsenic would be fatal in an adult?"

"From two and a half to two grains. A less quantity has been fatal, and more has been taken without producing death."

We know from the chemist's tests that he found nearly five grains of arsenic in Horatio's liver—more than twice the amount necessary to cause death.

"When persons die from the secondary effects, would arsenic be found if the parts were analyzed?"

"No, sir. I think not. Persons have died in eight days from the primary effects and no traces of the poison have been found on analysis."

"Assuming the testimony of Drs. Beardsley and Kinney to be true, in connection with the analysis, what, in your opinion, was the cause of death [for] Horatio Sherman?"

"Assuming the stomach and liver I analyzed to be those of Sherman, my opinion, in view of the symptoms stated, is that he died from the effects of a [lethal] dose of arsenic."

The professor went on to testify that Dr. Kinney had tested the bismuth and found no arsenic in it. Barker had also analyzed the bismuth found in the stomach of the deceased and found it to be pure bismuth. Then he mentioned the effects of arsenic on the lungs, heart, and bowels, and explained how pain followed from the various organs as poison progressed from the throat to the intestines. How faintness could occur, purging might also happen in some cases, and convulsions are exceptional, as was delirium.

But when cross-examined by Waterous, the chemist admitted he'd never witnessed a person die by arsenical poisoning, nor had he seen a patient under the influence of arsenic and had no experience as a medical practitioner. Barker had learned the symptoms he'd described from books and testimony of experts in other cases. The professor began his testing on November 6 and finished with Horatio's stomach on November 23, 1871.

When asked where he'd stored Horatio's organs, Barker said, "The liver was delivered to me [and] was in my laboratory from May 13th to November 6th, hidden behind some bottles in a sealed jar in a cupboard, and the cupboard was locked, and the laboratory was locked, and no one had a key but myself and the janitor. I completed the first analysis about the first of July. Students and persons in general are not allowed in the room. [I] told the janitor that the cupboard door was not to be opened by him or anyone else."

Waterous pressed the chemist hard on whether he was told to look for arsenic or if he'd conducted a blind test. Professor Barker admitted he'd been told the doctors suspected arsenical poisoning, but he didn't conduct tests to search for that specific poison. Rather, he tested for any metallic poison. As a damn fine defense attorney, Waterous haggled over the details. How could he not look for arsenic when Horatio's doctors pointed to that poison as the murder weapon? When the chemist stood firm, Waterous asked if any of the testing chemicals contained arsenic.

Professor Barker insisted he'd "used eleven chemicals [with] no means of telling their weight—water, hydrochloric acid, potassium chloride, hydrogen sulphide, nitric acid, sulphuric acid, ammonia, ammonia sulphate, sodium nitrate, sodium carbonate, sulphurous acid."

Previous use of the nitric acid showed that it did not contain arsenic, though it did "sometimes contain arsenic," he admitted. "That is not true of sulphuric acid."

To satisfy Attorney Waterous, the professor detailed how he'd arrived at the percentages of poison in the liver and stomach. At this point, one of the jurors, Mr. Jonathan Williard, felt faint and had to be removed from the courtroom. The court recessed for a few minutes to give Mr. Williard time to recover. When he didn't return, the justices sent a doctor to the jury room. Eventually, Mr. Williard returned to the jury box but still looked peaked from the testimony.

Professor Barker continued, "Chemists in the Wharton trial [referenced in the opening of Lydia's story] did not differ totally as to the existence of antimony in the body, but they differed as to whether the amount was sufficient to cause death. It is not uncommon to find arsenic in bismuth. My treatise does say that arsenic is found in bismuth, and it is sometimes."

Medical/legal book in hand, Waterous read an account of a man who took two drachms of bismuth by mistake, had burning and purging, and died within nine days. "Do you believe that [Professor Barker]?"

The chemist jutted out an opened palm. "Let me see the book." After perusing the details of the case, he said, "I do not believe it. It has been contradicted."

"Do you know whether arsenic enters into the combination of the beverages sold over the bar nowadays?"

"[I] do not know that. [I] know that certain coloring matter in beverages have been said to produce bad effects, something like arsenic. It is maintained by some toxicologists that arsenic will reach the liver if brought in contact with the body. After a sufficient lapse of time, arsenic applied externally will reach the liver. It is a fact that some solution applied to the head has poison, called Fowler's Solution. [I] have known one recorded case of a person dying by inhaling poison in a [green] papered room. [I've] seen recorded cases of two grains of arsenic causing death, and one case where two and half grains did it."

With regard to Horatio Sherman, Professor Barker "could not tell how long the arsenic had been in the liver. [Also] could not tell from the arsenic how long it had been in the stomach, or whether it had been put in there an hour before [death]."

Professor Barker admitted he'd preformed toxicology tests on several cases—in some he found arsenic, in others he did not. If Horatio swallowed poison on the Friday before his death, he would've been symptomatic before Monday, May 8. He also testified that he knew of only two recorded cases of death by nitrate of bismuth—in the first case, a reinvestigation proved the doctors hadn't prescribed bismuth; in the second case, Barker didn't believe the chemist's findings. Two leading authorities in their field, Wormley and Otto, didn't list bismuth as a poison, he said, and that was good enough for him.

6

UNHAPPY WIFE EQUALS END OF LIFE

The prosecution called Horatio's brother, George A. Sherman, to the witness stand. After the usual "state your name, address, and relation to the deceased," George said he last saw his brother on April 22, roughly three weeks before he died. But for a period of time George had lived with Horatio and Lydia, and it was that testimony—a peek behind the marital veil—the State planned to spotlight as a possible motive for murder.

Colonel Wooster asked, "What were the relations of the prisoner to the deceased as to kindness while you were there?"

"I noticed the first time I went there that they did not live happily together."

"State what you saw or heard."

"I heard [my brother and Lydia] talk angrily at each other several times, and hard words were used. It was in the basement where it occurred, at the [kitchen] table. I do not know what the words were. They were so disagreeable to me that I got up and left . . . I [even] heard loud words after I got upstairs. I mean, louder words than usual . . . [I] remember another occasion when they had angry words . . . [on Sunday, April 16]. I heard [my brother] tell her, she might take what things she brought and leave, or go, I forget the exact word. She replied, 'Very well.'"

Colonel Wooster could hardly contain his glee. "Will you state what you know about them not sleeping together?"

"During my last stay there [Lydia] called my attention to the fact that they did not occupy the same bed and asked me if I knew."

"Did she assign a reason for it?"

"When she first called my attention to [their sleeping arrangements], I judge, from what she said, that she wanted Nattie to sleep upstairs rather than sleep three in a bed, and my brother would not let [the boy] sleep away from him. [Lydia] said once that while unwell, she lay [on top of the covers] with her clothes on, and that my brother came into the room to go to bed. When he saw her, he reached over and got Nattie and carried him upstairs. [Lydia] slept downstairs that night."

"During the time you were there, do you know whether [Horatio] or the prisoner slept upstairs?"

"It is my impression that once in coming downstairs I called at an upstairs room and asked [Lydia] how she was. She complained a great deal about [my brother], that when she was unwell that my brother did not ask how she was. I remember on one occasion when she was talking about [Horatio], she said she had rather have him come home after he had been drinking, because he saluted her much more pleasantly."

Waterous interrupted. "You mean that she had rather have him come in drunk than sober?"

"Yes, sir. Not that she meant intoxicated, but after he had been drinking some."

"What [did you mean by] saluting?"

"[Lydia] said that at such times he called her Tiddie. I remember another time when she said that he treated her the worst when he was the soberest, and she did not see through it."

With Attorney Waterous satisfied, Colonel Wooster resumed his questioning of the State's witness. "Do you know what Mrs. Sherman's feeling was toward her husband about their going into society?"

"The remark was something like this. She was speaking about [Horatio] not taking her into society. [Lydia] said she knew that he did not love her, and did not respect her, and that he was ashamed to be seen on the street with her. [She and I] were in the sitting room alone when she said she supposed he was with other women. She talked twice that I remember about divorce, then she talked about who to get, and talking about the different lawyers. The occasion occurred in the sitting room. She said she didn't like to get a divorce on account of what people would say, as she had been told about [Horatio's womanizing ways]."

Waterous rose to ask for clarification. "[Told about other women] before she married him?"

"That is what I inferred from the remark."

Colonel Wooster led the witness toward another possible motive. "Anything else occur to you, anything about money?"

"On one occasion I recollect of her telling how much she let him have previous to the marriage, about $800, that she had [spent] about $1,800 [on the family, not including the initial eight hundred dollars]. The remark then was that she would not have had him at all if she had not let him have so much money. About a week before I went away for the last time before his death, my brother did not speak to the accused, only when he could not help it, and sometimes he did not pass her food at the table, [yet] did pass [the platter] to all others. This is what I observed. It occurred several times during that week."

"Do you know anything about the prisoner inducing the deceased to join the temperance society?"

George nodded yes. "He joined the temperance division the night I did. Mr. Hubbard came in and asked my brother if he would go down, and he said, 'No.' Don't remember that the accused said anything except to endorse what Mr. Hubbard said, 'You had better go,' or something like that. He finally [joined]."

The temperance society was a social movement against the consumption of alcohol. Members criticized alcohol intoxication by emphasizing its negative health risks, while promoting alcohol education and demanding a ban. These societal efforts led to Prohibition in the United States from 1920–1933. As a hardcore drinker, it's easy to see why Horatio wasn't thrilled with the idea of joining.

Colonel Wooster asked, "How soon were you there after your brother's death?"

"[I] came there on the 13th of May. He was buried on Sunday, the 14th."

"State if at any time while you were there [the prisoner] gave you any statement about [Horatio's] sickness and death."

163

"[Lydia] said that [my brother] came home from work, and he had eaten some fish that she had warmed up in the oven, that he drank some chocolate, one cup I think, and she remarked that he did not drink as much as usual, [which was odd since] he was very fond of it. After supper he went out into the yard and smoked awhile, and finally came to the door and asked if he should not get some spinach. [Lydia told me] that she [had] never seen him so pleasant before, and he had been so [nice] ever since he got back [from work].

"At that time she went on to tell [me] about how he used to order provisions; said he usually went down [the street] and ordered such things as he wanted, [then] sent them up, and that was the first she knew what they were going to have [for dinner]. [But that night,] he came back from down [the] street in about half an hour, and reported to her that he couldn't find any spinach, and that he came in and sat down on the sofa, leaned his head on his hand and said he did not see what made him feel so funny. Then [Lydia] went on to describe what occurred that night, I do not recollect it [other than] he got up and went into the yard and came in, and said he had been vomiting, and then went out again and came in, and said he had been vomiting again, and that it seemed to him that he had got[ten] rid of his supper and dinner too."

Knowing the public and jury craved juicy details, Colonel Wooster allowed George to ramble a bit longer.

"On another occasion she said that the day Barnum's show was there . . . she cleared the windows so that he could look out and see [the traveling circus], and that she propped him up so he could look out. . . . Once he was determined to get up . . . he got his feet and legs out [but] he fell back, and said he guessed he wouldn't get up [after all]."

Born in Bethel, Connecticut, Phineas Taylor Barnum first took his circus on the road in 1871 and passed right by the Sherman residence. At that time, it was called P. T. Barnum's Grand Traveling Museum, Menagerie, Caravan & Hippodrome, a traveling circus, menagerie, and museum of "freaks" which adopted many names over the years.

Colonel Wooster asked George Sherman, "What was said about a cup of tea?"

"Of her own accord [Lydia] said she thought a strong cup of tea would be good, and that she gave it to him."

"Did you hear anything said about arsenic?"

"I did," George confirmed. "I remember being near the cellar door, and of hearing my brother ask her where the arsenic was. She says to him, 'I have taken it, and taken care of it.' This was, I believe, during my first visit. The conversation was something about rats; heard someone say that they had tried [using arsenic] once on bread and butter."

As a slick defense attorney, Waterous couldn't wait to discredit the State's witness, evident by how quickly he leaped from his seat. "Nellie [Horatio's eldest son, Nelson] was at this time setting a trap in the cellar. Did [you] not hear [my client] say, 'The rats, I guess, have carried it off, paper and all.'"

"When I heard the angry conversation, I did not leave the table until I had finished my supper. Do not recollect anything that was said. The angry words on the 16th of April might have been about going to church; cannot say that she went to church Sunday afternoon. [I do] know that she went sometimes. [My brother] did not go that I know of. The prisoner said, 'I wish you would go to church sometimes,' and he might have made an angry reply."

"Except [for] those occasions, was not Mrs. [Lydia] Sherman a kind and considerate wife to your brother?"

"I cannot say that I saw much out of the way."

Referencing George's conversations around the time of his brother's death, before the prosecution tainted his memory, Waterous showed his determination to defend Lydia Sherman to the best of his ability. "Except these occasions, is it not true that Mrs. [Lydia] Sherman treated her husband kindly and with due respect, and have you not said so before and after his death?"

Resolute, George never flinched. "I have not said anything to perfectly endorse her. Except these occasions, [I] do not find that she acted very bad toward him. I don't consider that she did."

"Did you ever talk with Mrs. Hubbard about Mrs. Sherman?"

"I did after my brother's death."

"Did you not say that Mrs. Sherman was a jewel of a woman?"

George jolted to his feet. "Never!"

The outburst didn't faze Waterous. "And that she was not half appreciated there?"

"Never."

"And that there was not one woman in a thousand that would come there and do as she did?"

"I might have said that there was not many women that would come there and do as she did. I might have used the language without the word 'thousand.' I think I did not say it. I went on to tell Mrs. Hubbard what she did do, and said I thought she had done right [by my brother]."

"If you did not say a 'thousand,' how many women did you have in your mind?"

Laughter erupted in the audience.

"My impression is I did not use [that word]. I would not carry it up as high as that."

On a role Waterous next recalled Dr. Beardsley, who stated the prescription left by Dr. Kinney was composed of hydrocyanic acid dilute, one drachm's of subnitrate of bismuth, pulverized gum Arabic (a natural gum made of hardened sap from two species of the acacia tree), one ounce water and one ounce simple syrup, rubbed together, and that the dosage "was left blank for me to direct. I directed [the patient] to take a teaspoonful once in two hours if it would stay on his stomach."

After some back and forth about how many doses Horatio was able to keep down, the doctor explained that Horatio swallowed two doses, which equaled five grains of nitrate of bismuth and two drops of diluted hydrocyanic acid.

"The acid in the strong state is not used," said Dr. Beardsley. "In the United States [we use a] diluted [mixture] which has two drops of the strong [per] a hundred of the diluted. The preparation used [in this case] was the diluted [form]."

"Could there be any danger of death from poison from that prescription?"

"No, sir, not even if he took it all at one dose."

"How long would it take to feel a dose of arsenic?"

"From half an hour to three hours. I have seen the effect come on in less than half an hour in a case I had." The doctor confirmed that Horatio's symptoms matched arsenical poisoning.

Waterous played it cool. "Is the first vomit in such cases offensive?"

"My experience is that the subsequent vomit is more offensive than the first. In the case of Mr. Brock, the case I alluded to, the vomit was very offensive the second day." Beardsley admitted that he hadn't examined Horatio's bile on Friday morning and didn't notice it the night before.

"How do you know then that hydrocyanic acid was used?"

"I do not. I only give you the prescription. The presumption is—"

Lip curled, Waterous snarled at the witness. "Never mind the presumption, doctor. We can all guess. You do not know that the subnitrate of bismuth was not supplanted by arsenic?"

"I did not examine it. I could not have told by looking at it."

"If in the place of the five grains of bismuth there were five grains of arsenic, it would have caused death, would it not?"

"I think it would." The doctor smirked. "But he had the symptoms of death before he took that prescription."

"Is subnitrate of bismuth a poison?"

"I do not consider it a poison. . . . The case given has been contradicted, and it was proved that the dose was a precipitate of mercury. . . . Bismuth might be considered a poison only in the sense that a jackknife would be if it was swallowed . . . so might yellow earth and gravel. Taylor gives a case of poisoning by bismuth [with which] Wharton [is] one."

"Two," Waterous corrected, referencing the medical book authored by the toxicologist named Taylor.

"[I] would not give much for Taylor's opinion. . . . [Although,] bismuth does sometimes contain arsenic."

Waterous controlled his satisfied grin. "Did George Sherman ever find fault with you for having a postmortem?"

"Yes. He had a conversation with me. Cannot say that he found fault, but I might have inferred from his manner that he [did]. He said persons who took [another] person's liver [without permission] were liable to prosecution."

Attorney Foster rose from the prosecution's table. "If arsenic had been substituted for the two teaspoonfuls of bismuth, would it have caused death?"

"It would, for the man was nearly dead. He was almost *in articulo mortis* [at the point of death]."

Colonel Wooster interjected, "How large [of a] dose of bismuth have you given?"

"I have given a drachm [sixty grains or one-eighth of an ounce], and I consider it as harmless as chalk."

To regain control of the witness, Waterous said, "[In that case,] did the patient survive?"

"Yes, sir. He got well."

"How much arsenic is there in bismuth?"

"It is at the rate of less than half a thousandth of a grain."

"Have you not heard of cases where there was thirty percent of arsenic [in bismuth]?"

"I have not."

Once Waterous finished his cross-examination, Colonel Wooster told the court, "This closes our case for the State."

7

IN DEFENSE OF
LYDIA SHERMAN

Waterous called four witnesses, who testified that Lydia had doted on Horatio and his children. Then he called Mr. Lewis D. Hubbard, landlord, neighbor, and friend of the Shermans. Hubbard said he first knew of Horatio's sickness on Tuesday, May 9, when he saw Lydia carrying a bowl of vomit into the backyard. That day, Lydia showed him the bile.

"The appearance of the matter was dark," Hubbard testified, "and it had a very offensive smell. I made the remark at the time that it smelled like beer, and that I thought [Horatio] would soon be better." Hubbard visited Horatio on Wednesday, May 10. "I was called by him, and I think Mrs. [Lydia] Sherman came for me. When I went into his room, he shook hands with me and said, 'Mr. Hubbard, I feel as though I'm going to die. Are my dues paid in the lodge?' Meaning, the Knights of Pythias."

Hubbard reassured Horatio and offered him a receipt. He then asked if he wanted watchers from the lodge.

"Don't know that he made a reply, but he referred me to his wife. [I] asked her if she needed any assistance, and she told me she probably should. About ten o'clock I called again and asked [Horatio] how he felt. He said he felt more easy. [On] Thursday night about six o'clock, [Horatio's] appearance was worse, and he told me he thought he could not live long, and he wanted to have me stay. . . . He vomited during the evening. . . . I was up with him that night, also the old lady, Mrs. Sherman, and his wife . . .

[Lydia] principally waited on him. He preferred to have her mix the brandy slings, because she understood it. I was there when he died."

Waterous prodded, "Was there anything said about the little boy, Nattie, before Mr. Sherman's death?"

"About three o'clock the morning before he died, he expressed a wish . . . he said, 'You understand this matter, Lydia. We talked this matter over yesterday. What's in the house is yours. I want you to promise that you will take care of Nattie and bring him up.' I started to leave the room, and the old lady, Mrs. Sherman, called me back and said, 'I wish you to hear what Mr. Sherman said,' and I told her I did."

"State what the conduct of Mrs. [Lydia] Sherman was toward her husband during his sickness, so far as you observed."

"I saw nothing different from what is seen between any man and wife under the same circumstances. She manifested a great deal of feeling for him all the time during his sickness."

"Did Mr. Sherman say anything as to what he had eaten?"

"On Thursday night . . . I asked him what he had been eating or drinking to make him so sick. He said he had eaten very little except, I think he stated, lobster."

"To what did he attribute the cause of sickness, if anything?"

State Attorney Foster objected. "Leading."

"Overruled."

Without missing a beat, Waterous continued. "To what did he attribute the cause of his sickness?

"Don't think he said anything to me."

"What were his habits in regard to the use of liquor?"

"He had spells of drinking, probably to excess. Aside from that he was very attentive to his business when he was not off on these spells."

Hinting at an alternate cause of death, Waterous asked, "How frequent were these spells?"

"During the last few years he might have had them once a month, and then once in three months, not oftener than once a month. . . . On Saturday [May 5, I] had a talk with him. . . . The well was cleaned that day because a rat had got into it. Do not know of any rats being poisoned except those

I poisoned myself. I remember the prisoner bringing the slop pail with a rat in it and showing it to me. Think it was on Sunday [May 6], when Mr. Sherman was absent."

A discussion ensued between the attorneys about the effect of arsenic on well water, which the prosecution turned into: Who poisoned the rat that ran into the well?

State Attorney Foster said, "It is admitted that Mr. Hubbard did not poison the rat."

Sarcasm laced Waterous's tone when he replied, "Well then, we will put that down as admitted."

Hubbard offered more proof of rats. "In the fall of 1870, I purchased potatoes, and they were nearly destroyed by rats. Told [Horatio] to look at his [potatoes], and he found them in the same condition, and said, 'I can't stand this. I must get some poison.'"

State Attorney Foster cross-examined the witness, but the testimony consisted of repeating earlier testimony, until Hubbard added one crucial detail for the defense.

"On Thursday evening [May 11, Horatio] seemed low. He had pain, his voice was hoarse, he vomited, but only a little matter came up. I went that night for Dr. Beardsley, and I went to the drug store and got a prescription and some brandy. Gave him some of the prescription, and he vomited it up in about ten minutes. He took it only once, for he said it burned his stomach. When I gave it to him, he said, 'Oh, my God, my stomach. I don't want to take any more of that.' Dr. Kinney's prescription was the first one that stayed on his stomach . . . except brandy."

Foster asked, "Why did you ask [Horatio] what he had eaten?"

"Because after he had those sprees, he was not usually sick. . . . [This time,] he seemed so different."

The court adjourned until 2 p.m., when Waterous called Horatio's drinking buddy, Ichabod Allen, to the stand. Ichabod had known Horatio for fifteen or sixteen years and saw him the Sunday before he died.

"Between ten and eleven o'clock, [I] saw him part of the time in Captain Healey's saloon. While there the party [of men] had three or four drinks, and [Horatio] . . . walked with me to my gate, and we talked awhile [before] I left. . . . Should not say the man was intoxicated, and I should not say he was sober. He appeared to have been drinking some. He seemed despondent. The general run of his conversation was the [bar patrons] had tried to kill him [or] injure him, and that he would show them that he would yet come out [on] top of the heap and beat them all. [I] have often heard him talk that way."

"What have been his habits as to the use of liquor?" inquired Waterous.

"Oh, he used to have his sprees pretty often."

"What was his state of mind when he came out of them?"

"Never saw him when he was coming out of them; saw him in them."

"What was his state of mind in them?"

"Sometimes he was despondent and sometimes not."

"Did you ever hear him say, within a few years, that he had as lief be dead as not?"

The question made Ichabod squirm. "I should not like to say that."

"State what is your impression."

"I don't recollect anything about [his happiness]. He has talked so much [about people trying to kill him] that I didn't pay attention to it."

"Did you ever tell anybody . . . ?"

Foster blurted out, "What, [now you're] going to contradict your own witness?"

Ignoring the outburst, Waterous explained, "What we want, Mr. Allen, is your best impression."

"My impression is that when some parties [Dr. Beardsley and an associate, Dr. Hotchkiss] were talking I [repeated what Horatio had said] . . . but I told the party I could not swear to it. I don't want to give it in evidence. I have an impression that he [talked about death threats], for he used to say it a great deal."

This interaction between Allen and the two doctors occurred at the Bassett House, a pub in Derby, Connecticut. "When [Horatio] was sober he was reserved. When intoxicated it set his tongue going, but he was not always good natured. I kept a saloon there myself and he used to trouble me a good deal. . . . Guess they were ten cents a drink all round. Think he drank spirits . . . [even] pop once. He called for [more] drinks . . . a pony glass of ale, [and] I told him that I guessed no one was trying to beat him any worse than he was himself, and that if he would keep to work and be steady he [would] get along well enough. Mr. Gardener [Waterous's second chair] came to me and asked about this matter."

"We rest," Waterous said, "if the Court pleases."

Foster proposed to include evidence from other cases which had already been ruled inadmissible. The defense claimed Horatio's poisoning was accidental—an arsenic-filled rat in the well water—or he died by his own hand. In Waterous's view, the State hadn't proven their case.

The Court asked if the State had any other evidence. Foster said no.

Waterous said, "Then it is understood that the evidence is closed?"

Foster agreed. "It is, I believe."

After closing arguments, Judge Park spent fifty minutes charging the jury, with a strong plea for the State. "But," he said, "Connecticut statute requires at least two witnesses before you can convict of murder in the first degree, therefore, you must find the prisoner guilty of murder in the second degree."

The jurors deliberated for less than an hour. When they returned, a hush fell over the courtroom as Lydia stood before the twelve men who would decide her fate.

Justice Park said, "Gentlemen of the jury, have you agreed upon a verdict?"

"We have," replied the foreman, who then turned toward Lydia. "We find the accused guilty of murder in the second degree."

Lydia raised the back of her hand to her forehead and collapsed in her seat. Soon after, she was chatting with friends as though nothing had transpired. Had she been acquitted, a Middlesex County sheriff was standing by to arrest her for Hurlburt's murder.

"A vast crowd" blocked the street as Jailer Webster escorted her to the coach. Lydia "stepped into the open buggy, which whirled her off to jail," according to eyewitnesses.

In her cell Lydia fell "into a swoon, recovering from which she indulged in a long spell of weeping, expressing her disappointment over the result of the hearing."

Even though sentencing was not yet imposed, Lydia foresaw her future, evident by her actions the following winter.

8

CRISIS OF CONSCIENCE

Alone in her cell, Lydia penned a full confession that began with the murder of her first husband, Edward Struck.

[Sergeant Mc—] advised me to put [Edward] out of the way, as he would never be of any good to me or to himself again. I asked [the sergeant] what he meant, and he told me to get a certain quantity of arsenic, and he told me how much to give him, and where to get it. I thought of it for a few days . . . [but Edward] was getting worse and worse. . . . Finally I went to Harlem and purchased [arsenic] at a druggist's, and paid ten cents. . . . I came home and made some oatmeal gruel, and put in about half a thimble full of arsenic, and stirred it in well. Then I gave it to my husband to drink, and he drank of it several times during the afternoon. He was then taken sick with purging.

Edward died May 26, 1864.

It was May this occurred, and I continued to keep house. I had nothing to live upon, and I became discouraged. The children could do nothing for me or for themselves. The 1st of July [1864] I moved into another house in the village. I had two little children, Martha Ann, six years old, and Edward [Jr.], four years old. I thought that I could not get along and support them, and I came to the conclusion that it would be better for them if they were out of the way. I was much discouraged and downhearted.

Every time Lydia became "discouraged" or "downhearted" someone close to her died.

I gave [the children] only a little [arsenic] at a time, and after I gave it to them, I was afraid they would die, and I sent for Dr. Oviatt. When he came, he told me that they had gastric fever, and he doctored them for a few days. Then I sent for Dr. Jackson. He told me that they were very sick, and he thought they would not live. Next morning Martha Ann died. She was taken with vomiting soon after I gave her the arsenic. . . . The doctors said nothing to indicate that they knew what was the matter.

[Four-year-old] Edward was affected in the same manner. He was sick at the stomach and vomited frequently. In the evening Edward died. He was a beautiful boy and did not complain during his illness. He was very patient. The afternoon before he died my stepdaughter, Gertrude Thompson, came in to see the children, and she spoke to him.

'Eddy, why, are you sick?'

He said, 'Yes.'

'You will get better,' Gertrude assured him.

'No, I shall never get well.'

The doctors had no suspicions in this case either.

Lydia had the nerve to gloat after murdering two of her children on the same day, July 5, 1864.

I continued to keep house and had with me four children at the time. I got work by nursing and sewing. At this time my son, George Whitfield, was fourteen years old. He was employed [as a painter] . . . and was able to earn $2.50 a week.

175

In the latter part of the Summer, I think in August [1864], he was taken sick, and I sent for Dr. Oviatt. He called to see him, and said he was sick with the painter's colic, and he could not work at the painting business any longer. He did not improve, and as he was continually growing worse, I got discouraged. I thought he would become a burden upon me, and I mixed up some arsenic in his tea.

Her callousness had reached an all-new high.

I think he died the next day. He was afflicted like the others, but during all the time the doctor thought he had the painter's colic, and that he died of it. I gave him the arsenic because I was discouraged. I know now that that is not much of an excuse, but I felt so much trouble that I did not think about that [at the time].

After the burial of George, I went to [Dr.] Oviatt's, and he recommended me to places to do nursing, and I went out to this work all the time. I left Ann Eliza home part of the time, and Lydia [her namesake] at home a portion of the time. She was at work in a dry goods store in Harlem . . . at this time eighteen years old. She boarded with me, and it was so far for her to walk that she could not stand it and gave it up. Then she got a situation to do work on bonnet frames sent from New York, and we worked at home together.

A young man named John Smith kept company with [my daughter] Lydia at this time and called upon her quite often. My little daughter, Ann Eliza, was with me, and I thought if I could get rid of her that Lydia and myself could make a living. This was in March [1866]. I do not remember the date. We had had a hard Winter. I had no one to leave her with. I was discouraged. She had been unwell with chills and fever and was continually sick from time to time. I was downhearted and much discouraged. I had some of the arsenic in the house I purchased in Harlem, and I got some medicine for her at the druggist's and mixed some of the arsenic in it and gave it to her. I think I gave it to her twice. She was taken sick as the others . . . [for] four days. I sent for Dr. Rosenstein, and he attended her. He said she had a fever. [But] died about noon [March 9].

As if it made a difference, Lydia claimed, "[Ann Eliza] was the happiest child I ever saw. . . . The arsenic I used at all these times was part of what I got at Harlem for my husband [Edward Struck]."
Lydia swore she did not murder her namesake, Lydia Struck.

I never gave this daughter anything except what the doctor ordered me to. She died a natural death.

This coldhearted murderess also claimed not to poison old man Hurlburt, though she admitted in her confession, "there may have been arsenic in the saleratus which he put in his cider, but if there was, I did not know it."
Even with her past history, Lydia still said Horatio wanted baby Franky "shuffled off the mortal coil." But the court testimony contradicted this point in her confession. For Horatio to plead with his wife to care for young Nattie after his death, in this author's opinion, showed a father who loved his children.

I was full of trouble, and, not knowing what to do, I was tempted to give him (Franky) something to get him out of the way, for I thought he would be better off. They had arsenic in the house. The old lady [Franky's grandmother, Mrs. Jones] had used it before to poison rats with. I put some of it in some milk, and only gave it to [Franky] once. He, being quite feeble [less than a year old!], began to be sick at the stomach and to vomit.

Dr. Beardsley was sent for, and when he came he said he had never thought the child [was] out of danger, although he was better. This was in the forenoon. [Dr. Beardsley] gave [Franky] something to settle his stomach and came again in the evening and found him sinking very fast. He said he could not live much longer. [Franky] died that night, about eleven o'clock. This was on November 15, 1870.

Odd that she recalled the exact date Franky died but not when most of her biological children took their last breath. Lydia soon learned a valuable lesson.

> Instead of making matters any better everything grew worse. The old lady [Mrs. Jones] said she was going to leave, but that she would not do so until she had received the money due on the piano. [Horatio] Sherman said he did not have it, but that as soon as he got it, he would pay her.
>
> The old lady and Mr. Sherman jawed so much that the neighbors heard them. [Horatio] went upstairs, and I went up and asked him what the trouble was. He said the old lady was 'mussy' about the piano. I told him she must have the money, as I could not live [this way]. About this time Henry Tayler bought my place for $1,100, and paid $300 down, and I gave Mr. Sherman $100 and told him to pay her. He paid her and left.
>
> Mr. [Horatio] Sherman was drinking all the time and was not doing any work, and I supported the family for about six months. During this time the old bills came in and I had them to pay [as well]. I found that Mr. Sherman had not paid many of his bills, and I paid about three hundred dollars out besides keeping the family. Then came Christmas time, and Ada devoted a great deal of time in trimming the church and preparing for Christmas. I furnished her with all her clothes and paid her dressmaking bills. I made her a Christmas present, and [my husband] also received presents from me.

On Christmas Eve a young lady, Katy Hill, came to stay with Ada. Just before dark they went down the street and bought some confectionery. Upon their return, young Nattie tottered into the room said Ada was sick.

Like any doting mother, Lydia sent for Dr. Beardsley. The family physician prescribed a brandy sling, but Horatio "drank every drop of alcohol in the house." When he stormed out of the house to drink more, Lydia's bitterness and anger turned lethal. So, "she mixed arsenic in Ada's tea," and the teenager died the next morning, December 31, 1870. The crafty murderess bought another pint of brandy. This time, she added arsenic to the alcohol in the hopes of making Horatio sick enough to stop drinking, or so she claimed. Instead, her husband "kept drinking the brandy" and died May 12, 1871.

A 2001 study found that because female serial killers have a quieter "technique," they tend to get away with murder for much longer than their male counterparts. On average, a female serial killer's "career" spans eight to eleven years, whereas a male's often only lasts two to four.

The court sentenced Lydia Sherman to Wethersfield State Prison for the rest of her natural life. *The New York Herald* didn't shy away from voicing their disdain for the latest American Borgia or the jurors who refused to impose the death penalty.

The verdict assured her that her neck could not be broken on the gallows, as it should be, had she a thousand spinal columns within it. Hence, she makes her confession. Meek-faced, pious to the last, she excuses this confession on the ground that Christ called her to sorrow for her sins. She flung herself on her knees at night, and in the morning, she says, 'I felt the burden was gone and I was forgiven.'

It may be futile now to ask, when the evidence was so clear, when the man's blood was, as it were, red upon the woman's hands, how a jury could be found to bate her doom one jot. It was, perhaps, a mistaken spirit of feeble humanity which led them to do it; but we venture to say that when these jurymen read in the *Herald* of to-day the litany of horrors that Lydia Sherman coolly confesses to, they will shudder to their fingertips that the iron of the Hebraic law was not in their souls when they agreed upon a verdict.

In the early years of Connecticut, the only state or colony facility for housing prisoners was the New-Gate Prison in Simsbury (known today as East Granby), where convicts were held underground in a former copper mine. But by the early nineteenth century, New-Gate Prison was considered inhumane. In June 1827, they trucked twenty inmates to Wethersfield to construct a new prison. Two months later, August 20, another twenty inmates joined the construction crew, then eighty-one more on September 29, for a total workforce of 121 prisoners.

"Among them were four women and Prince Mortimer, an African-American prisoner who was 103 years old," according to Connecticut historians.

Wethersfield State Prison was considered to be a place of rehabilitation rather than punishment. The prison's workshops produced a variety of goods, including shoes, boots, clothing, furniture, pewter "Britannia ware," clock parts, spectacles, canned goods, and even firearms.

A French diplomat, Alexis de Tocqueville, traveled to the United States to study its prisons and returned with a wealth of broadened observations that he codified into *Democracy in America* (1835). Tocqueville marveled at the low cost of operating Wethersfield State Prison and the fact that its prolific workshop turned a profit for the State of Connecticut. But what he didn't see was the prisoner abuse and mismanagement occurring within its walls. On April 30, 1833, two years after Tocqueville's visit, the inmates fought back and killed a night watchman during a botched escape.

On September 12, 1835, another inmate tried stabbing the warden to death. Fortunately, he didn't succeed. But other wardens weren't as fortunate. A total of two wardens and four prison guards lost their lives. In 1872, the prison commission recommended building a new prison at a new site, but the legislature rejected the plan. Instead, they upgraded the existing facility.

Lydia Sherman arrived at Wethersfield State Prison on January 11, 1873, and in June 1877, she escaped due to "the negligence of the Matron who had charge of her," as one journalist opined.

But being out, with all the world before her, with some friends to help her and with some money [she'd stolen fifty dollars from the matron] in her pocket, she leaves Hartford only to be arrested in Providence, Rhode Island.

And sent back to prison. Roughly five months later,

She was stricken with cancer in 1878, and unlike her victims, was forced to suffer through till her demise on May 16, 1878.

Even her death could not lessen the outrage.

[*The New York Herald*] have used the word woman in her regard; but it would degrade the name of the vilest beast or reptile whose [screech] has made it an enemy to be killed at sight, by comparing her to it.

PART III:
NELLIE WEBB

1

THE BUGBEE-
TOWNE AFFAIR

The quaint village of Lancaster, New Hampshire, nestled into a rural countryside, with high sloping hills and rich forestry, in the northern White Mountains and southernmost part of the Great North Woods in the county of Coos (after Coös, an Indian name for "crooked"). Although the town stood in the "northern seat of legal lore" and was home to many of the county's most distinguished professionals, its outskirts remained agricultural.

In 1823, a journalist for the *Gazetteer of New Hampshire* described residents as "poor, and for all that appears to the contrary, must always remain so, as they may be deemed trespassers on that part of creation destined by its author for the residents of bears, wolves, moose, and other animals of the forest."

Despite that crude remark, prosperity and growth increased "in the land of bears and moose," and the Town of Lancaster stood on its own. A bronze monument of a fox poised on a boulder in Centennial Park, set there in 1914 on the town's 150th anniversary, commemorates the men and women "who redeemed Lancaster from the wilderness." The process wasn't easy, though. Agriculture in particular remained difficult. Settlers had almost abandoned the village due to harsh weather destroying their crops. But the town persevered, and by 1874 Lancaster became the twelfth most productive agricultural region in the state.

One such farmer was a man named Barton G. Towne, husband of Harriet (Patience) Towne and father to Colonel Francis Town (he dropped the

Key players in the Bugbee-Towne Affair: Barton G. Towne, Harriet Towne, Colonel Francis Town, and Dr. Frank Bugbee *Courtesy of Lancaster Historical Society & Town Recreational Dept.*

"e"). Shortly after a prominent physician, Dr. Frank Bugbee, married the Townes' daughter, Maria, on March 4, 1863, Barton G. Towne retired from farming and the two families purchased side-by-side homes on High Street. The Towne family moved into a striking three-gabled home—known today as the House of Three Gables—and the Bugbee newlyweds settled into the large Colonial next door.

No one could have predicted what would happen there. One hundred and forty years later, local historians still talk about the Bugbee-Towne Mystery, formally known as the Bugbee-Towne Affair in polite New England society.

In the summer of 1880, the two families began their downward spiral when fourteen-year-old Hattie Bugbee—Frank and Maria's only child—returned from hosting "a child's picnic" on Saturday, July 10. By nightfall, Hattie complained of minor body aches and a slight sore throat. When Frank Bugbee examined his daughter, he spotted a grayish-white membrane covering her tonsils. Somehow, his beloved Hattie had contracted a nasty strain of diphtheria.

Hattie Bugbee *Courtesy of Lancaster Historical Society & Town Recreational Dept.*

Even with Frank's expertise as a family physician—one of only three doctors in town—he couldn't loosen the death grip around his precious Hattie. By the next morning, Hattie's prognosis turned grimmer. On Monday night, July 15, Richard P. Kent and his wife, Emily, called at the Bugbee home, because their two granddaughters, Bertie and Annie Kent, were worried about their friend.

Choking back tears, Frank told them Hattie had "diphtheria of the most virulent type."

After returning home, the Kents tried to prepare their granddaughters for the worst by breaking the sad news—Hattie would probably not survive the disease.

Richard P. Kent was a prominent local businessman who moved to Lancaster in 1825 and started a journal that would span more than fifty years. That night he wrote in his leather-bound diary:

> Hattie Bugbee sick with diphtheria. Emily & myself went to the house in the evening and came home at 10 o'clock.

He also recorded another event that took place on the same night.

> Free Lindsay, while driving a six horse train with nine passengers down the carriage road from Mount Washington to the Glen House, upset the carriage in driving round a turn in the road, one lady killed instantly & most of the passengers injured. Lindsay striking his head & [is] supposed to be injured fatally. The telegraphic account in the Boston papers say Lindsay had been drinking & was tipsy.

The following day, while Maria clung to her daughter's bedside, Frank Bugbee sent his stable boy to the South Groveton home of Cornelius Regan to fetch Regan's daughter, eighteen-year-old Hannah. The Bugbees would often call on Hannah when they needed hired help.

Horses tugged the coach toward the Regan house while Hannah watched from the kitchen window. As the stable boy stepped down out of the coach, an icy tingle shimmied down her spine. When Hannah learned why he had come to the house, a grave premonition washed over her, a vision that showed if she left with him that day, she would never come home again.

Without sharing her premonition, Hannah rattled off one excuse after another for why she couldn't take the job. When skirting the issue didn't work, Hannah broke down, trembling and crying.

Lizzie, her mother, couldn't understand why her daughter was so upset. "Stop acting so foolish, girl," she said. "Go with the man. You know we need the money."

With her arms wrapped tight around her mother, every inch of Hannah warned her not to leave home. But a good daughter obeyed her parents.

When the stable boy and Hannah reached the Bugbee residence, Frank hedged her off at the door. "As you know, Hannah, diphtheria is very contagious. If being in this house bothers you in any way, you may feel free to leave whenever you wish."

Confirming with a nod, Hannah agreed to stay.

To assist in the care of his daughter Frank had also enlisted the help of Nellie Webb, a twenty-two-year-old girl who lived next door with Frank's in-laws. Nellie came from a single-parent home in Guildhall, Vermont, across the Connecticut River from Lancaster. Nellie's father had died in the war and her mother allegedly burned down a neighbor's barn.

Soon after, Nellie went to live with a family friend, Abigail Webb, wife of Colonel Edward H. Webb. Though the Webbs never formally adopted young Nellie—born Nancy French—she assumed their surname. No records exist as to why she'd changed her first name to Nellie, or when this occurred, because "Nellie" was not a common nickname for Nancy.

Living with the Webbs allowed Nellie to receive a better education than local schools could provide. In fact, most reports state her mother sent Nellie to the Webbs for this purpose.

After graduation, Nellie expressed her desire to become a teacher. Thrilled with the idea, Abigail Webb arranged for her to live with her good friends, Barton and Harriet Towne, so she could attend Lancaster Academy. Abigail and Harriet were spiritual sisters in the Methodist Church, and after Nellie graduated from Lancaster Academy, they extended their generosity one more time by paying for teacher training at Plymouth Normal School.

Nellie taught school for two years and then turned her attention to taxidermy, assisting Hattie Bugbee in stuffing birds and making hats for an elite clientele.

When Hannah came to the house that day, Frank explained she would work under Nellie's supervision. Hattie Bugbee's condition was worsening, and by Wednesday, July 15, the diphtheria had weakened her heart and attacked her nervous system. Hattie wouldn't survive for much longer.

During a brief respite from the pain, Hattie asked to say goodbye to her two best friends, Annie and Bertie Kent.

A heartbreaking account of Maria Bugbee watching her daughter die appeared in the *Gazette*.

> Devoted to her daughter, she remained by [Hattie's bedside] with assiduous watchfulness from the commencement of her alarming disease, and worn down by care, watching and grief, [Maria] could not resist the attacks of the malady that fastened upon her [daughter].

On a cool afternoon, Wednesday, July 14, Frank slid his arms under his daughter's thin frame and carried her to the window to fulfill her final wish. Richard P. Kent memorialized this touching moment in his diary.

> Hattie Bugbee, sick with diphtheria, with no hope of recovery, from her chamber took leave of Bertie and Annie, who were in the yard below, precluded from visiting her room from fear of contracting the disease—a striking instance of coolness in the midst of suffering.

At peace with her grave condition, Hattie passed away the following night, July 16, at 11 p.m. Because of the contagions associated with diphtheria, the family buried her the next day in Summer Street Cemetery.

The dawn of each new day brought a joyous chance to collect one's thoughts, to appreciate the sounds and smells of all God's creatures while busying the hands with the day's chores. The reverent peace fed the soul, allowing a closer connection to the earth. Indeed, Richard P. Kent must have felt this way, as he began each new diary entry with the weather and often his morning routine.

In his diary entry dated Friday, July 16, he wrote:

Mercury at 6 a.m. 53° above zero—clear and hot till from P.M. when it clouded up with a mild shower at 5 ½ P.M. Orville Moore brought load [of] hay from G. P. Hartfords—reaching my barn just as the shower commenced in earnest.

Funeral of Hattie Bugbee at house at 2 p.m. Short service by Rev. D. J. Smith. Some twenty carriages in precession followed the casket which was carried in Doct. Bugbee's carriage to the New Cemetery. Emily, Addie, Annie & myself rode in carryall with Edmund driving. From the infectious character of the disease— people did not enter the house from fear of contagion.

The poor little thing was conscious through all her dreadful suf- fering, sending messages to her playmates and friends, and talking to her agonized kindred and attendants. The interment occurred in Summer Street Cemetery on a Friday afternoon. The services were strictly private, but a large number of friends of the family followed the Doctor's carriage to the grave—a sunny spot on the pleasant hillside—less chilling in its garniture of pure and choicest flowers.

That same day the *Gazette* offered a poem to express the community's grief over Hattie's passing.

Tenderly down in the grave we have laid her;
Robed its portal with garlands and flowers;
Safely we leave her, with God who hath made her—
His the lost darling, the memory ours.

Sadly, the deaths in the Bugbee household did not stop with Hattie. But did they die of natural causes or from something far more sinister?

2
DEATH TOLL RISES

Grief-stricken, Maria Bugbee fell ill after Hattie's funeral, evident by the last line of the Kent diary dated Saturday, July 17.

> Mercury at 6 A.M. 62° above zero—partially cloudy with shower at 5 P.M. . . . Mrs. Bugbee sick with diphtheria—attacked yesterday.

The following day, July 18, Kent noted, "Hannah Regan, Irish girl, housemaid at Doctor Bugbee's—attacked with diphtheria."

With both his wife and Hannah sick, Frank did everything he could to save them. Nonetheless, on July 21, Maria became "unexpectedly and alarmingly worse." But not before trying to soothe her husband's fears by assuring him that she'd found peace.

"I place my trust in my Savior," she said, "and submit to his will."

Once again, Richard P. Kent wrote in his diary, an entry dated Wednesday, July 21, 1880.

> Mrs. Maria [Bugbee], wife of Doct. Frank Bugbee, died of diphtheria, attacking Friday 16th—the daughter Hattie having died of the same disease [on] Thursday 15th. Mrs. Bugbee buried at 4 ½ P.M., died at 9 ½ A.M. —twenty carriages followed the body to the grave. Weather very dry & beautiful. Mercury ranging 75 to 80° above zero.

That same day, the *Lancaster Gazette* wrote a beautiful tribute to Hattie:

The death of Hattie Bugbee, only child of Dr. and Mrs. Frank Bugbee of Lancaster, which occurred on Thursday, July 15th, of malignant Diphtheria, is accompanied by circumstances of peculiar sadness. This bright and beautiful child, about fourteen years of age, was a general favorite; in whom was centered the love and hope of parents and grandparents.

On Saturday, the 10th, she was apparently in perfect health, entertaining her companions at a child's picnic. That night she complained of a slight sore throat, on Sunday the trouble increased, and on Monday it assumed a most malignant character, baffling the skill of the faculty and the love of those around her.

Even with a diagnosis of diphtheria, many townsfolk believed poor drainage in the house caused malaria, which in turn triggered a bilious attack, killing young Hattie in days. Frank also had a brief bout of sickness but recovered with the help of Nellie Webb.

The Towne family's home *Author photo*

The *Gazette* once again offered condolences:

When we referred last week to the sad death of Hattie Bugbee, we were unprepared for the painful event that speedily followed, bringing double bereavement to the already desolated home. Tuesday evening Mrs. Bugbee became unexpectedly and alarmingly worse, expiring at about nine a.m. on Wednesday, of the same disease—Diphtheria. She was buried on the afternoon of the same day, beside her lost daughter, whom she thus joined in death.

Forty-two-year-old Maria Bugbee had been "a consistent and exemplary member of the Methodist Church," and so was Nellie Webb. "It is seldom that a sadder event afflicts a community than this sudden and fatal illness in the family of Dr. Bugbee, who, with Mr. and Mrs. Towne, will have to a marked degree the sympathy of the community."

But the darkness hadn't passed. On July 23, Hannah Regan crossed into the afterlife, confirmation of the premonition that shook her to the core days earlier.

Richard Kent wrote only one sentence that day.

Maria Bugbee *Courtesy of Lancaster Historical Society & Town Recreational Dept.*

Hannah Regan—housemaid at Doct. Bugbee's, died this morning of diphtheria, the third death from the same disease at that place within a week—buried in the afternoon at 4 ½ P.M. at the Catholic cemetery.

With three deaths in a short period of time, Nellie's friends worried the Bugbee house wasn't safe. They urged Nellie to leave, but she insisted she felt no fear about remaining because she knew the Lord would look after her. Plus, she may have felt obligated to look after Frank. Or did she have an ulterior motive?

To the dismay of parishioners at the Methodist church, Nellie wore Maria Bugbee's coat to Sunday services about a month after the funeral. She also wore Maria's watch and chain. When questioned, Nellie went on the defensive, stating Mrs. Bugbee gave her the coat and watch before she died. Frank had gifted Nellie the chain because it went with the watch. Simple as that.

Nonetheless, by staying in the Bugbee home, muffled whispers about Frank and Nellie's alleged romantic entanglements swept through the town. Didn't matter that Frank, forty-three, was twice her age and Nellie was engaged to Burt Mayo, a young brakeman for the Boston, Concord, and Montreal Railroad. To compound matters, Frank was then seen driving his carriage down South Lancaster Road to the home of Honorable James W. Weeks, a former probate court judge and close family friend. The rumor mill wrongly assumed, as it often did, that Frank was calling on Weeks's daughter, Clara, regardless of the fact that Clara was an invalid and her grave condition was worsening by the hour.

As a family physician, perhaps Frank was treating Clara.

Racked by grief and probably more than a little fed up with local gossip, Frank packed a suitcase in late August and traveled to Derby Line, Vermont, to visit his two brothers, Abel and Marquis De Lafayette Bugbee, who were also physicians. While there, he bought a demijohn of whiskey. This purchase was not unusual in and of itself. Vermont had a higher quality whiskey which Frank couldn't find in Lancaster.

On Friday, September 3—"Mercury at 86° above zero at 9 P.M.," according to Kent—Frank told Nellie he wasn't feeling well. That evening, he retired early. Nellie fixed him a "liquid preparation" which included some of the whiskey. Within hours, Frank experienced violent and persistent vomiting, and by morning, he could no longer keep anything down. By Sunday, September 5, Frank was slipping in and out of consciousness.

Many local physicians were called in to examine him, including his brother, Dr. Ralph Bugbee from Littleton, New Hampshire. But pinpointing what was causing Frank's symptoms seemed to baffle all the doctors in attendance. No one had to tell Frank how grim the future looked. Early Monday morning, he updated his will and included directions for what should be done after his death.

Then, to the surprise of everyone in the room, Frank bolted upright in bed. "I wish I knew what is killing me!"

Dr. Adams, one of the attending physicians, asked Frank to self-diagnose his symptoms. "What would you say if you had a patient in your own condition?"

"I should say that it was arsenical poisoning."

But the doctors did not agree. With diphtheria tearing through the household, they attributed Frank's death to bilious fever (a fever associated with excessive bile or bilirubin in the bloodstream and tissues) and blood poisoning. The immediate cause of death they attributed to "the infusion of blood around the heart." The doctors believed Frank had contracted malaria (the most common cause of bilious fever) from poor drainage in the house. Kent wrote in his diary that day:

> Mercury at 6 A.M. 54° above zero & at noon 82° above zero. Rode with Emily an hour after breakfast. Doct. Frank Bugbee who has been sick of bilious fever the week past, died at 9 o'clock A.M.—made & executed a will, which was commutated only an hour before his death.
>
> His daughter Hattie died July 15th & his wife [died on the] 21st, both of diphtheria—& the housemaid Hannah Regan also died of the same disease July 25th [official records state July 23, as did Kent's diary entry that day]—making four deaths in seven weeks & comprising the entire family. Emily Kent came [home] on a visit from Old Orchard Beach by the 4 ½ P.M. train. Cut my left thumb quite badly while trimming a dry Codfish for use.

The funeral of Frank Bugbee was quite an affair, as Richard Kent noted in his diary the next day, Tuesday, September 7, 1880.

Mercury at 7 A.M. 50° above zero—the air filled with smoke [days later he attributed the smoke to forest fires in lower Canada]. Wind from the north & quite cool in the afternoon. Funeral of Doct. Bugbee at 3 P.M. [held] at his late dwelling, house—prayer at the house by Rev. D. J. Smith, Methodist. A very long precession, prowled by the Knights Templar in full regalia with the brass band—a Masonic carriage at the grave—that was after 50 carriages in the precession.

A week later, James W. Weeks announced he'd been appointed executor of the estates of Frank and Maria Bugbee. And on October 2, Reverend D. J. Smith quietly united Nellie Webb and Burt Mayo in marriage.

To outsiders, with four dead in the Bugbee household and only one left standing, it looked like Nellie had murdered them all. The question was why. Frank left Nellie five hundred dollars and a few "small gifts" that didn't amount to much. Hardly enough incentive to murder an entire family.

3

DARK DAYS CONTINUE

Needing a respite from the grief, seventy-year-old Harriet Towne and her seventy-one-year-old husband, Burton, took a carriage ride to the quaint town of Bethlehem on Thanksgiving Day. Upon their return, Mrs. Towne didn't feel well. Nellie, who continued to care for the Townes while her husband was on a rail run, assisted Harriet into bed and mixed up a "liquid preparation" that included some of Dr. Bugbee's whiskey.

Just like in Frank's case, the symptoms came on hard and fast, with violent bouts of vomiting. The attending physician treated her for "a disordered functioning of the liver." But as her condition worsened, all of Harriet Towne's organs began shutting down.

On Friday, December 10, Kent entered the sad news in his diary:

Mercury at 7 A.M. 10° above zero—morning cloudy, stormy in the hills—Mrs. Barton G. Towne died at half past three in the morning.

Cause of death listed as "chronic difficulty and bilious fever."

As if five deaths in less than five months weren't enough for one family to bear, word reached Lancaster that Frank's father, Dr. Ralph Bugbee Sr., age eighty-four, had died at home in Waterford, Vermont—one month and a day after Harriet Towne's funeral. The funeral for Mrs. Towne was "a swift affair" due to the fear that she, too, might have contracted diphtheria.

On December 11, Richard Kent dipped his pen in the inkwell to journal the day's events.

Very cold this morning—Mercury 16° below zero at 7 ½ A.M. & quite clear. Wrote to Ezra R. Rogere with copy of note $98. . . . Mrs. Barton G. Towne buried in the afternoon—funeral at the house. . . .

A special dispatch to the *Boston Journal* reported, "[Mrs. Towne's] quick taking off was considered to have resulted from the same cause which made so great mortality in the Bugbee family, but in the case of Mrs. Towne, no diphtheria membrane was formed in her throat. She was a lady of fine physique and possessed a strong constitution."

Two months later, on February 21, 1881, Barton Towne joined his family in heaven after a brief and sudden illness.

On that day, Kent wrote:

Morning cloudy—indication of approaching storm—Mercury at 7 A.M. 15° above zero. Lent $1,000.00 to Henry O. Kent, taking his note at this date for the amount. Mr. Barton G. Towne died, aged 73 years [seventy-one years, according to his gravestone]—his disease at first presented as a bilious attack, the physician at a later stay called [it] blood poisoning. Similar to the disease which carried off Doct. Bugbee.

Still fearful of diphtheria, they buried Barton Towne the day after he died. On Tuesday, February 22, Kent recorded the event.

Morning cloudy—Mercury at 7 A.M. 22° above zero—Very clear & mild through the day. Mr. Barton G. Towne buried in the afternoon, the funeral a private one—it not being considered best to risk the effects of possible contagion by having people go to the house, the scene of such sad occurrences.

The only surviving member of the two families was Colonel Francis Town, a surgeon in the United States Army who hadn't been home since the Civil War. A prominent and well-respected gentleman, Colonel Town served with the Army of Cumberland from 1861 to 1863. He organized the Harvey

General Hospital for the State of Wisconsin at Madison (1863–1865) and served as chief surgeon in Kentucky after the war. Continuing his military service, Colonel Town worked as a post surgeon in Montana, Maine, and Oklahoma, even across Europe, and finally landed in Walla Walla, Washington, where he received cables of his sister's death, along with Hattie, Frank, and both his parents.

After absorbing such an extreme blow, Colonel Town sent word to Dr. Ezra Mitchell Jr. of Governor Bell's staff—please exhume his father's body. The request ran through the proper channels, and on May 25, Attorney General Tappan's office directed Deputy Sheriff George M. Stevens to disinter Barton G. Towne from the grave. Dr. Mitchell and Dr. Emmons F. Stockwell, another Lancaster physician, removed the stomach. Then Dr. Stockwell hand-delivered the organ to Professor Edward Stickney Wood at Harvard Medical, a pioneer in toxicology and the same chemist who would later discover morphine and atropine in the victims of Jane Toppan.

On August 5, 1881—"Mercury at 6 A.M. 58° above zero"—Professor Wood's report showed high levels of arsenic in Barton Towne's stomach contents and liner. But not ordinary non-soluble arsenic, most commonly used to kill rats. Rather, he found Fowler's Solution, a medicinal arsenate solution that contained arsenic trioxide, dissolved in potassium carbonate solution, and flavored with lavender extract to prevent misuse.

Dr. Thomas Fowler introduced arsenic into medicine with his treatise entitled *Medical Reports of the Effect of Arsenic in the Cure of Agues, Remitting Fevers, and Periodic Headaches*, published in 1786. Along with apothecary Mr. Hughes, Dr. Fowler had devised his own medicinal arsenic recipe from white arsenic (the most toxic of all arsenate compounds) and potash, which became widely used. Fowler's Solution remained in pharmacopoeias for 150 years. In nineteenth-century New England, its use ventured beyond purely medicinal, rising in popularity as an aphrodisiac, and labeled as "a tonic for tired businessmen."

*"Social isolation—loneliness—might be argu-
ably the most common characteristic of the
childhood of serial killers. Male or female."*

—Peter Vronsky,
author of Female Serial Killers

The Boston Journal covered the Bugbee-Towne Affair, headlined as "A New Hampshire Sensation" with three-tier sub-headings: "Mysterious death of several persons in Lancaster. A young woman suspected of wholesale poisoning. To secure a paltry sum of money."

In the article dated August 8, journalists leaped to the conclusion that Nellie Webb must be a murderess.

> A great sensation has been caused in Lancaster and vicinity over the discovery of what is expected to prove that a terrible tragedy has been committed in that town. It is believed by the officials of the law that the evidence which is fast accumulating will show that one person, and it is not known how many more, have been willfully poisoned in Lancaster. . . .
>
> As would be expected, Miss [Nellie] Webb, who has since become the wife of Burt Mayo, a conductor on the Montreal Road, stands in a peculiar position. She is a woman of good personal appearance and a member of the Methodist Church in Lancaster and was formally a schoolteacher. . . . Last Friday Dr. Stockwell had a serious talk with Mrs. [Nellie Webb] Mayo, informing her of the result of Prof. Wood's analysis, and remarked that she was the only person under suspicion, and that she should probably be arrested. Mrs. Mayo frankly declared her innocence and stated that she was ready to meet the charge at any time. Immediately afterward she consulted with friends, and also secured able counsel.

A father-and-son legal team agreed to represent Nellie. The article continued:

> From the Bugbee estate Mrs. Mayo received $500 and some presents, and from the Towne property only some furniture. There is

no suspicion that there was anything wrong in connection with the death of Mrs. Bugbee or her daughter or the servant. As would be expected the excitement in Lancaster . . . is intense, and the matter is the talk in all directions. There seems to be no explanation of the death of Dr. Bugbee, excepting upon the ground that he was poisoned. If that crime was committed, there was a motive for it, but in the interests of justice we are not allowed to give the points now in the possession of the officers, which will soon be woven into one of the most remarkable criminal cases that has ever occurred in our State.

The implications in that article outraged local editors, and they retaliated in kind.

The sensational reports published in Boston and other papers, we understand were sent from Concord and ought to have been suppressed. Additional facts are every day coming to light regarding the Bugbee-Towne case, which we sincerely hope will soon place all suspicion at rest.

The executor of the Bugbee and Towne estates, James W. Weeks—who later became a notable senator that sponsored legislation to create the White Mountain National Forest in 1910—was not convinced of Nellie's innocence. Quite the opposite. In Concord, Weeks met with Attorney General Mason Tappan, and later that afternoon (August 11), the sheriff's department received word to exhume the bodies of Harriet Towne and Dr. Frank Bugbee. The autopsies were held in the back room of the Parker J. Noyes building on Main Street.

Gossip continued to circulate. "While living at the Bugbee Home Mrs. [Nellie Webb] Mayo assisted the daughter [Hattie] in preparing birds of preservation, in which work they made use of arsenic," the *Boston Journal* declared. "Sheriff Pike of Coos County, who is in Concord this evening, admits that the case is a mysterious one, and says that nothing will be left undone to secure a searching and impartial investigation of all the circumstances connected with the supposed crime."

Five days later, August 16—"Morning clear. Mercury at 6 A.M. 48° only above zero"—after the authorities found the remains of Mrs. Towne and Frank Bugbee in such a remarkable state of preservation, Attorney General Tappan assumed they had died from arsenical poisoning. That day, he ordered the exhumation of Maria and her daughter, Hattie. Lizzie Regan couldn't bear the thought of disturbing her daughter's grave. She refused to allow Hannah's exhumation for more than a year.

4

THE MYSTERIOUS WHISKEY

After Barton G. Towne died, Nellie gave Frank Bugbee's whiskey to John W. Weeks. He'd stashed the bottle in his safe and forgot about it until the spring of 1881, when Frank's body was exhumed from Summer Street Cemetery. At that time, Weeks sent half the whiskey to Parker J. Noyes, a local druggist, chemist, researcher, and inventor of the first sugar-coated pill; he also invented the first precision food pellet for laboratory animals. The remaining whiskey Weeks sent to Professor Wood at Harvard.

Both Noyes and Wood found Fowler's Solution in the whiskey. Which meant, the poisoner would have to know that common white arsenic didn't dissolve like medicinal arsenic, thereby pointing toward a more cunning killer. Perhaps someone with a medical background.

The *Gazette* ran an update on the case:

No new developments have been brought to light in the Towne-Bugbee affair, except the finding of arsenic in the whiskey used during the sickness of Dr. Bugbee and Mr. and Mrs. Towne, a small quantity of which was analyzed by Mr. P. J. Noyes. This is considered, by many, as a very important point, but as [of] yet it only tends to show that poison was the cause of the last three deaths.

The reports which appeared in the *Boston Journal* last week . . . [allegedly] sent to that paper by its special reporter, created much indignation here, as they were very unjust and wholly uncalled for, as no one in this town, as far as we have been able to learn, has thought that any particular person did the deed. . . . The internal organs will be sent to Prof. Wood of Harvard in sealed packages as soon as possible, probably tomorrow, and his report will be awaited with much anxiety by our people.

What if when Frank visited his two brothers in Derby Line, Vermont, where he'd purchased the whiskey, a family argument ensued? Frank brought that bottle back to Lancaster, and from it, "liquid preparations" were made. Who's to say Fowler's Solution wasn't added to the demijohn before he'd left Vermont? Perhaps the poisoner only meant to kill Frank.

Before any conclusions could be made, authorities would need to wait for Professor Wood's report. But that didn't stop the press from voicing their opinions. The *Gazette* ran the following:

The general belief in Lancaster is that Dr. Bugbee was poisoned, and that the deed was not done from any mercenary motive. Dr. Watson of Northumberland, now a member of the House of Representatives, was one of the physicians to [attend] Dr. Bugbee. It is admitted by Dr. Watson that there were symptoms of arsenical poisoning, but as some members of the family had died of diphtheria, the physicians naturally attributed the cause of Dr. Bugbee's death to blood infection.

The deaths of Mrs. [Maria] Bugbee [and her] daughter and servant [Hannah Regan] were believed to have been caused by bad drainage, but Mrs. [Nellie Webb] Mayo, who now resides in the house, says she has no fears in living there.

On August 10—"Slightly cloudy but mostly clear and quite warm," according to Kent—Deputy Sheriff Stevens interviewed Nellie about the case. Nellie explained how Frank bought the demijohn of whiskey in Vermont, that he'd transferred some of the whiskey into a smaller bottle, but while cleaning, she'd bumped into the demijohn and it shattered on the floor. When asked about the original bottle, she said she'd tossed the broken glass in the trash. But, she said, this wasn't a secret. Barton Towne knew about it.

A dead eyewitness didn't help the investigation.

Nellie did admit the whiskey tasted bitter. The one time she'd indulged, it had made her sick, too.

On September 7, the first of three toxicology reports arrived in Lancaster. Professor Wood found no traces of arsenic in Maria Bugbee's organs. Thus, he concluded Maria and Hattie had indeed died of diphtheria (as did Hannah Regan, which the public later learned). One week later, on September 21, Professor Wood sent his findings for Harriet Towne and Frank Bugbee. Like Barton, they died of arsenical poisoning. Which aligned with the theory that someone poisoned the whiskey bottle, and the killer perhaps never intended to murder the Townes.

But who was the culprit?

Meanwhile, an anonymous source in Littleton sent a letter to the *Boston Globe*.

"The Lancaster poisoning case is still attracting a great deal of attention here," the unnamed author wrote, "and nearly everyone has a theory."

Before the toxicology reports of Dr. Bugbee and Mrs. Towne came back,

Many people questioned whether a series of murders had really taken place. All the evidence went to show that whiskey . . . was taken from a bottle which was probably replenished from the demijohn in which Dr. Bugbee brought the whiskey to Lancaster.

Rather than believe in the fiendishness of someone who must have been often in and about the house during the sickness of these three persons, these people were willing to believe that by some terrible mistake or blunder a bottle which had contained Fowler's solution of arsenic had been used [in] the whiskey. This theory, however, is overthrown, and the fact is undeniable that a series of awful murders took place, and that the deaths of Dr. Bugbee and Mr. and Mrs. Towne occurred as the direct result of poison.

Since the letter writer never came forward, how much weight should be given to his or her theory? The town where the letter originated also seemed suspect. Frank's brother lived in Littleton, so this could be the ramblings of a grief-stricken relative.

Unanswered questions divided the town. Half the residents cried out for justice; the other half believed in Nellie's innocence.

Attorney General Tappan scheduled a grand jury hearing for October 18, 1881, where he would lay out his case in the hopes of securing an indictment for Nellie Webb Mayo. On Friday, October 7, he met with "county authorities and local physicians concerning the Towne-Bugbee poisoning affair. The object of his visit [was] . . . to examine the evidence already accumulated and determine in which manner to bring it before the court."

On October 17, the day before the grand jury hearing, Richard Kent didn't seem concerned with the chaos in town. Rather, he had romance on his mind.

Cloudy & mild. Mercury 44° zero—get up at 6 o'clock (Emily and myself alone in the house).

Later that day, Richard and his wife left for a trip to New York, with stopovers in Concord and Boston. Thus, Kent only mentioned the grand jury hearing in the last line of his diary entry dated Tuesday, October 18:

Rainy morning—feeling pretty tired, we do not rise very early—go down to breakfast at 8 o'clock. Rained incessantly during the day till sunset having amassed last night about dark. I went out in the afternoon to the State House where workmen were engaged taking up the marble flooring . . . to make repairs. Spent some time viewing the old battle flags carried by the N.H. Regiments during the war, which are reneged in cases on the walls—some of them very much tattered & discolored by hard service . . . Court commenced session at Lancaster.

As the grand jury listened to arguments on day two of the proceedings (October 19)—"Fine weather this morning, the wind having shifted to the north in the night & dissipating the clouds," according to Kent—the rest of New England focused on the testimony.

"The Coos Co. (N.H.) Superior Court commenced its session at Lancaster Tuesday, Judge W. H. Allen presiding," the *Boston Journal* noted on October 18. "After disposing of several matters of minor importance, the Towne-Bugbee poisoning case was taken up in hearing testimony, and a large number of witnesses are yet to be summoned."

While the grand jury hearing was well underway, the invention of electricity bedazzled Richard Kent, evident by his diary entry on Thursday, October 20:

> Very cloudy this morning with appearance of approaching rain but clearing off in the afternoon & weather quite mild. This house has three electric lights, two to light the dining room & one [for] the office—the former going out at supper, making it necessary to light the gas lantern but startling into life again after a short delay.

By the evening of October 20, the grand jury had reached a decision.

5

VERDICT STUNS
THE PUBLIC

Even with the secrecy of the jury room, word leaked out that the grand jury would not indict Nellie Webb, finding the evidence "insufficient and circumstantial." Thus, no formal charges were ever brought against the alleged murderess.

With this ruling, the *Boston Morning Journal* changed their tune.

Mrs. [Nellie Webb] Mayo, the accused, has always borne an excellent reputation, is prepossessing in appearance, well educated, having been a successful school teacher, and has for many years been a member in good standing of the Methodist Church. Public opinion has all along been strongly in her favor, and there is a general feeling of satisfaction at the result.

But that wasn't necessarily true. The verdict didn't sit well with some Lancaster residents, especially John W. Weeks.

Richard Kent noted this in his diary dated December 15, 1881.

Mr. J. W. Weeks made a lengthy call at our house and talked over the incidents connected with the poisoning of the Towne and Bugbee families. He has no doubt of the guilt of the suspected party, although the Grand Jury failed to indict her.

Others, however, sided with Nellie. A notable fiction writer, Mary R. P. Hatch, from Stratford, New Hampshire, wrote her own ending to the mystery in a novel entitled *The Upland Mystery: A Tragedy of New England* that mirrored the case. Published in 1887 by Laird & Lee Publishers of Chicago, the story is of Dr. Charlie Carber (Colonel Francis Town's character) of Upland (Lancaster) who returns to town after learning of his family's tragic end.

Parents, sister, brother-in-law, their daughter, even the servant girl; all were dead; not one left to welcome him.

Colonel Francis Town was a proud, distinguished, and accomplished gentleman who didn't think much of the novelization of his family's destruction, especially since his character and Nellie's character, Marah Connell, developed a romantic relationship.

When the novel released, Colonel Town took extraordinary measures to suppress local sales by purchasing "crateloads" as workers unloaded the books at the Lancaster depot for local markets. He also advertised to buy any and all copies in circulation. All the novels he purchased, he destroyed. As a result, today copies of *The Upland Mystery* are quite rare. Only two exist in Coos County, one of which is kept under lock and key at the Weeks Memorial Library and available to read by appointment only.

Even though Colonel Town never married, he didn't allow his family's tragedy to dictate his life. Much like Richard P. Kent, Colonel Town never lost the love for his hometown. But perhaps he dropped the "e" to separate himself from the Bugbee-Towne Affair. Who could blame him?

Years later, Colonel Town died of natural causes in 1922. In his Last Will and Testament, he wrote a touching tribute to Lancaster:

Living during the warmer portions of each year, and until drawn to a southern climate by wintery days, At Lancaster, New Hampshire, encircled by hills and mountains of wonderful scenic beauty, this charming locality is still greatly beloved by me; the same having been the home of my childhood and youth. Here I also desire to be buried finally, near the remains of the other members of my father's family, all of whom, except myself, have long years since departed from earth.

The act of a generous man devoted to the preservation and enrichment of the community, Colonel Francis Town bequeathed his entire estate to worthy causes, such as his alma mater, to whom he left "Two Hundred and Fifty Thousand ($250,000) to the trustees of Dartmouth College . . . to have two (2) annual prizes . . . to be given to two meritorious, and deserving students at the end of their Sophomore year, in the scientific course of the college."

He also donated stocks and securities to the Protestant Orphans Home and the Salvation Army Rescue Home in San Antonio, Texas, where he rented a winter home. In addition, he left the Texas homeowner everything within the San Antonio property, with the exception of "oil paintings and books in the same; these said Oil Paintings, and the books over two thousand in number," which he donated to the Carnegie Library in the same city.

Close friends and descendants of his late uncle James (Barton G. Towne's eldest brother) also inherited from Colonel Town. But the largest portion of the estate he bequeathed to the Town of Lancaster, with specific instructions for a bright future. Two hundred shares of stock for the Lancaster Hospital Association

to the Town of Lancaster. . . . The lot of land, and the buildings thereon, now owned and occupied by me, and located on High Street [Colonel Town lived in the former Bugbee house] . . . and all the entire contents of the said buildings [unless] heretofore been otherwise given, and bequeathed to other parties in any of the prior Clauses. . . .

Hence, I hereby give, and bequeath, to the said Town of Lancaster, New Hampshire, all the Oil Paintings owned by — at the time of my decease, which have been gradually picked up at moderate cost during past years, and it has afforded me much pleasure in these past years to hunt about in various cities for them. These

Oil Paintings should be preserved, and accessible to the public, as I think pretty much all of them have some merit as works of art, and some of them are interesting old works. Some of these Oil Paintings might be hung in the High School Building . . . [to benefit] liberal education.

Colonel Town further bequeathed "any and all securities, or monies" [today worth close to three million dollars] to the town "forever held in Trust, and shall thereby become a perpetual Trust Fund. But the net income from this said Trust/Fund is to be always expendable . . . [for the youth and as] assistance in the support of the public library."

All he asked was for nine thousand dollars to be used to erect a "headstone made of granite" for the family burial lot, "where the remains of my father's family now lie, perhaps there is room for my remains [to be buried with them]."

Which is exactly what the town did. With the trust fund, Lancaster transformed Colonel Town's residence (the old Bugbee home) into a community center for kids, complete with its own bowling alley, pool tables, and auditorium. The Colonel Town Recreational Department hides a secret floor that's been perfectly preserved in time, with the original furniture, trinkets, statues, and other furnishing from the era, along with stunning oak-and-glass bookcases stocked with priceless first editions. It's a lovely way to honor the two families who met such a tragic end and to celebrate the life of the lone survivor who turned a gut-wrenching tragedy into a beautiful legacy.

As for Nellie Webb, her name would forever be scarred by one burning question—did she poison the Townes and Dr. Frank Bugbee? After the grand jury hearing, Nellie and Burt Mayo left New England and never looked back. The rumor is they settled somewhere in the Midwest, but there's no evidence to support which state they landed in. Once Nellie left Lancaster, she vanished. No records exist of her life, marriage, or death in the Midwest.

Did she adopt a new alias? After all, she'd changed her name before. Why not do it again? Nobody can even locate her grave.

To compound the mystery of the Bugbee-Towne Affair, the Coos County Courthouse burned down at 2 a.m. on November 4, 1886, a fiery blaze that destroyed all the grand jury transcripts—history forever lost among the ashes.

Today, uncertainty still veils the town in mystery. Did the sheriff accuse an innocent girl of unspeakable crimes? Or did Nellie Webb commit the perfect murder? We may never learn the truth.

PART IV: SARAH JANE ROBINSON & HARRIET E. NASON

1
A SINISTER SCHEME

What if two New England women claimed to experience visions of death and destruction—often in dreams—and then were accused of committing a string of murders? Now suppose one lady was a poor blue-collar worker and the other "stood well in society" and possessed great influence. Would the courts and the public treat these two ladies as equals under the law, or would their fates run in opposite directions?

> "Women are more likely to be given softer, gentler nicknames—like Jolly Jane or Tiger Woman—where men are given monikers that reflect the brutality of their crimes, like the Kansas City Slasher."
>
> —Marissa Harrison, Associate Professor of Psychology at Penn State

On a brisk Friday evening, February 20, 1885, after a long hard day of dressmaking at R. H. White & Co. department store (later bought by Filene's), Sarah Jane Robinson slogged up the stairs to her third-floor tenement on Hughes Street in Cambridge, Massachusetts. A blonde who dressed impeccably, almost forty-six years old, with a "refined and intelligent face," Sarah had barely gotten through the door when a family member handed her a postal card. Annie Freeman, Sarah's only sister, had pneumonia. Come quick.

Sarah raced down the stairs to her neighbor on the first floor, pounding a fist against the door. The lady of the house answered.

"I must go to my sister," Sarah said, winded. Would she be kind enough to watch her family till she returned?

Once the neighbor agreed, Sarah "took the next car and went to South Boston," she would later testify. Arriving at the Freemans' F Street apartment, Sarah found an unfamiliar nurse tending to her sister, Annie.

I thought [my sister] was very sick, but I thought I had seen her often as sick before.

Annie asked about her husband. "Where is Prince?"

After calling for her brother-in-law, who was in the adjacent kitchen, Prince darted into the bedroom.

We both— I think I was sitting at her bed, and he stood, for probably three or four minutes before [my sister] said anything.

In a hoarse voice, Annie mumbled, "I want Sarah to have the control of the children. Have you any objections?"

"None at all." After all, Prince didn't know where else they could go, according to Sarah. At the time, Prince's father was also very sick, so his mother was in no position to care for the children.

One problem. Sarah had to work in the morning.

I told her I couldn't [take the children that night], that there was no one to take care of them on Saturday, but I would send for them. I went to work that Saturday, and after I got home Lizzie [Sarah's eldest daughter] had got home. Bertha Gardner [Lizzie's friend] and she went for the baby [Annie's infant, Elisabeth]. I wanted to go over on Sunday but Lizzie and Willie [Sarah's eldest son] objected to my going for fear that I should take the pneumonia from my sister.

[Instead] Willie went over and brought Arthur [nicknamed "Tommy," Annie's six-year-old son] home with him. I went to work on Monday as usual.

Between three and four o'clock that day, Prince Arthur Freeman stopped by the store. After his visit, Sarah claimed,

> I went to the manager of the store, the room, and asked him for a leave of absence to go to see my sister, and he gave it to me.

Prince escorted Sarah back to the apartment.

Greeting her sister, Sarah "didn't think [Annie] had changed any from what [she] saw [of] her on Friday." Still, Sarah asked the nurse where the Freemans' family physician lived.

> I wanted to talk with him, and I went and saw the doctor [to] find out about my sister's condition.

On that visit, Dr. Archibald Davidson told Sarah, "The symptoms subsided, the fever subsided, and thirst, and to all appearance [Annie] was over the dangerous part of pneumonia."

But the good news didn't lighten Sarah's mood. Quite the opposite. She returned to Annie's bedside, and asked if she would like her to stay.

"Sarah, you know I would," said Annie, "but you would be down sick if you stayed."

"No, Annie. I shan't leave you again."

The two sisters were very close. Born in Newton Hamilton in Northern Ireland, Sarah Tennent (her maiden name) was only fourteen years old when her parents, a poor farming couple, died within months of each other. Before their deaths, Sarah's older brother had moved to America.

When "mother died in December, and father died the following June," Sarah packed up nine-year-old Annie and set off to America on September 23, 1853, in a "steamer" ship. The two girls met their brother in Boston, and he welcomed them into his Cambridge home. Sarah had learned the trade of milliner or dressmaker in Ireland, so she immediately went to work while Annie attended school.

Four or five years later, Sarah met Moses Robinson "at the Baptist Church in Old Cambridge." They dated for "a little over a year, perhaps two," before they married.

> I was twenty [in May of that year], and I was married the following July.

The newlyweds moved in with Moses's father in Sherborn (today known as Shirley, Massachusetts) for a short stint before relocating several times, finally settling in Chelsea. Meanwhile, Annie was working as a nanny in Natick, when she met and married a carpenter with the last name of McCormick. She had two children, but both died in infancy shortly before Annie lost her first husband, after McCormick sliced open his hand with a saw-blade and succumbed to "blood poisoning." Now a widow, her sister, Sarah, insisted that she move in with her and Moses. Sarah later testified to this event:

> Three years and a half after we were married, Lizzie was born [while her sister was living there]. I suppose my home was always [Annie's] home. She of course didn't stay there. She had to earn her living, but she always called my house her home, kept her clothes there, come there on Sundays. She came there very often.

Soon, Annie found love again when she met Prince Arthur Freeman. The couple married in South Boston. "They had but two children during their marriage," said Sarah, that being Thomas "Tommy" Arthur Freeman and baby Elisabeth. Sarah, on the other hand, gave birth to eight. Lizzie was the oldest, then Willie, then twin girls, who died of natural causes within days of each other, the first living to only "eight months and sixteen days."

But the tragedies didn't end there.

On July 23, 1882, "[Moses] got overheated and then drank too much ice water" and dropped dead. Thankfully, he'd taken out a life insurance policy with the New England Relief Association for two to three thousand dollars, but they refused to pay the benefits to his widow. At Sarah's behest, Attorney David F. Crane brought suit, claiming "the assessments" were paid to an insurance agent, but he never turned the money over to the company.

What else could she do? By this time, Sarah had five children to feed at 183 Brookline Street in Cambridgeport—Lizzie, Willie, Charley, Emma May, and Gracie—and very little income. Charley worked at "Mr. Holmes's store" in Cambridge. Lizzie "kept house," taking care of her siblings when they got home from school.

By the time Annie fell ill, Charley had left school to work at Cupples and Upham's Bookstore on the corner of Washington and School Streets. Yet, even with the two eldest boys and Sarah working full time, the Robinson family still struggled. The lawsuit never gained traction, which meant Sarah wouldn't receive the payout from Moses's insurance.

Cupples and Upham's Bookstore, where Sarah's son Charley worked
Courtesy of Historic Boston Inc.

Out of desperation she mortgaged her furniture and anything of value with three different lenders (some reports say five) by using her own name and two aliases. Clever ruse, considering before a mortgage on personal property could be signed off, the mortgagee would check with the city's clerk office to ensure no previous liens existed. By not seeing Sarah Jane Robinson's name on the list, each creditor presumed they held the first mortgage.

Mr. Desmond was one such mortgage holder. On several occasions Desmond trekked to Sarah's apartment to see about repayment of his loan. Each time, Sarah promised to pay him from the proceeds of Moses's life insurance, even though the court had ruled against her in the lawsuit.

Prince Arthur Freeman, a laborer who made six dollars per week and spent half his salary on transportation, had also made provisions for his family by joining the Order of Pilgrim Fathers, a social group whose sole purpose was to provide cheap life insurance to blue-collar men and women. He insured his life for two thousand dollars, "payable to Annie for the care and support of her and their children."

Annie had no such policy on her life.

 Male and female serial killers tend to choose their victims and commit their crimes in different ways, which may be due to thousands of years of psychological evolution, according to a 2019 study by Penn State researchers.

The nurse stayed at Annie's bedside Monday night, February 23, and left in the morning. Why waste good money when Sarah could care for her sister?

Numerous friends visited during Annie's sickness, including Mrs. Mary J. Wright, who lived downstairs on the first floor of the tenement. According to Mrs. Wright, "[Sarah] felt as though she ought to come and take care of her sister, that she had had a terrible dream, and she knew her sister would never get any better, and that whenever she had a dream like that there was always one of the family [who] died." Regardless of Dr. Davidson's prognosis, "she knew [Annie] would never recover." But until the day Sarah arrived,

"[Annie] seemed to get better, and [then] all of a sudden she seemed to sink very fast."

During this time, Mrs. Wright had a strange conversation with Sarah.

"Mr. Freeman comes down to your place quite frequently." Sarah waited for her to agree. "If he should say anything about where he was going to stay if anything should happen to Annie, use your influence [to get Prince to move in with me and the children]."

Later that night, Sarah instructed Prince to "go into the chamber" where his wife was, and Sarah followed. When Sarah returned to the kitchen, she told Mrs. Wright, "There, I have fixed it all right now. Any little rings, or anything that Annie has, I have had her distribute so that there will be no trouble if anything should happen to her, and the children are to come to me."

"Well," Prince interrupted, "she has made provisions for the children but not [for] me."

Sarah curled her upper lip. "Oh, you are only half-baked. Annie knows well enough that you will follow the children."

Friends continued to roam in and out of the Freeman house. One such friend was Mrs. Susan Marshall, a former nurse. When Sarah had first arrived at the house, Mrs. Marshall was sitting with Annie, who looked like she was feeling better. Even her coloring had improved.

With her body propped up on the pillow, Annie greeted her sister with a warm smile on Monday, February 23. But Sarah seemed oddly dismayed. After quizzing Annie about her health, Sarah asked to speak with Mrs. Marshall in private.

As the two women strode into the kitchen, Sarah shared her fears. The night before she'd had a terrible dream that Annie grew sicker and sicker "until she wasted into a skeleton." Sarah dried her alligator tears. "I just know she'll never get any better."

Were they talking about the same patient? "But she is getting better."

No matter what Mrs. Marshall said to the contrary, Sarah remained steadfast in her opinion. "Whenever I have a dream like that, there is always one of the family who dies."

Days later, on February 24, Mrs. Marshall received a note from Sarah, asking her to return. Mrs. Marshall arrived the following day.

"I am so glad you have come." Sarah enfolded her in a warm embrace. "I want you to stay and take care of my sister and let me go to my home. I have stayed as long as I can."

"Sarah, you mustn't make any dependence on my staying nights, I can't do it. I will come over and do anything to assist you in the affairs of the day, but I can't sit up nights. My health is feeble, and I don't feel competent to the task."

"Well, it doesn't make any difference. Ann has been calling for you a great many times and she won't be satisfied, and I should think you might stay a little while."

"I can't," Mrs. Marshall said for the third or fourth time. "That is imperative."

When Mrs. Marshall entered the sickroom, Annie didn't seem stricken with "any ordinary natural sickness." Her condition had changed, her coloring "was of a dark hue. Her features were very much bloated," and her complexion looked like death wasn't far away. Annie's throat became so constricted, she could barely speak, though she did plead for something cold to drink to ease the dreadful burning in her stomach. A blinding headache squinted her eyes, exacerbated by overwhelming nausea.

Then a deeply puzzling symptom manifested itself—binding cramps in both calves. Even the opium Dr. Davidson had prescribed didn't seem to help. Annie remained in a constant state of agony, writhing in pain.

Sarah brought ice cream to Annie, dutifully feeding her sister one spoonful at a time. But the ice cream worsened Annie's nausea and vomiting until all she could throw up was thin, blood-streaked fluid.

Sarah stormed out of the room, and Mrs. Marshall darted after her.

In the kitchen Sarah said that Annie was being "fretty," and she refused to wait on her another moment.

"Don't make any such remark as that," Mrs. Marshall admonished, "for you will regret it. I don't think Ann will live for any length of time." Aghast by Sarah's attitude, Mrs. Marshall wondered aloud about the sudden reversal in Annie's condition.

"We have been doing all we can for her. But I do not expect that she will ever leave her bed." Sarah heaved a sigh. "It is happening just as in my dream."

The next day while Mrs. Marshall was leaving, Dr. Charles Beers strode through the door and handed Sarah a bottle wrapped in newspaper "about the size of any ordinary pint bottle. It was a round bottle with a long neck like any common wine bottle." Thing is, Dr. Beers wasn't one of Annie's physicians. He'd been fawning over Sarah ever since Moses died. With piqued interest, Mrs. Marshall hung around a little longer.

Dr. Beers told Sarah, "You will find that strictly pure."

"Dr. Davidson had been in previous to Dr. Beers's coming," Mrs. Marshall recalled, "and had left a prescription."

At the time, Sarah said, "I haven't the money to have that prescription filled now."

But on this day, Mrs. Marshall bustled into the kitchen a few moments later to find Dr. Beers and Sarah "in close proximity."

After he left, Sarah grinned. "Now I have the money to have the prescription filled."

The following day, February 26, Mrs. Marshall planned to return to Annie's bedside. In fact, she had promised to bring her more ice cream, as Annie requested, "But I was very much inconvenienced that morning, and did not leave even as early as usual, and thinking the patient was very sick the thought came across me that perhaps she never will want the ice cream, and I did not detain myself to go downtown and get it, but I pursued the method of going directly to the house."

When Mrs. Marshall climbed the stairs to the third-floor tenement, she found Sarah and Prince chatting in the parlor.

Sarah said, "It seems, Prince, as though Annie will not live to see [Mrs. Marshall], doesn't it?"

"Well, it does."

Appalled, Mrs. Marshall urged them to lower their voices. "Be quiet. Don't let her know I am here, because I promised to get her some cream." Mrs. Marshall slapped the coins in Prince's hand. "I will let you take this money and get some."

After Prince returned with the "cream in a pail," he handed it to Sarah, who scooped a spoonful or two into a saucer.

Mrs. Marshall strolled into the sickroom and "bade Mrs. Freeman good-morning," saying, "Well, Ann, I have come, and here is your cream."

"I don't want it now." Annie looked even more physically spent. "Why didn't you come before?"

Mrs. Marshall handed the saucer to Sarah. "You take it. Perhaps she will take some from you by and by."

After five or ten minutes, Annie drifted asleep. That was Mrs. Marshall's cue to leave the room.

Along some hour or two after that, Mrs. [Sarah Jane] Robinson took some [more] cream in a saucer and carried it [into the sickroom]. I couldn't say that [Annie] ate it. I don't know. I only saw [Sarah] go into the room with the cream in a saucer. She came out with it empty and said her sister had eaten it, and upon coming out she put the saucer into the sink.

Then, out of the blue, Sarah said, "Ann wants some of that wine."

Startled, Mrs. Marshall jolted back in her chair by the stove. "What wine?"

"The lady downstairs [Mrs. Wright] offered to give her all the wine she wanted while she was sick."

"Well"—Mrs. Marshall slapped her thighs and rose—"let me take a cup and go down and get some."

"No, I will go." Flashing a flat hand, Sarah insisted, "I will go."

If she preferred to fetch the wine, Mrs. Marshall wasn't about to stop her. "She took a cup and went down."

Earlier in the day, Prince had complained to Mrs. Wright, "[Sarah] prevented in every way [of my] being in the room with [my] wife." His sister-in-law told him, "[You] better go to work." They could get along very well without him around.

Racked by grief, Prince didn't want to leave. "Mrs. Wright, what would you do?"

She said she "thought it necessary for him to stay at home; his wife was very ill."

And so, Prince took her advice. All day long, however, Sarah kept sending him on errands.

When Sarah came down for the wine on Thursday, February 26, she asked, "Mrs. Wright, if Ann should die, do you know of any underclothes, good underclothes that would be likely to be used in such a case?"

Mrs. Wright explained that when little Elisabeth was born Annie had stored a trunk with some underclothes in [it]. If anything was to happen, Annie asked her to please tell her sister about the trunk.

Sarah thanked her and brought the cupful of wine upstairs.

Mrs. Marshall was still seated by the stove in the kitchen when Sarah "came up and walked past the stove into the [sick]room." A god-awful noise followed—"denoted by a person with an empty stomach and sick, as we would naturally say a gulping sound, hollow, which indicated to me that she was drinking the wine, although I couldn't see it, or drinking something which purported to be wine."

When Sarah returned to the kitchen, she set the cup in the sink, turned, and cupped Mrs. Marshall's hands in hers. "You should have seen how voraciously she drank that wine, drained it to the dregs."

A gurgling sound emanated from the bedroom—the death rattle—and Sarah sprinted into the chamber. Moments later, she called out, "Annie is dying! Come in!"

2

DON'T COME
BETWEEN MOTHER
AND DAUGHTER

Miles away in Rutland, Vermont, E. L. Hatch hustled down the street
to Mrs. Harriet E. Nason's house, after her daughter, Maud, had
called for him in a panic. Somehow, sixteen-year-old Maud had swallowed
a pin and it lodged in her throat. E. L. had known Maud's new husband,
twenty-two-year-old Donald C. Parker, for years. They'd played in the same
band and moved in the same social circles. So, when Don's new bride called
for him on Tuesday, February 17, 1885, he came right away.

While at the house, Mrs. Nason—"a woman of rather nervous temper-
ament, but resolute and energetic, and not particularly attractive in personal
appearance"—told E. L. Hatch that Don was a very sick man. The chances
of survival, she thought, weren't good.

"The house was fated," she added.

Fated for what? E. L. charged into the sickroom and found his friend
in a bad way. Don complained of a burning sensation throughout his
body. "His thirst was insatiable and severe contractions of the limbs almost
amounted to convulsions." E. L. knew something like this would happen if he married Maud Nason, "a young woman of quite noticeable personal charm." Hence why he and his friend Nicholson had protested the
wedding.

Don Parker was a popular, intelligent young man and well-liked in society. "About a year ago, he began paying attention to Miss Maud," after boarding at Harriet Nason's house for two years. Although both were young, the courtship was a brief one. On October 13, 1884, the two lovebirds tied the knot and "kept house" with Mrs. Nason, a widow of four years. "Everybody agreed that it was a happy household. Don manifested a genuine affection for his mother-in-law as well as for his wife," and life went smoothly until Don scored a high-paying job in Boston. As an expert stenographer, his skills were in high demand. "He was about to start with his wife for that city when he was taken suddenly ill."

Harriet Nason asked E. L. to tell the attending physician, Dr. John A. Mead, that Don had experienced "such spells" while boarding at his house several months earlier.

E. L. refused, "because it was not true." He had never seen Don in this condition. "Mrs. Nason prepared all the food taken by the sick man, and Don could retain none of it." E. L. stayed the night, watching over his friend till dawn.

In the neighborhood where E. L. Hatch's family and the Nasons both lived, many regarded Harriet as "peculiar at times" but with "remarkable powers in the way of prophesying fires." Some even said, "She's a witch, and has predicted the exact time of various fires." Like Sarah Jane Robinson, Harriet claimed to obtain the information in dreams.

"Mrs. Nason's house on Grove Street burned in accordance with her prediction about three years ago," a neighbor told a reporter for the *Rutland Herald*. "Subsequently, she had another fiery vision. This alarmed another family in the same block and a watchman was employed. But the second fire occurred on scheduled time, though not until Mrs. Nason had been notified by the owners of the property to vacate."

When E. L. Hatch returned on Wednesday, February 18, Don kept clutching his stomach and abdomen. If only he could get rid of whatever was in there, he said, he would be all right.

Mrs. Nason told E. L. that she had prepared all of Don's "nourishment" because he wanted her to do it. But now, "Don was delirious half the time, rolling about in bed with convulsions and drawing up the limbs, and seemed in great agony."

Mrs. Parker, Don's mother, was also at the house. Early on in his sickness, she had leaned over the bed and whispered, "I pity you, Don, if you have got to live with that woman all your life."

"Wait till I get well, Mother. Maud and I will have a house of our own and I'll be boss then."

Unsure of whether to trust Dr. Mead—her son seemed to be sinking fast—Mrs. Parker called on Dr. Sanborn, who "gave her a powder and some medicine in a vial." Back at the house she "administered it in accordance with the instructions," even though the powder never lasted long on Don's stomach. On a follow-up visit, Mrs. Parker begged Dr. Sanborn to examine her son, but he said he would only prescribe the same medicine. Nonetheless, he agreed to stop by.

Once Dr. Sanborn examined the patient, he prescribed beef extract. Mrs. Parker prepared the dish for her son.

> But Mrs. Nason tipped it over on the stove and prepared some more herself. When Dr. Sanborn asked to have the contents of the stomach saved when [Don] vomited, it was put away in a basin, but Mrs. Nason threw it away once because she said she didn't know [the doctors] wanted it, and another time because she said that it would make them all sick if [the vomit] was left standing.

E. L.'s mother, Mrs. Hatch, was also in the kitchen when Mrs. Nason knocked over the beef extract. Once, she said, Mrs. Nason asked her to guard the door of the sickroom and not let anyone in, not even Don's mother. "Mrs. Nason then remained with Don, but I didn't know what she was doing inside."

"On Wednesday [February 18,]" Mrs. Parker said, "he threw up a singular substance that looked like a piece of coarse beef. He eagerly picked it out, saying that he guessed that was what caused all his trouble. He even thought that it might be a piece of some dried beef that he ate the night he was taken sick. This was carefully saved to show to the doctor," but she forgot about it. Then "Mrs. Nason said she had showed the doctor and he thought it might be slippery elm, as he had taken some when he was first sick to allay the irritation."

 *Slippery elm is a tree. The inner bark is still used today as medicine for coughs, sore throat, colic, diarrhea, constipation, hemorrhoids, irritable bowel syndrome, bladder and urinary tract infections, syphilis, herpes, and expelling tapeworms. It's also used to protect against stomach and duodenal ulcers, colitis, diverticulitis, GI inflammation, and to cause abortion.*

That same afternoon Mrs. Parker returned to the house, but Harriet Nason hedged her off in the kitchen with a tumbler of water. Don wanted some drink, she said, and she got it for him.

When Mrs. Parker asked about her son, Harriet said, "Oh, he's asleep," and turned and walked away.

Mrs. Parker hurried after her. "Give me the water and I will let him drink it when he wakes." But Mrs. Nason immediately emptied the glass. During his illness, "Don liked to listen to the after running in the adjoining room," according to his mother. When liquid was poured down the sink, the sound soothed him. "But Mrs. Nason stopped it, saying that she would have to pay for it."

"I don't believe that Don is as sick as he thinks he is." Harriet batted her hand. "He is very nervous."

Puzzled by Don Parker's case, Dr. Mead administered a counterirritant of potash and soda, aconite, oxide corium, and injections of hydrate chloral.

[I] detected no signs of poisoning while treating the patient, and [I] think that the great number of blue pills he took may have been converted into [a] corrosive sublimate in the acid in the pickles, of which [I] ate, too, freely.

But the nurse, Warren McClure, knew better.

When [I] first got there, I told the friends [E. L. and Nicholson] that unless [Don] Parker rallied soon, he would be a dead man in 48 hours. [The patient's] mouth was raw, he was suffering from intense thirst and seemed to be burning up inside. The muscles of his arms and legs would contract convulsively and he would beat his breast with his hands and roll restlessly in bed.

Although McClure asked for Dr. Mead to wait and see him about pre-scribing medicine, when McClure returned from his meal, the doctor had been and gone.

[I] had only a few powders to give the sick man and no narcotics to induce sleep.

When asked about the powdered medicine at trial, McClure testified:

[I] tasted the powders before administering them. The room was cold and the patient's body seemed clammy to the touch. [Don Parker] struggled for breath and had to be fanned constantly. . . . On Wednesday night, I stayed with him and gave him occasionally a powder, which was the only medicine left by [Dr. Sanborn]. The patient was restless and suffered intense pain all through the night. He seemed to be burning up inwardly and I had to give him water to drink every ten minutes and fan him constantly.

[Don] had every symptom of being poisoned. His mouth, chest, and stomach appeared to be sore and inflamed. He had no disease and yet he was dying by inches.

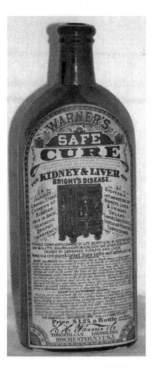

Warner's Safe Kidney & Liver Cure *Public Domain*

Harriet Nason told Dr. Sanborn that Don had a habit of taking medicine, and showed him a bottle of Warner's Safe Kidney & Liver Cure. "Do you think this could have poisoned him?" She and Maud had taken doses of it, she said, and it had made them both sick.

Hulbert Harrington Warner was a New York businessman and philanthropist who made his fortune off patent medicine. When he developed a severe case of Bright's disease (kidney disease), he drank a vegetable concoction developed by Charles Craig, and soon his health was miraculously restored. Warner was so amazed that he purchased the formula and the product rights. In 1879, he introduced Warner's Safe Kidney & Liver Cure, sold in amber bottles with a safe imprinted in the glass and on the label. Warner went on to develop Safe Nervine, Safe Diabetes Cure, Safe Tonic Bitters, Safe Rheumatic Cure, and Safe Pills. By 1884, his company was churning out a staggering seven thousand gallons of Safe Cure medicine per day.

What were the ingredients in the mystery cure that Don Parker drank almost daily? Bungleweed, wintergreen extract, glycerin, alcohol, water, and potassium nitrate (better known as saltpeter), which is a common food preservative and additive, oxidizer for fireworks and rockets, and one of the principal ingredients in gunpowder. But the real culprit Harriet Nason might have alluded to was liverwort extract, also known as *Hepatica Americana*. Even though it's an herbal medicine, large doses can produce symptoms of poisoning.

Dr. Mead called a colleague to consult on the case, and it was this physician, Dr. Goldsmith, who first mentioned Don Parker might be suffering from poisoning, even though when he first examined him he thought he would recover. "There were no noticeable symptoms of fever, but [Don] Parker suffered from distress," which Dr. Goldsmith attributed to simple indigestion. "The symptoms seemed more alarming Wednesday [February 18], and he gradually sank until death Friday." (Since Don died a minute before or after midnight, some records show he passed on Thursday night, February 19; others show he died in the early morning hours of Friday, February 20.)

Maud told Dr. Goldstein her husband had been taking "some white bismuth powders," and her mother, Harriet, added, "she wondered if those powders could have been anything besides white bismuth."

At trial Dr. Goldstein testified:

> Mrs. Nason said something about looking for some of the powders to examine them. The first indication of approaching death was noticeable in the pulse, and he continued to sink until the end, attended by the same symptoms noticed earlier in the case.

Rumors ran rampant in town. Did Harriet Nason poison her son-in-law? If so, how did Dr. Mead miss the telltale signs?

The first to bring up the necessity for an investigation was E. L. Hatch, but he wasn't prepared for Dr. Mead's reaction.

> Dr. Mead took me into a room, locked the door, and put the key in his pocket. Then he called me to account for what he had heard I had said about him [that Dr. Mead had missed the symptoms of arsenical poisoning]. He wanted me to understand that he held a prominent position.

"You had better not carry this thing too far," Dr. Mead warned. "I know Governor Ripley very well, and you will lose your job at the Rutland Opera House if you do not stop this talk. Everybody knows that [Don] Parker's death was from enlargement of the heart."

When Don died, Mrs. Nason fainted, according to Mr. Nicholson who was at his friend's bedside when he gasped his final breath. In fact, it was he and E. L. Hatch who brought their concerns to Mrs. Parker.

The furious mother demanded an autopsy.

But no one could've predicted what Harriet Nason would do next.

3

THE FOUNDATION
OF LIES CRUMBLES

Back in Cambridge, three months after the death of Annie Freeman, Mr. Desmond took another trip to Sarah's door, insisting, "Now, I must have that money, Mrs. Robinson."

With desperation in her eyes, Sarah pleaded for more time. "Mr. Desmond, I am going to have money pretty soon, and I will pay you."

But, he said, there was something peculiar about *the way* she said it. "Why, Mrs. Robinson, what is all this mystery about?"

Even after asking numerous times, he never got a straight answer.

She resided on Hughes Street, I think. I had two or three conversations with her in that house. I went there once when I was out to ride in a sleigh with a friend, and she said, 'Mr. Desmond, we have had another death in the family since I saw you.'

He had trouble recalling which family member died, but he thought it was a child. The next time Desmond spoke to Sarah,

She lived on another street, I don't remember the number. The fifth day of May 1885, I had a long conversation with her, when she lived in the house on Boylston Street, Cambridge. It was the longest conversation I had ever had with her. I went there . . . [but] she was not in when I called. I waited till she arrived home. She gave me five dollars, the last and the only money she ever gave me with her own hand. She told me there had been another death in the family—I think she told me that every time I called at the house.

Sarah invited him into the parlor to chat.

"Mrs. Robinson," Desmond said as he sat, "you must have had a pretty numerous family. You have had so many deaths. It can't be possible. I never have seen your family, you don't allow me to see them. I never knew you had any family, any more than yourself."

"Well," she said, "my family has increased now. My brother-in-law has come to live with me, and, really, my family is made up of two families now."

Then she explained that her brother-in-law had died. But before Desmond left the apartment, Sarah corrected herself. Her sister had passed, not her brother-in-law.

We had quite a conversation about her changing what she had told me.

Doubting her story, Desmond used a brash tone. "It is very singular you are having so many deaths in your family. Can it be possible?"

"Yes, I think I shall lose them all. I think they will all die, all go in the same way."

"Why?" Desmond's eyes widened. "What appears to be the matter with them?"

"I think they are in a general decline."

Desmond asked if the lawsuit to recoup Moses's life insurance had been tried in superior court.

Staring at the floor, Sarah admitted the court had ruled against her.

Later, Desmond recalled this conversation. Once she came clean about the verdict, Desmond said she added this clarification:

But her counsel had assured her that the law point was in her favor, that the action would be reversed, and she thought she would recover the money finally.

Unbeknownst to Sarah, Desmond had spoken to her attorney.

While it was possible she might [obtain a reversal], I had very serious doubts whether she would ever recover on that policy.

Sarah asked for his views on insurance companies. Specific policies, she said, "where, in the case of death, each party pays in money."

"You mean these companies that have sprung up recently, called mutual companies?"

"Yes."

"I always have heard a good report of them. I don't belong to any of them myself, but I understand they are good reliable companies."

When Desmond inquired whether she was counting on the lawsuit's reversal to pay her bills, Sarah said, "No, I am going to get a large sum of money. I am going to be all right shortly. I can see my way clear now."

"Why?" Desmond cocked an eyebrow. "Where is this money coming from?"

"Oh," she said, "I am going to get it. It is all right. I shall have plenty of money to pay you off. You have been very kind and waited for me, and I shall pay you all your money, principal and interest. I shall also pay Mr. Tobin [another creditor] and other parties previously."

"Well, you are very fortunate. Where is it coming from, Mrs. Robinson?"

"Well, I cannot tell you that," she flimflammed, "but you will get your money."

"How much are you going to get? How much money?"

"It will be several thousand dollars."

"About how much?"

"Well, it will be thousands."

"How many thousands?"

"Well, it will be two, three, or four thousand, not less than two."

"Well, now, Mrs. Robinson, why not tell me where it is coming from? You have got my interest awakened. You are owing me a good deal of money, you have told me false stories several times, why not tell me where it is coming from?"

"I cannot tell you, Mr. Desmond. The parties do not wish me to say anything about it."

As Desmond was leaving, he stopped and turned back. "Mrs. Robinson, what is this mystery about you and your house? It has continued since I first saw you up till this very time, and to-day it is mystery upon mystery. Pray tell me what it is."

Still seated in her chair, Sarah casually rested her hand on the armrest. "What mystery?"

"That is what I want to know. What mystery? I cannot tell, but there is some mystery that I have not been able to ascertain."

Desmond's loan was for seventy-five dollars. With principle and interest, Sarah needed to repay $146. But how?

Lizzie's friend Belle Clough recalled going in the carriage with Mrs. Robinson and Lizzie to Annie's funeral. She'd known the family for eight years, visiting almost daily.

> During the carriage ride, Mrs. Robinson asked her daughter to use her influence upon her uncle to come and live with her, as [Lizzie] had a great deal of influence over [Prince].

"You need not worry about that," Lizzie told her mother. "I will have uncle come all right. He would do anything for me."

During the mercy meal in South Boston, Sarah seemed anxious to have Prince move in at once. And he said that he would, just as soon as he could get things squared away at his house. Then Sarah asked if the life insurance beneficiary was changed yet. Prince said he hadn't done that yet (they'd buried his wife less than an hour ago), but he would get to it posthaste.

This infuriated Sarah. It must be done right away, she demanded, or his mother and sister might try to get custody of Tommy. After all, Prince's family never bothered with him, she claimed. But now? Now, they knew about the insurance.

On almost every visit to the house, Belle overheard "Mrs. Robinson mumbling about the insurance, that she was afraid [Prince] would not make the insurance over to her, that he was going over to his folks every Sunday, and she thought they had a great deal of influence over him." Prince's attitude toward Sarah had changed. "He was not as pleasant at the house and was not pleasant with her."

Every Sunday when Prince attended church with his folks in South Boston, Sarah urged him to take Tommy, "but he always refused." The reason she wanted Tommy to go, she told Belle, was so she could drill him with questions when he got home. Perhaps "Tommy might tell [me] about things that happened while he was away."

It wasn't until early April that Prince finally moved into Sarah's third-floor tenement at 54 Boylston Street. Three weeks later, baby Elisabeth developed a sudden case of intestinal catarrh (inflamed mucous membranes of the intestines). Sarah nursed her niece with the same tender care that she'd lavished upon her sister. Nonetheless, within a few days, little Elisabeth succumbed to her illness. They laid her to rest next to her mother in the Robinsons' family plot.

Later, District Attorney William B. Stevens cautioned the jury about her passing.

> I have not anything to say about little [Elisabeth]. There is no evidence that she was killed. She was a little infant, and you are not to presume anything against Mrs. Robinson about her. It is presumed she died a natural death.

But did she?

Devastated by another death in his family, Prince changed the beneficiary on his life insurance policy to Sarah Jane Robinson on May 13, 1885, "for the care of Thomas Arthur Freeman."

One month later, the evening of June 21, Prince and his seventeen-year-old nephew, Charley, hiked to the Boston Common where thousands gathered for spiritual guidance. Reverend Bates conducted the one-hour service and had gazed down during the event to see Prince cradling his face in his palms and looking "very pale, very white, cast down, sad."

After the service, Reverend Bates checked on the keening widower and father. "What is the matter?"

Prince said he wanted to take some air and had come to speak with the reverend.

"What did you want to see me for?"

Prince said he wanted comfort, that he'd been sick and disheartened ever since his wife died.

The reverend laid a soothing hand on his shoulder. "Be brave and fight the battle. A great many men had had bereavement as hard and severe as [you], and God had given them deliverance."

On the way home Prince and Charley trekked across the West Boston Bridge on foot. At the halfway point, the grieving widower broke down. "I have a good mind to jump overboard. I have nothing to live for. My wife and child are both dead. There is nothing for me in life."

"You better not," said Charley.

Those three words ended the suicide nonsense.

While outwardly affectionate and kind toward Prince in public, behind closed doors—"when he was not there, when she was among her own family and the inmates of her own house," according to Belle Clough—Sarah showed her real feelings toward Prince, calling him "a worthless fellow."

Over dinner one night, Sarah said, "[I] never would have had him move in if it had not been for the insurance. . . . He could not earn his living. . . . [I] got him a job in Mount Auburn, because he was too lazy to get a living. . . . He could not earn enough to support himself. . . . He earned only six dollars a week in South Boston, and spent more than half he earned in car fares. . . . He was a poor, worthless fellow. . . . [I] wish he was dead . . . that he better die. . . . [I] wish somebody would give him a dose and put him out of the way."

After a brief pause, Sarah added, "[I] wish he could have died instead of [my] sister." Swiveling toward Lizzie, hope sparkled in her hollow eyes. "Would you talk with him and make him feel more contented and more at home?"

"Oh, he's all right," Lizzie said. "He [will] stay."

"He's no good anyway." Sarah's face reddened. "I wish he was out of the way. I wish someone would give him a dose and *put him* out of the way."

Then she "kind of stopped a minute," according to Belle, "then she got real nervous, and looked over her shoulder and we thought she was going to fall."

"What is the matter, Mother?" asked Lizzie. "Has Father come to you again?"

"Yes, I thought your father tapped me on the shoulder."

"Oh, [has] Father come for Uncle, Mother?" Meaning, in a vision. The whole family believed Sarah possessed the gift of prophecy.

"Yes," she confirmed. "I should not wonder but something would happen to your uncle soon."

On the morning of Wednesday, June 17, Sarah told Prince to visit his mother in Charlestown, "because he might not live to see her again."

Five days later, Monday, June 22, Prince headed out the door after breakfast. He'd made it to South Boston when he vomited all over the road. "On Pleasant Street, between Shawmut Avenue and the Providence Depot," he ran into a member of his "Colony" of the Order of Pilgrim Fathers. Mr. F. J. Hayes took one look at Prince—"awfully weak, pale"—and asked him what was wrong.

"Mr. Hayes, I feel awfully queer in the stomach. I don't feel well. . . . I have just thrown up my breakfast."

"Well, Mr. Freeman, if I was you, I would turn 'round and go home."

"I can't," Prince insisted. "I have just buried my wife, and I am only getting six dollars a week, and I have to look out for my family." Then Prince inquired about his insurance papers. "I applied a good while ago for them." Matter of fact, he'd planned to attend the Colony meeting that night to make sure everything was in order.

"Come, Mr. Freeman, if you are able, but I guess they are all right."

Later that day, Prince ran into Maggie Smith, who also asked him what was wrong.

"I am very sick. I have been vomiting all day."

Struggling at the Norwegian Steel and Iron Company in South Boston, where Prince spent his days immersing iron bars in an acid bath (a process known as "pickling"), his supervisor noticed something wasn't right with Prince and sent him home.

Once Prince arrived at the third-floor tenement at 54 Boylston Street, Sarah acted as though she'd expected him to leave work early. But how? Had she experienced another vision?

Slinging Prince's arm around her neck, Sarah assisted him down a long hallway that ran down the middle of the apartment, with a kitchen and parlor on one side and two bedrooms on the other.

As Prince crawled into bed, Sarah sent word for Dr. John T. G. Nichols—the same physician who misdiagnosed Jolly Jane's victims—to come right away. That same night she sent Lizzie and Belle Clough to the officers at the Colony to "ascertain whether the insurance was all right or not."

When the two girls returned, Lizzie's answer didn't quell her mother's anxiety. Obsessed over one or two "trifling assessments," Sarah sent more messages to the lodge during that week. Without receiving an adequate response, she pleaded with Mrs. Florence Stanwood, the Colony's treasurer, to come to the house so they could speak in person.

Even after Mrs. Stanwood assured her the assessments were paid, Sarah said she had no money to pay any arrears. Prince was worthless. He had fifty cents to his name. "I have gone without food on my table to keep these assessments paid up."

Considering Prince had "enjoyed good health all his life," the statement struck Mrs. Stanwood as odd.

Later, District Attorney Stevens would call attention to this conversation.

It would be, as the government say, a remarkable statement for her to make, unless she was going to get some benefit out of this insurance.

Nonetheless, Mrs. Stanwood paid the past-due assessments out of her own pocket.

But then, Sarah spat out another off-the-wall remark—please don't tell Mrs. Melvin (Prince's sister) that he'd changed the beneficiary.

Wanting no part of butting into family affairs, Mrs. Stanford agreed she would not say a word.

Later that afternoon or early evening, Dr. John T. G. Nichols arrived. After a thorough examination, he noted that Prince suffered with several different symptoms.

Headache, vomiting, pain in the abdomen, thirst, a quick pulse, and low elevation of temperature. [The patient] showed no sign of disease in the lungs, nor in the heart, nor were there any physical signs—signs that were evident to [his] senses in the abdomen. The abdomen was not distended . . . not tender.

"I don't know what ails him," Dr. Nichols told Sarah. "I can't tell."

"If you don't know his case," Sarah said, "bring in another physician, call any man you see fit, call any physician, and let them make the examination."

At trial, Dr. Nichols couldn't recall what he'd prescribed for Prince, except "the principal things used at that time." External applications included "mustard, and milk, and lime water, and soda water, and opium, in doses sufficient to relieve his pain."

Prince explained to the doctor "that he went to his work that morning and was taken sick on his way to his work, with vomiting and headache and pain, and that those symptoms increased to such an extent that he was obliged to leave his work and come home, as he did."

Dr. Nichols wished him well. The following day, Tuesday, June 23, he returned.

His condition hadn't changed materially, and his symptoms were not severe enough . . . to make him a second visit on that day.

On Wednesday, the doctor visited twice, "because his symptoms were worse." The vomiting persisted and "the pain continued . . . there was some diarrhea . . . his pulse was extraordinarily weak. All this while his mind was clear . . . no fever, as shown by the temperature rising."

At Sarah's insistence, Dr. Nichols invited Dr. Driver of Cambridge to consult on the case. Dr. Driver conducted a thorough examination.

[Prince] was again carefully examined [and] still no evidence could be found of any organic disease. The lungs were carefully examined, and the heart was carefully examined. The sound was very feeble, but no disease could be detected by the ear, nor could there be any disease detected in his lungs or in his abdominal cavity, except as it was indicated by pain and vomiting.

Dr. Driver found no obstruction in the abdomen.

No evidence of any localized inflammation could be felt, nor was there any evidence of general inflammation, because the patient could move without any considerable pain, and there was no noticeable tenderness. The intestines were active, as shown by the diarrhea and the rolling and rattling . . . no albumen in the urine . . . examination showed that there was some acid, to a specific gravity, which was normal.

Neither doctor felt a microscopic examination was necessary at that point.

In the interim, a family friend, Mr. Charles Chandler, stopped by the apartment to lend a hand. Sarah said Dr. Nichols had ordered a hot bath for Prince and asked if he wouldn't mind bathing him.

"I told her I would, and I did," Chandler recalled. "And the next time I went up [Friday, June 26] she told me I had scalded him to death. I told her I didn't think I had."

"Well," Sarah said, "you have."

Chandler hustled into the sickroom, and Sarah followed.

I asked him how he felt. He said he didn't feel any better.

"But," said Prince, "I will get around all right."

"Mrs. Robinson said I fixed you with a hot bath."

"I guess you did. I am all right, or will be in a few days."

Sarah made "some passing remark" and left the room. When Chandler met her in the kitchen, she said, "The insurance had been made over to [me] to take care of Arthur [Tommy], and if anything happened to [Tommy, I am] to have it." Then she claimed her dead sister visited her in a dream "and told [me] that Mr. Freeman was not going to live."

"What have you done to them all that they are coming back to you?"

Sarah stumbled over to the lounge and collapsed.

"I guess she fainted," recalled Chandler.

The two physicians continued to check on their patient. Dr. Nichols later testified:

The question came up of the possibility of irritant poison. After we had considered that subject, which was broached to the patient and to Mrs. Robinson. [Prince's] occupation was considered. . . . It involved working in the presence of . . . sulphuric acid [fumes], and the possible handling of sulphuric acid. We determined that even if there were fumes of sulphuric acid in the room it would be impossible, in our opinion, for the symptoms . . . to be caused by the inhalation of the fumes. [Though] I can't profess to be an expert in pathology.

Next, the doctors discussed arsenic in particular,

and we considered the different methods by which a considerable quantity could be got into the system—the principal one being the possibility of household utensils being a way to get it into the system.

It wasn't unusual for folks to spread arsenic on bread to lure rats.

[After examining] one or two of the household utensils, [we con-cluded there was] no reason to suspect that arsenic could have got into his system from any such cause as that.

I must say, too, that those inquiries were answered in a most natural manner both by the patient and by Mrs. Robinson. There was nothing in the behavior of either of them, or in the answers of either of them, to warrant the slightest suspicion on our part . . . to pursue our inquiries more closely. . . . I began to be apprehensive about Wednesday, from the continuance of the symptoms, rather than any change.

Later that day, Sarah tried to convince the two physicians to speak on her behalf, as noted by Dr. Nichols.

Mrs. Robinson wished us to say something to Mr. Freeman in regard to the disposition of his boy, Thomas Arthur, the reason being that she was afraid the sister or the mother and father—or, at all events, his friends—would claim the boy, and she felt that he would be much better off with her. . . . She could give him better care. . . . She had had [Tommy] a good while, and that [his] relations with her were altogether pleasanter than with his own friends.

This request didn't raise any suspicions in either physician. So, Dr. Nichols explained, "Dr. Driver and I asked [Prince] Freeman that day what his desire was with regard to the disposition of his boy."

Prince said, "I wish [Tommy] to be in the care and in the hands of Mrs. Robinson."

On Thursday, June 25, Sarah asked for the Freeman family physician, Dr. Davidson, to consult on the case, as he might make Prince more com-fortable since he'd treated Annie. Dr. Nichols raised no objection.

Later that evening, Dr. Davidson prescribed bismuth for Prince.

Dr. Nichols noted on Friday:

His condition through the day hadn't materially changed, and that evening he was weaker, he was restless, his pulse was 120 and feeble, the sound being very feeble, the second sound being especially indistinct.

During that day he had hardly any pain, and no elevation of temperature, the vomiting continuing. He got some brandy and tincture of *nux vomica* [a homeopathic medication derived from the *Strychnos nux-vomica* tree, also called the vomiting nut or the poison nut tree, because the seeds contained strychnine and brucine—both toxic in large doses] two drops every hour, hoping to check the vomiting. He was so sick that I saw him three times [that day].

In Charlestown, Prince's family received an urgent postcard from Sarah. Catharine Melvin, Prince's sister, had been spending the summer in Nantucket. When her mother first wrote to her on Monday, June 22, she hustled home. But by the time she reached the house, a second postcard had been delivered.

"The doctor considered him out of danger," Catharine recalled, "so we didn't hurry." Sometime "towards night" Catharine and Mrs. Melvin, her mother, arrived at 54 Boylston Street to find Prince "ill and drawn out."

Sarah said that Prince left work on Monday. "He was very sick and had been vomiting."

"He was vomiting when I arrived," Catharine retorted.

"[I] felt all day that he would come home sick, and had told [my] daughter several times, 'Uncle is coming home sick.' [I] had been looking for him, and not surprised when he came home."

"Well, probably he will get over it." In Catharine's heart of hearts, she felt her brother would make a full recovery. But Sarah insisted that she knew better.

Catharine and Mrs. Melvin stayed all night. During that time Prince told his sister he was hungry, which was encouraging, but she didn't dare give him anything until the doctor arrived in the morning.

When Dr. Nichols examined Prince on Saturday, June 26, he remarked, "I don't know what it is, but you seem to be very much better." He turned toward Catharine. If he felt like eating, feed him.

"Then he suggested a specific food and how to prepare it," Catharine recalled.

Dr. Nichols had suggested Liebig's Extract of Meat—also called Liebig's Fleisch Extract ("Fleisch" meaning "meat" in German)—which was a thick, dark, syrupy beef extract paste sold in glass bottles and later sold in tins as well. It first gained popularity as a food for the poor, until it wormed its way into middle-class kitchens as an ingredient.

During the last few hours of Catharine's stay on Saturday, her brother seemed restless and complained of a "great thirst." At trial she testified, "I gave him ice continually; kept cracked ice by him." She offered to stay again that night, but Sarah was expecting two Colony members to act as "watchers" while Prince slept.

"It would be better for you to go home to Charlestown and return in the morning," Sarah said. "[You] are not very strong. [Get some rest, then you will] be better prepared to take care of him [tomorrow]."

Catharine never saw her brother alive again.

4

THE LETTER

———————————————

Harriet Nason was appalled by the ugly rumors that she, an upstanding
member of society, could possibly be a murderess. One night, she
tried to dispense such disgraceful talk by writing a letter to Don's mother.
By the flickering glow of an oil lamp, Harriet dipped her pen into the ink
well on her desk.

At Home, Tuesday Afternoon.

Dear Mrs. Parker:

My heart is so sad to-night I can scarcely write, but I feel that I must
see Mr. Parker [Don's father], and have a talk with him. I hear that
he has said that my poor boy, Don, was poisoned, and that I know
about it. A great many other terrible things have been said connected with it. Now, I don't believe Mr. Parker said one-half of what
I hear he did, but if any evil-minded person has told him anything
of that kind and he believed it, why didn't he come to me?

It seems to me perfectly ridiculous for him to believe any such
thing, much more to report it. You both know very well how I
loved Don, and he loved me, as he often told me. It seemed that he
thought as much of me as he did of his own mother. I feel just as
bad to lose him as I would my body, and God in heaven knows I
did all I could to have him get well, and he said so the night he died.

Now, supposing that his medicine should have poisoned him,
which I don't think for a moment it did, why should I be blamed?
Supposing what he took that night when he was taken sick should

be poison, why should I be to blame? Supposing if any of the physicians should give him anything through a mistake, am I to blame for it? You only stop and think for one moment what a terrible thing to say that I was to blame for Don's death. It just drives me wild, and I think now, as God is my judge, that it will drive me crazy. Ah! If poor Don was only here, if he could only speak, how quick he would say,

"Never mind ma; you are good to me."

Among other things I know that if what Don took that night was poison he never knew it. He never would take it on purpose. He was too happy with his darling wife, and it seems so hard to see my poor Maud now grieving her life away day after day. She feels her loss more to-day than ever before. Her health is all broken down. God only knows how it will end with her; I don't. Tell Mr. Parker I want to see him this week; if he can come up he must.

Please write.

Mrs. N.

On the evening of the autopsy Albert Parker, Don's father, called on Mrs. Nason, and she said she hoped he did not blame her for his son's death.

"Mrs. Nason," he said, "I hope nothing is wrong—I *hope* nothing is wrong—and I only want to know that all was right. I do not know whether anyone was guilty. The Lord knows, I hope not."

All efforts to hush the ugly stories or to smother an investigation were unavailing. Don Parker's body was examined, but the postmortem did not reveal the cause of death. The autopsy only showed general internal inflammation and slight enlargement of the liver. The medical examiner sent the stomach and its contents to Professor R. A. Witthaus of Buffalo, New York, for chemical analyses.

Muffled whispers continued around town. The fuse had been lit. No amount of denial could stop the stampede of questions for Harriet Nason. The authorities dug into her past. Henry Nason, Harriet's husband, died four years earlier on September 15, 1882, after a brief and sudden illness. Mrs. O. H. McKeen's infant son, Don (named after a paternal uncle), died in December 1885 while Harriet was visiting her sister in Gorham, New Hampshire.

The *Boston Globe* reported:

> The terrible suffering of the child and his peculiar symptoms caused the physicians to think he had been poisoned, but there was no reason for attaching suspicion to anyone.

Mrs. C. S. De Britton of Portland, Maine—Harriet's "well-to-do" friend—also died under suspicious circumstances a month earlier (November 1885). The two women visited each other frequently, and no known falling out occurred between them; however, Mrs. De Britton's sickness was also very peculiar.

Later, the *Boston Globe* opined,

> Mrs. Nason was her most intimate friend, and frequently dined and supped with [Mrs. C. S. De Britton]. Many times after eating with Mrs. Nason she was taken very ill, an unaccountable sick headache and pains in the back and legs.

At the time, suggestions of poisoning got tossed around between De Britton's attending physicians, as her symptoms aligned with arsenical poisoning, but the inquiry was quickly quashed due to the lack of a plausible motive.

Folks now questioned if Harriet had killed them all.

Despite the rumors, Dr. Mead stood firm in his beliefs.

> No such inflamed appearance on the autopsy [of Don Parker] as arsenic would naturally have caused. So far as the other deaths in the Nason family are concerned, where foul play is now suspected, Mr. [Henry] Nason died in 1882 of contraction and hardening of the liver, and Mrs. De Britton was suffering from heart disease aggravated by typhoid, and her death was consequently due to these complications.

Not everyone agreed.

A few days after Don's funeral, E. L. Hatch ran into Harriet, who seemed agitated about the current rumors about poisoning.

"If he did die of poison," Harriet said, "how are they going to prove it? Supposing they find a coal hod [bucket-like container] full of poison, how would they prove that I gave it?"

E. L. just ignored her. In his mind, this woman had murdered his friend. The *Sunday Globe* agreed with Hatch.

[The news] soon came to the ears of Mr. Kendall, the State's attorney, that other relatives and close friends of Mrs. Nason had died in a sudden and mysterious way. He was so impressed by the similarity of symptoms in these cases that he obtained leave to exhume the bodies of the dead.

A life insurance policy on Henry Nason paid out "several thousand dollars" to Harriet after the loss of her husband. She and her two children, Maud and Guy, lived on the proceeds until "about a year ago, when the money ran out." Don Parker had a one-thousand-dollar policy with Equitable Life. Was that enough incentive to murder her son-in-law?

The *Essex County Herald* shared their opinion.

There is no evidence that there was the slightest domestic discord or unhappiness in the [Nason-Parker] family. Mr. [Don] Parker had an insurance of $1,000 on his life, but this would seem but a small incentive for murder. Besides, he was her main support, as [Mrs. Nason] has but little property of her own, and it is difficult to assign a motive for the crime.

Maud agreed to an interview with the *Daily Globe*, and insisted her mother knew nothing of the one-thousand-dollar insurance on her husband's life. "It had been kept a secret between [my] husband and I. Don had never been well [since they wed in October 1884]. He was troubled with biliousness and was forever taking medication."

When the reporter asked if the rumor of suicide could be true, she said, "Why, it can't be possible. He loved to live too well. He had a long, hard struggle to get an education, and was just beginning to feel that he was fairly on his feet and free from debt. He received word by telegraph the Saturday before his death [February 14] of a position as stenographer awaiting him in a large Boston house, which he was to accept immediately. He replied that he would go Monday [February 16]."

"Did you intend to go to Boston with him?"

"Oh, yes, indeed. I expected to be ready to follow him Wednesday [February 18], and mamma would go later, after making arrangements to live with us in Boston."

Did Harriet think she was losing her daughter? What if, after the newlyweds moved away, they decided to live alone? Harriet would be left behind. That she could never allow.

Before State Attorney Kendall had the chance to investigate all the suspicious deaths within Mrs. Nason's inner circle, Professor Witthaus sent him a telegram on the evening of April 21—large quantities of arsenic found in Don Parker's stomach. State Attorney Kendall ordered Deputy Sheriff Stearns to arrest Harriet Nason on the sole charge of murdering her son-in-law.

As the deputy explained to Harriet why she was being arrested, she scowled, outraged by the accusation. "Why am I accused? For what reason [would I have to kill Don] any more than any other person? Why not attribute it to the white powder Dr. Sanborn sent up in the night? Why not arrest him as well?"

Meanwhile, State Attorney Kendall dug into the other mysterious deaths. A solid motive became a little trickier to pinpoint. Unless, of course, Harriet had "a mania for poison."

Mrs. Nason is afflicted with a most dangerous and insidious form of insanity, and that all the results of her secret work are not yet known.

5

SUSPICIONS GROW
IN MASSACHUSETTS

I n Cambridge, Catharine Melvin was understandably devastated by her
brother's death.

> I went the next morning as soon as I got the first horse-car that went
> over [to 54 Boylston Street].

Prince Arthur Freeman expired a few minutes after midnight, on Sunday, February 28, 1885. At trial Dr. Nichols testified to his patient's final days.

> His mind was wandering some in the afternoon [on Saturday].
> The sound of his heart was very indistinct, the second sound being
> absent. [Around midnight] his pulse was very weak, and he died.

Careworn and consumed with grief, a million things raced through Catharine's mind at once. "Do you think the insurance on his life would be paid?"

"I doubt it very much," said Sarah.

"If the insurance *is* paid, his funeral expenses would be paid out of that."

True, but Sarah said she hadn't received the papers from the Colony, that the papers were still waiting to be transferred.

Catharine wrongly assumed she meant the beneficiary had been changed to her nephew, Tommy. "In that case, I would be responsible for his expenses (meaning the cost of the undertaker's services)."

With a curt nod, Sarah agreed. But when the undertaker arrived, he insisted on following proper procedure. Rather than bill an individual, he needed to submit the invoice to the estate.

Once Mrs. Florence Stanwood (treasurer for the Colony) cut the insurance check, she traveled to the Robinson house to deliver the money in person and spend the afternoon.

Later that day, Lizzie arrived home.

When she strode through the door, Sarah showed her the check. "Now, Lizzie, that we have got the money, you can join the Order. You shall have some gloves and little extras, as soon as [the check clears]." A new membership cost $5.25.

Why this didn't concern Lizzie, no one knew.

With cash in hand, Sarah paid her creditors and moved her family into a nicer home in Somerville. In November of that year, Sarah treated herself to a trip to Wisconsin to visit her brother. Soon after her return, in February 1886, Lizzie suddenly fell ill.

As Colony collector, Mrs. Florence Stanwood rode the added miles to check on the well-being of the newest member of the Order of Pilgrim Fathers. The new home was a major upgrade from the third-floor tenement on Boylston Street.

A change for the better, decidedly. In the carpets, furniture, [and new] piano.

"What a pretty carpet," Mrs. Stanwood remarked.

"Yes," said Sarah. "It is one I had before Moses died, and it has been in storage all this time. Hasn't it kept nicely? It just fits this room."

The carpet looked new, but Mrs. Stanwood kept that detail to herself.

Lizzie grew sicker and sicker—with identical symptoms to Prince and Annie—and died within a week, on Monday, February 22. But she had insured her life for two thousand dollars when she joined the Order, at her mother's insistence. Lizzie, however, was not a stupid girl. In the event of her death, her brother, Willie, would receive the payout.

Being excluded as beneficiary on her daughter's policy simply would not do. So, Sarah put a new plan into motion by encouraging Willie to join the Order of Pilgrim Fathers. Not only was he the oldest now but with so many deaths in the family, it was the right thing to do. And so, he followed his mother's advice. In the interim Sarah played the grief-stricken mother role.

> After Lizzie died, I was very sick. Dr. Stevens was my attending physician at the time. Miss [Belle] Clough was taking care of me. Dr. Beers called one afternoon, and I was very much worse after his call. Miss [Belle] Clough asked me to write to him [and tell him] not to come on Sunday, and I don't remember whether I wrote the note or [she did] . . . and sent it by Charley [Sarah's son] to the doctor."

But was she grieving the death of her daughter, or had something else sent her swooning onto her bed?

When Charley returned that day, he told his mother that Dr. Beers wasn't in. While there, though, he had a strange interaction. Sarah recalled the conversation with her son.

> Charley told me that he went to the door, and I don't know whether he said a gentleman or lady came to the door. . . . He said to someone who came to the door—he asked if the doctor was in, and [the person] said no, but his wife was in.

Until that day, Sarah believed Dr. Beers was a widower. After all, he'd been courting her for many years. One night he'd even dropped to one knee and presented her with a ring—a promise "not to marry anyone but him."

How could he have a wife? Sarah was so shaken by the news, she confronted Dr. Beers, who insisted Charley must be mistaken. Nothing of the sort occurred at his door. Regardless of the sincerity in his voice, Sarah saw through his lies. She also couldn't come to grips with his infidelity. Somehow, she needed to find the truth.

"Mother,"—Willie rested a soothing hand on his mother's shoulder—"I don't want you to worry over this. I will find out for you." He turned toward Belle and asked when the doctor might be returning to the house. Belle had no way of knowing that. So, Willie called at Dr. Beers's home. And like before, the same thing transpired—the person who opened the door said the doctor wasn't in, but his wife was. Unlike Charley, Willie was older and wiser and insisted that he wasn't leaving till he spoke with Mrs. Beers.

Dr. Beers hustled to the door and said he and his wife were divorced but she'd stopped by for a visit.

After this incident, Dr. Beers stopped calling on Sarah.

A few months later, Annie appeared to her sister in a dream. Tommy would be the next to perish. "No, oh, no," Sarah screamed, "[you] could not have him." But, she said, Annie just flew away.

"I had [several] conversations with her about dreams," Charles Chandler testified, "when the others of the family died. She would say that she dreamed so and so [came to her], and one of them was going to be sick, and all stuff like that. I cannot just say the way she put it. And they died."

District Attorney Stevens asked, "What did you say?"

"I told her she had better not dream that about me."

Little Tommy Freeman never received a penny from his Aunt Sarah. In fact, after his father died, she acted as though she couldn't stand the sight of him. Visitors to the Robinson household were often shocked by Tommy's forlorn appearance. But if anyone questioned Sarah, she would excuse Tommy's condition by saying, "The poor boy missed his parents dreadfully."

"Sometimes," Sarah confessed to a neighbor, "[I think] he would better be dead than alive. He was likely to follow in the footsteps of his father if he lived to grow up."

Sure enough, on July 19, little Tommy fell ill, with uncontrolled diarrhea, vomiting, and abdominal pain for four straight days until death finally ended his suffering. When Tommy gasped his final breath on July 23, 1886, Charles Chandler was sitting at the head of the bed, gazing down at his lifeless body.

"Sarah," he said, "how is it they all look alike, have the same symptoms, take the same medicine, with different diseases?"

Narrowing her eyes at Chandler, she stared at him for several minutes. Then she lowered her gaze to Tommy and draped a cloth over the contortion on his face. "I don't know." Irritation laced her tone. Sarah stormed out of the room.

Later that day, Catharine Melvin asked Sarah if Dr. Nichols was Tommy's guardian.

"What do you mean?"

"You told me some doctor in Cambridge was his guardian."

Sarah denied it. "The policy was made out to me. [Tommy] had nothing to do with it, the money was mine. I have paid Prince's bills with it, and after his bills were paid there was not very much left. The money would be mine anyway, because I adopted [Tommy]."

Catharine rocked back on her heels. "I don't see how you can have adopted him without Mother and I knowing it."

"It was not necessary, for [the adoption notice] was advertised."

Suspicions circulated about the train of deaths in the Robinson household. One of the many attending physicians spoke with Somerville Police Chief Parkhurst. But without solid evidence, there wasn't much they could do. Even so, Chief Parkhurst assigned Sergeant Cavanaugh to shadow Sarah's every move. Perhaps they could prevent a future death.

Three weeks after Cavanaugh took the assignment, on Wednesday, August 4, Willie was working at a commercial warehouse when a wooden crate fell off a high shelf, striking him between the shoulder blades. Even with the box empty, the accident knocked the wind out of him. Fortunately, he wasn't seriously injured. Yet, within an hour or two, nausea rose from his gut and he vomited up the breakfast his mother had prepared for him that morning.

Over dinner that night Sarah fixed Willie a cup of her "special tea." Even though the tea had a strange bitterness, he drank every drop. By the end of the meal he was even more nauseous, so he took to his bed "with racking cramps and constant vomiting."

In the morning Sarah sent for Dr. Emory White, a local physician associated with the Order of Pilgrim Fathers. Knowing about the series of deaths in the Robinson family—several members insured by the Order—Dr. White kept a close eye on Willie.

Nonetheless, normal medicine wasn't working. Willie continued to sink, so Dr. White bottled a sample of Willie's vomit and shipped the evidence to Professor Wood at Harvard Medical—the same toxicologist who found poison in the victims of Jane Toppan and Nellie Webb. Dr. White also shared his suspicions with Chief Parkhurst, who told him Sarah had been under surveillance for weeks.

In fact, Parkhurst said, "[I] always believed Mrs. Robinson poisoned Prince Arthur Freeman, and wanted the body exhumed [then]."

Two days later, Professor Wood sent back his report. Arsenic saturated Willie's vomit. From the sheer volume of poison, he doubted any traditional medicine could save the young man.

Dr. Durrell, a colleague of Dr. White, broke the sad news. "Now, William, that you know you cannot recover, who administered the poison to you?"

"My mother and Mr. Smith poisoned me, and I knew it at the time, but I thought I could be cured. Since I have been sick, I have taken neither food nor medicine from anybody else. All I have had they gave me."

The Order sent F. J. Hayes to the house in Somerville.

I went there Monday morning and saw Mrs. Robinson, and shook hands with her.

Then he went to check on Willie. When he left the sickroom, he told Sarah, "The people want some money."

"Mr. Hayes, I haven't got any money."

"They are much in need of money and they sent me to see if you had any."

"I haven't any," Sarah lied. "All the money there is, William has."

"William is not in any condition to speak."

"Why?" She softened the hard edge from her tone. "Is he dead?"

"Yes."

"Well, Mr. Hayes"—this news didn't affect her—"I haven't any money at all."

"Mrs. Robinson, I know you have received four thousand dollars from the Pilgrim Fathers [after Prince and Lizzie died], and it looks as though you might have money enough to pay the funeral expenses of one person."

Sarah crossed her arms on her chest. "Well, I haven't got a dollar."

A reporter for the *Watertown Republican* wrote about Willie's death.

> In his last hours, William suffered terribly from the convulsions. Chief of Police Parkhurst was notified . . . Mrs. Robinson had an interested friend and counselor, Thomas R. Smith, and it was prudent not to arrest the woman until the whereabouts of the man were determined.

Newspapers across New England churned out headline after headline: "Bay State Borgia," "A Woman's Awful Crimes," "A Modern Lucretia Borgia," "A Criminal Sensation," "The Boston Borgia," "Killed for the Insurance," "Eleven Persons Poisoned by a Woman."

Sometime over the next two days, Thomas Smith accompanied Sarah to the Garden Cemetery in Chelsea, as he often did.

> I was with her there placing flowers or plants upon Lizzie's grave.

"Mr. Smith," said Sarah, "there is no one living that Lizzie would rather have place flowers upon her grave than you."

After he set out the plants, he rose, laid his hands on the sides of Sarah's upper arms, and stared into her eyes. "Mrs. Robinson, that plant, if it lives and does well another year, will bear a beautiful white rose."

"I know it."

"Lizzie lives to-day in a land where flowers bloom but not fade."

"I know it, and I wish I were with her, and that my body was to be placed to-day in the grave with hers. Then I should be rid of the horrid feeling that I have all the time."

"How long have you had this horrid feeling that you speak of?"

Sarah's gaze fell to the family plot. "Ever since my husband died."

"Don't you think that the anxiety for the living and the sorrow for the dead causes that feeling?"

"No."

"I know that your sorrows are many, your afflictions are great."

"Oh, I know what sorrow is. This is not sorrow—this is horror, and I never shall be rid of these feelings until I die." Knees buckling, she looked like she might faint.

Not wanting to intrude on her suffering, Thomas Smith patted down the soil around the plants.

Out of the blue, Sarah said, "I know when any member of my family is going to die. I knew when [four-year-old] Emma May was going to be taken [in 1884], for Mr. Robinson came to me and said, 'I am coming for Emma May.' [I also] knew when Willie was to be taken away, for Lizzie came and said, 'Mother, I am coming for Willie.'"

What could he say? This wasn't the first time she'd claimed to have visions. But it might be the last.

6

EVIDENCE MOUNTS
IN VERMONT

With Harriet Nason behind bars in Rutland, the Commonwealth had a duty to investigate all the mysterious deaths, but some claimed they were tiptoeing around evidence because Harriet was a woman of influence. Those who knew her best described her as "peculiar at times, but incapable of committing such a terrible crime, and hoped to see her proved innocent."

The entire community didn't share that sentiment. Many were outraged. If the authorities wouldn't convict her, the press would.

The *Vermont Caledonian* wrote:

The frequent postponement of the Mrs. Harriet Nason poisoning case causes much unfavorable comment and criticism. Some charge the delay to the government's attorneys, who, it is said, are influenced by persons who would rather not have the case continued farther. It is claimed that embalming fluid was poured into the body of Mr. [Henry] Nason so that an analysis for evidence of poison would be useless, but others claim the embalming fluid was only used upon the surface of the body. So, the State's attorney is led to say that he doubts whether it would be of use to exhume and analyze these bodies suspected of being poisoned by Mrs. Nason.

This case morphed into national news, with journalists unable to agree on Harriet's guilt. The *Daily St. Paul Globe* claimed,

So far there is absolutely nothing to explain the presence of arsenic in [Don] Parker's stomach.

Closer to home, papers like the *Portland Daily Press* touched on the community's emotional unrest.

The affair has created a great sensation on account of [Don] Parker's standing. He was an expert stenographer, commanding a good salary and stood well socially. Mrs. Nason's anxiety to get Parker to marry her daughter was regarded with suspicion.

What truly baffled the community was the lack of motive. Why would Harriet Nason murder her son-in-law?
Even the *Caledonian* couldn't make sense of it.

Donald C. Parker, a prominent Rutland young man, died February 19 under suspicious circumstances, and arsenic in large quantities was found. Mrs. Harriet E. Nason, Parker's mother-in-law, was arrested on a charge of murder. . . . [Don Parker] had $1,000 insurance on his life, but money is not considered the motive of the crime, as Mrs. Nason has acted strangely for some time.

Mrs. Harriet Mussey "had for a year lived in the same block as Mrs. Nason" and before Don died, had a bizarre conversation with her neighbor.

Mrs. Nason stated that when her husband died she had poison under her pillow. Her feelings were such that she intended to take it but was prevented from doing so. Mrs. Nason said to [me], 'No man should come between [me] and my daughter. If he did, [I] would kill him.'

Miss Bertha Mussey lived with her mother, and she confirmed the conversation. Even in Maud's presence, Harriet Nason repeated, "No man should ever come between mother and daughter."

Miss Bertha asked how she could possibly prevent that from happening. With a deadpan expression, Harriet said simply, "I will kill him."

The public demanded justice. Due to the pressure State Attorney Kendall ordered the exhumations, but he stalled for over a year. About April 29, 1886, the *Burlington Free Press* reported on two of Harriet's alleged victims.

> The body of Mrs. Nason's husband [Henry Nason] was exhumed at Gorham, NH, as was that of Mrs. Nason's nephew, the infant son of O. H. McKeen. Notwithstanding the long time after death, [Henry] Nason's remains were found remarkably well-preserved and the liver and parts of the other organs were taken, sealed, and will be submitted [for] chemical examination.

The preliminary hearing of Harriet E. Nason opened at the House of Corrections in Rutland on Tuesday, May 4, Justice Wayne Bailey presiding. Three days later, State Attorney Kendall ordered the exhumation of Mrs. C. S. De Britton; her body was disinterred from the grave.

The Sun voiced their opinion about the latest murderess.

> Strong circumstantial evidence, slowly accumulating during several weeks, has at length laid at the door of a woman of this city [Rutland] a series of horrible crimes. Mrs. Harriet Nason, suspected poisoner, is now accused of the murder of her husband, her son-in-law, her nephew, and her most intimate female friend. There are ugly rumors, too, that the list of victims may be still further increased on investigation, but if half of what is already told be true, the woman has few equals even among the famous practicers of the poisoners' art.

In the jail chapel, where the hearing was held, a reporter from *The Sun* attended the pretrial.

> She borne the ordeal calmly, though her imprisonment [was] beginning to tell upon her, and she continues to steadfastly assert her innocence. . . . Her case has come before Justice Bailey for examination on several days since [her arrest]. . . . There has been the most intense interest in the matter in this community, and the court room has been crowded chiefly by ladies at each sitting.

To show motive, the Commonwealth put forth that Harriet had exhausted the proceeds of her husband's life insurance and needed money. "Much more evidence the State's attorney claims to possess, which he will not use until the final trial." In the meantime, the Commonwealth was still investigating the other mysterious deaths. Though, upon exhumation, all the bodies showed a remarkable state of preservation, a fact in and of itself that could indicate the presence of arsenic.

State Attorney Kendall ordered the medical examiner to send portions of the stomachs and intestines to Professor R. A. Witthaus of Buffalo, New York, a well-known toxicologist who specialized in chemical analysis of poisons for the past ten years, and who had testified at the trial of Emeline Lucy Meaker, the first woman executed in Vermont.

In the spring of 1879, a child welfare worker approached Emeline Meaker and her husband and asked if they would consider taking custody of Mr. Meaker's eight-year-old niece, Alice, and her brother, Henry. The two children had been living in an overcrowded orphanage since the deaths of their parents. When the case worker offered four hundred dollars to care for Alice, Mr. Meaker agreed, but they could not accept Henry, too.

Even with this stipulation, Emeline was not pleased.

"Mrs. Meaker conceived a violent dislike for her," a local journalist noted, "and determined to be rid of her."

Rather than care for the orphaned girl, she beat and starved Alice on a regular basis.

By 1883, Emeline decided to rid herself of this burden once and for all. So, she ordered her son, Almon—"a weak-minded youth of seventeen"—to obtain a lethal dose of strychnine from the apothecary.

One sultry summer evening, Emeline loaded Alice and Almon in the carriage for a long, peaceful ride. "On the way she mixed the strychnine with sweetened water and gave it to Alice." A few moments later, she pulled over and threw a sack over Alice's head, dragging her to a remote area outside Burlington.

When Emeline arrived at a clearing by a stream, Alice was thrashing in agony. So, Emeline held her down, with a hand over the young girl's mouth to silence her cries till the convulsions stopped. Between the poison and the smothering hold of her foster mother, Alice died. Once she did, Emeline ordered her son to bury the body "in a swamp-hole under a log."

Later, the jury returned a verdict of guilty for both Emeline and Almon. A capital murder charge came with a death sentence. But Almon qualified for protection under the Vermont Legislature of 1882. Officials commuted Almon's sentence to life imprisonment, because his mother's influence had over-powered him that fateful night. The court shipped Emeline to Windsor Prison, where she threw "violent outbursts" almost daily.

As her execution date drew closer, Emeline quieted, as if she'd found inner peace.

Executing a woman was big news. Every reporter in New England vied for the story.

Prison officials granted access to the *Vermont Phoenix*:

Mrs. Meaker slept soundly last night and rose about sunrise and ate a hearty breakfast with much relish. She was then dressed by the matron in the clothes in which she will be executed, and manifested considerable interest in her brand-new costume, which is of black cambric. She was visited about nine o'clock by Chaplain Hull but refused to say anything about the murder. At her own request she was taken out to see the gallows by Sheriff Amsden. She walked out and up on to the scaffold with a firm step and curiously inspected its trap, rope and build. She asked if she should have to ascend the stairs alone and said she could do so if necessary.

After returning to her cell, Prison Director Charley Thatcher, Washington County Sheriff Frank Atherton, and Superintendent Rice paid her a visit.

"Do you want to say anything different from what you said yesterday?" asked Thatcher.

"No, I have nothing more to say. They can murder me if they wish to, but they will have to answer for it."

Superintendent Rice tried to cheer her up. "You are looking well to-day."

"The matron says I look sweet sixteen." Emeline grinned. A moment later, she asked about her daughter, Nellie, and her husband. "Tell them I walk on to the scaffold without help. Tell Nellie to be a good girl and always do right."

Throughout her incarceration Emeline showed indifference toward her death sentence. On this particular morning, she remained even more cool-headed as she enjoyed "several good smokes from an old black pipe."

I shall smoke to the last!

At 1 p.m. sharp, the prison admitted ticketholders. About one hundred people passed through those gates, including Warden Dodge of New Hampshire, ex-Warden Earle of Massachusetts, and a number of visiting sheriffs.

At 1:15 p.m. Sheriff Amsden and deputies proceeded to Emeline's cell to bind her. A local reporter covered the execution.

The dreadful death procession appeared, two deputies walking beside Mrs. Meaker, having hold of her arms but not sustaining her. She stepped promptly up the scaffold stairs and took a seat on the gallows with calm self-possession. Prayer being offered, Sheriff

Amsden held up a written slip in his hand for the condemned woman to read. [Emeline had gone deaf.] The paper asked if she had anything to say about why the sentence of death should not be executed upon her.

As though dazed, Emeline stared at the note for several seconds. "May God forgive you all for hanging me, an innocent woman. I am as innocent as that man standing there," indicating a deputy.

The hangman slipped "the fatal noose around her neck" and drew "the black cap" over her head.

In an instant, and without warning, Sheriff Amsden put his foot on the spring, the drop fell, and Mrs. Meaker was ushered into eternity. Her body showed no convulsive motions, and in a few minutes, life was pronounced extinct. Her neck was broken by the fall.

No one from the Meaker family attended Emeline's execution. Her husband even refused to take custody of her body for burial.

Would Harriet Nason meet the same fate?

7

THREE ARRESTS IN
MASSACHUSETTS

On Wednesday, August 11, Sergeant Cavanaugh spotted Thomas R. Smith entering the Robinson residence. Time to move in. Accompanied by Officer Oliver, Cavanaugh rapped on Sarah's door. Once inside, he announced that Thomas and Sarah were under arrest for the murder of Willie Robinson. Sarah fainted on the spot.

"She went as rigid as death," Officer Oliver recalled. Thomas Smith—a pastor at the Park Avenue Methodist Church in Somerville—begged to pray over her, and Oliver agreed. "Smith knelt down over the woman and made as fervent a prayer as [I] ever heard."

At the arraignment on August 13, Sarah seemed "completely broken." Beside her stood her alleged accomplice, Thomas R. Smith. Both prisoners pleaded not guilty. Justice Field set bail at $25,000 for Sarah and $3,500 for Smith.

Neither had any money.

When the news of her arrest reached her former civil attorney, David F. Crane, who had represented her in the lawsuit against Moses's insurer, he told the *New Haven Daily Morning Journal and Courier*:

> I cannot believe that she would get her children's lives insured and then commit wholesale slaughter. If she be the woman they say she is, she has a gift for deception unequalled. The death of her daughter [Lizzie] last spring I know was a source of great grief to her

and also her husband's death. I always supposed her to be a good woman, above reproach. She has reliable friends in Cambridge and is thought a good deal of.

In the weeks that followed, authorities exhumed the bodies of Moses Robinson, Annie Freeman, Prince Freeman, Tommy Freeman, Lizzie Robinson, and her former landlord, Oliver Sleeper, who died in August 1881. After Sleeper's death, Sarah submitted a fifty-dollar invoice for nursing services, which the family paid. They were more concerned about the thousands missing from his account.

Professor Wood found arsenic in them all.

Later, authorities also arrested Dr. Charles Beers as an accomplice. A local reporter noted:

Another startling chapter in the notorious Robinson-Smith poisoning case developed this morning [August 21] in the announcement of [Charles] Beers of Boston, on the charge of murdering in conjunction with Mrs. Robinson, the latter's daughter Lizzie A. Robinson, by administering poison to her.

On December 12, 1887, the first trial began in the Supreme Judicial Court in East Cambridge. All the press was in attendance.

Mrs. Robinson was attired in black and very pale as the proceedings began with the work of impaneling the jury. She betrayed no nervousness, however, and seemed interested in the legal controversies. A large number of jurors were challenged by both sides, but the panel was finally completed. . . . Judge Field informed the jury that as the trial would probably last some days, they might retire in the custody of officers to write home to their families.

After reading the indictment, charging all three defendants with first-degree murder, Clerk Hurd stunned the public with, "The government has decided to *nol pros* [common abbreviation of *nolle prosequi*, Latin for "we shall no longer prosecute"] the counts against Smith and Beers, to retain the first count only against Sarah Jane Robinson, which charges her with the murder of her son, Willie J. Robinson."

Incompetence combined with a monotone, rambling prosecutor worked against the State. The trial lasted six days and resulted in a hung jury, after jurors had deliberated for only twenty-four hours. The prosecution didn't dismiss the charges, however. Sarah remained behind bars for the murder of the others.

On July 2, the *New York Tribune* announced,

> Mrs. Sarah Jane Robinson of Somerville, who is accused of having poisoned her husband and several of her children, was visited by Dr. Kelly of the McLean Insane Asylum, at the County Jail, East Cambridge, to-day. Since her first appearance in court on the several charges of poisoning, the belief has become current that she must have been insane. Her counsel never entertained the thought, much less those who meet her daily. In order to set public opinion right in the matter, Dr. Kelly has been engaged to make a thorough examination of her mental condition. He called upon her about 4:30 o'clock and remained until 6. They talked over various subjects and particularly of the crime with which she is charged. She expressed the most hopeful opinion as to the ultimate result of her trial.

Dr. Kelly "was much struck by her cheerful appearance, and from the observations of yesterday is firmly of the opinion that there is nothing insane about her."

Even Sarah said she didn't want "to try the insanity dodge."

Sarah's second trial took place on February 6, 1888, Justice Field and Judge Knowlton presiding. This time around, the Commonwealth accused her of capital murder, for the death of Prince Arthur Freeman. According to the official trial transcript,

> The prisoner was placed at the bar and the jury was impaneled to try Sarah J. Robinson. The clerk then read the indictment, to which the prisoner pleaded Not Guilty.

District Attorney William B. Stevens represented the State, along with Attorney General A. J. Waterman. For the defense, John B. Goodrich, Esq., acted as senior counsel, Attorney David F. Crane as associate counsel.

Justice Field allowed the prosecution to introduce the other murders only to show one piece of an overall "scheme" which Sarah had concocted long ago. But, he cautioned, "you shall not submit the evidence of one crime to prove another."

District Attorney Stevens addressed the jury:

This insurance had been made out, payable in case of the death of Prince Arthur Freeman to his wife Annie, and the first step that was necessary for the purpose of enabling Mrs. Robinson to get the insurance was to get Mrs. [Annie] Freeman out of the way. . . . Mrs. Robinson, during this time, was pressed by creditors—she had mortgaged her property to at least [three] different people under different names; she had been threatened with arrest on account of having obtained money by false pretenses; she was sorely pressed by her creditors, and the money was received by her finally from this insurance.

The deaths of the Freeman family occurred as part of a "fatal web" she weaved "at least as long ago as 1885, during the sickness of her sister," District Attorney Stevens continued.

There was a master at the end of the wires, and every figure had moved in its proper place. . . . She commences to dream dreams and to see visions. She is haunted by the spectres of those who have gone to the land of shadows. . . . Her acts rise up like ghastly ghosts against her, verifying the truth that exists so often in the history of great crimes, 'Whom the gods would destroy, they first make mad.' It is of the highest consequence, gentlemen, that this should not [result in] a mistrial. I pray you, in this case do your duty well.

The Commonwealth sought the death penalty.

During closing arguments, Attorney David F. Crane warned the jury that a guilty verdict came with consequences.

> The verdict of a jury cannot be recalled or revoked, however much you might desire it in subsequent years. The doors of the cells in yonder cells may open and let the inmates out at the bidding of one man, but the doors of the grave never open to let the innocent pass out.

In the end, the jury found Sarah guilty of capital murder and sentenced her to hang on November 16, 1888. Oddly enough, public opinion turned in her favor by the end of October that same year. A petition for clemency gained over five hundred signatures, including seventy-six ministers and seven of the jurors who'd sentenced her to death. On November 15, 1888, the day before her execution, Governor Ames commuted Sarah's sentence to life in solitary confinement.

The *Clarksville Evening Chronicle* announced,

> Sarah Jane Robinson, Massachusetts' notorious female prisoner, will not hang, but her fate will be hardly less terrible. It took the governor and his council over two hours to reach a decision Monday afternoon. The result was a surprise to everyone, for it was quite generally believed that the death sentence would be executed. The commutation provides for the woman's solitary imprisonment for life in the state prison. Only one other case of this extreme kind is recorded in the state's history—that of Jesse Pomeroy.

> *"Female serial killers murder for the same basic reason males do—for power, profit, lust, thrills, or revenge. But they're far more cunning than their male counterparts. They feel no need to take trophies, Polaroids, or engage in necrophilia. The act of murder is their ultimate reward."*
>
> —Peter Vronsky,
> author of *Female Serial Killers*

The public had mixed feelings about Sarah's commutation. A journalist from the *Clarksville Evening Chronicle* said it best:

> The terror of it is even worse than death, for it implies endless solitude and darkness. Already the murderess has been removed to her living tomb, from which her counsel, jubilant in their success in saving her neck, confidently declare their hope of securing her liberation. . . . Never has the exercise of mercy been so tardily indorsed as in the case of this modern Lucretia Borgia, only the doubt shadowing the evidence warrants the plea for clemency, and yet the community is relieved and breathes easier now that the affair is ended.

By June of 1901, Sarah could be found quietly spending her time in the East Cambridge prison—just a short distance away from where Jolly Jane murdered Mattie Davis.

Sarah Jane Robinson spent twenty years in solitary confinement. In her final years, she arranged for her own funeral, even though in 1904 she sought a pardon, claiming, "I have been unjustly sentenced." Since she never confessed or displayed the least bit of remorse for her victims, the governor denied her request.

Two years later, on January 3, 1906, Sarah died from "complications of a prolonged illness." She was sixty-seven years old.

8

PRELIMINARY HEARING OF VERMONT BORGIA

The State's first witness, Professor Witthaus, took the stand in the Harriet Nason case on Tuesday, May 4, 1886. He explained in careful detail the method used to find arsenic. As he testified, "Harriet's face flushed occasionally as she leaned forward, intently listening to the testimony," according to eyewitnesses. In the audience sat Maud and her nine-year-old brother, Guy.

While the chemist shared details of his analyses, one journalist watched Harriet's daughter to gauge her reaction.

> Maud took pains to carefully arrange her elaborate mourning garb from time to time, and pouted or smiled as the evidence seemed to please or displease her.

Professor Witthaus testified to the presence of arsenic in Don Parker's organs:

> On March 16, [I] received a box in which was a second box, the edges of which were protected by tape and sealed with the stamp of the Supreme Court of Vermont. The inner box contained four glass bottles and two fruit jars, which enclosed a human stomach, a

portion of the upper intestines, a fragment of the liver, a kidney, a bladder, part of the rectum, and the spleen.

Witthaus explained how he'd sliced pieces off the stomach and liver "to examine separately for mineral and organic poisons. The latter analysis he had not finished" in time for the preliminary hearing. He could say, without reservation, that he did not find strychnine.

About one-third of the liquid found in the stomach was used in the analysis, and after being put through certain processes, sulphuric acid was applied. In ten minutes there was a marked and distinct metallic mirror. On examination the substance forming the mirror was found to be deposited in octahedral crystals. There is no substance which will produce a metallic stain on these crystals under such circumstances, except arsenic.

He then took a portion of the liver and subjected it to the same rigorous tests and received similar results.

A part of the liver taken from another jar was subjected to a different process but produced the stains of arsenic in about the same proportion.

In total he conclusively deduced that Don Parker ingested a lethal dose of white arsenic, 2.5 grains found in the liver alone.

The undertaker, George P. Russell, was in charge of the remains after Don died.

[I] made no use of embalming fluid in the preparation of the remains for burial until the next day [Saturday, February 21], when [I] applied some on the face with a cloth and left directions with Mrs. Nason and her daughter to keep the cloth moist.

When asked if the fluid used on the face contained arsenic, he said, "[I] could not tell whether there was any arsenic in the fluid or not."

Equitable Life agent W. H. S. Whitcomb of Burlington testified to "Don Parker's holding a $1,000 policy in the company, which he paid to his widow on January 18, 1886," almost one full year after her husband died.

Mr. Nicholson, who worked as a taxidermist, said Harriet asked him during Don's sickness to describe the effect of poison upon the human system.

The details of the autopsy came next, and Mr. Seamans, the medical examiner, told the jury how "they went at Parker as if he had been a beef critter, and sawed his skull open to look over the brain."

At that precise moment, "Mrs. Parker [Don's mother] gave way to her feelings in an outburst of tears," noted the *Herald*.

Mrs. Nason looked stoically on, however, without exhibiting the slightest indication of feeling, excepting, perhaps, an occasional twitching of the mouth. By the side of the accused woman sat a friend of hers from Brattleboro—a straight, slender, cynical-looking maiden of 50 years, wearing gold-bowed spectacles. On her Mrs. Nason leaned at times, and she had pencil and notebook in hand, with which she occasionally jotted down parts of the testimony. A bell rang often during the hearing, calling the warden or keeper to the door below to admit some spectator or witness, who had to be ushered upstairs through the hospital and past S. M. Waite's cell to the chapel above.

S. M. Waite was a popular financier convicted of embezzlement, who was mistakenly pardoned (but never released) when the pardon clerk confused his case with another.

After several more witnesses took the stand, the state recalled Professor Witthaus and asked about "the stringy piece of beef" that Parker had vomited. He testified:

Persons suffering from arsenical poisoning often threw up parts of the coating of the stomach. Such pieces were often reddish brown and might resemble pieces of beef.

To update the jury on his progress with the other tests, the chemist said he found no mercury in the analysis.

Blue pills are made of metallic mercury.

Character witnesses all testified to "Mrs. Nason's strange conduct during her son-in-law's sickness."

The *Vermont Phoenix and Record and Farmer* covered the case in great detail.

Mrs. H. E. Nason of Rutland, who is under arrest and in jail on a charge of killing her son-in-law last February with poison, was for five or six years a resident of Brattleboro 10 or 12 years ago. Her husband was in the employ of the railroad. They had a daughter and son and lived in a house back of the Brattleboro house, and also on Canal Street. The son, Guy, died soon after they left here, and another son, also called Guy, was born afterward. While living here Mrs. Nason seems to have been that sort of woman who had a few friends and intimates who believed in her, while the majority who knew her regarded her with a certain distrust and aversion.

This running theme developed in the papers, but *Spirit of the Age* (Woodstock, Vermont paper) took it one step further.

Already judgment has been passed upon her by those of her own sex, while the men are asking, is there evidence enough to warrant the justice in holding her for trial? The women have almost without exception pronounced her guilty and sentenced her to death on the scaffold, while occasionally one of stern aspect wishes that the accused might expiate her awful crime by suffering death from poison—the means alleged to have been used to dispose of [Don] Parker.

A notable physician, Dr. George Fox, testified, "[Don] Parker's symptoms were those of perfect collapse, and exactly similar to a case [I] had some time ago of a man who died after taking Paris green." Although, he admitted, similar symptoms could also accompany heart disease.

The State brought in more witnesses to repeat "threats which Mrs. Nason had been heard to make" about a man coming between her and Maud. Even with these witnesses—most of whom lived in Harriet's neighborhood and knew her well—the public wondered if the testimony was enough to send an upstanding citizen to prison for murder, and that question played out in newspapers across the country.

The *Savannah Morning News* wrote:

> There was some vague testimony in reference to what took place in the sick room, but nothing on which the charge of administering poison could be substantiated.

This mindset worked in Harriet Nason's favor. Even after all the witnesses testified to her "strange behavior," along with damning statements about murder, combined with experts who all agreed Don Parker could only have died from arsenical poisoning, Justice Bailey ruled that he did die from arsenic, but the State hadn't proven who poisoned him. So, with "insufficient evidence to hold Mrs. Nason in custody till the Grand Jury hearing," he released her from jail. A grand jury hearing should've been held the following September but wasn't. Postponement after postponement allowed the case to gradually fade from the courts.

Harriet Nason walked free on May 22, 1886. Once she did, the public lost interest. The rest of her life, burial site, and date of death remains a mystery to this day. All that can be substantiated is that she was not buried with her husband, Henry Nason, in Gorham, New Hampshire. At thirty-nine years old, it's possible she remarried, changed her name, and moved out of the area. What we do know is, unlike Sarah Jane Robinson, Harriet got away with murder on at least four occasions and her victims and their families never received justice.

9

DEATH CERTIFICATION
REFORM

The murderous acts of the five female serial killers depicted in this book shook the foundation of medical and legal communities across New England. Most notably, the rampages of Jane Toppan and Sarah Jane Robinson, which incited a reform in death certification, as well as a ban on arsenic in embalming fluid.

On Thursday, April 24, 1902, the *Boston Medical and Surgical Journal* released a "Reform in Death Certification—Life Insurance Reports—Medical Notes," which reads as follows:

> Recent developments in connection with the Toppan case are of such a character as to call attention to the necessity of decided action to prevent the occurrence of similar cases in the future. The Robinson cases are still fresh in mind, and as a consequence of those murders Mrs. Robinson has been confined in jail for about fifteen years at the public expense.
>
> These deaths, together with those which have been attributed to the acts of Miss Toppan, make nearly a score of Massachusetts citizens who have at some time or other lost their lives in consequence of the acts, whether criminal or otherwise, of these two women, and have given to the State an unenviable notoriety, which demands investigation to determine whether there is not something wrong in the present symptom of death certification which may,

in part at least, value in the settlement of claims for life insurance, pensions, property rights in families, and especially in cases of disputed survivorship.

(2) They are of much value to the genealogist, who is in search of questions pertaining to family history.

(3) Taken collectively, they constitute an extremely valuable source of knowledge in the study of the causes, prevalence and distribution of diseases.

(4) They often furnish valuable aid in the detection of crime.

It is to this latter object alone that we desire to call attention. The subject has attracted the notice of the British Parliament, and in 1893 an investigation was made at which Sir Henry Thompson, Dr. Ogle of the registrar general's office, and other noted physicians testified, and urged the necessity of improved methods. The following quotation from the report of the committee shows that the necessity for reform existed:

Among the class of certified deaths are to be found many deaths attended by unqualified assistants and certified by qualified practitioners who may never have seen the cases; deaths certified by medical practitioners who have not seen the patient for weeks or months prior to death, and who only know by hearsay of death having occurred; and deaths in which the true cause is suppressed in deference to the feelings of survivors.

Such cases are numerous, but in addition evidence was given as to cases accidentally brought to light of deaths registered, with a view to insurance of other frauds, of persons afterward discovered in some cases to have been murdered, and in other cases to be still alive; and deaths registered under circumstances suggestive of fraud, regarding which it was not known whether the subjects had or had not died, and coffins buried alleged to contain corpses, the deaths of which had not been registered, and concerning which all that is known is that no such persons as those alleged to have been buried had died at the address given to the burial authorities.

Sir Henry Thompson, in testifying before the Parliamentary Committee, urged the necessity for greater precautions to prevent the concealment of crime, and Dr. Ogle stated that one of the chief objects of the death certificate was to prevent foul play and murder.

It is evident that, so far as the certificate of death is concerned, every possible guarantee of protection to the community should be given, by surrounding the certificate with the proper safeguards for making it as definite and as accurate as possible.

ACKNOWLEDGMENTS

Special thanks to all the individuals, agencies, and resources who helped with my research:

State Library of Massachusetts
UMass
Bourne Historical Society
Diane Ranney, Jonathan Bourne Public Library
New England Historical Society
New Hampshire Historical Society
Halie Grobleski, Bourne Historical Society
Stephanie Krauss, Harvard Library, Special Collections
Francis A. Countway Library of Medicine, Harvard
Smithsonian
Murder by Gaslight
Supreme Judicial Court of Massachusetts Archives
United States National Library of Medicine
Library of Congress
Psycho USA: Famous American Killers You've Never Heard Of by Harold
    Schechter
Fatal: The Poisonous Life of a Female Serial Killer by Harold Schechter
Tales Told in the Shadows of the White Mountains by Charles J. Jordan
Female Serial Killers: How and Why Women Become Monsters by Peter Vronsky

Female Serial Killers: Up Close and Personal by Christopher Berry-Dee

Psychology Today

Abimael Medina Jr. of Lancaster Historical Society and Weeks State Park
  Association

Betty Newel, Lancaster Historical Society & Museum

Colonel Town Recreational Center

NCBI Resources

NHCurrency.org

Poison Fiend! Life, Crimes, and Conviction of Lydia Sherman by George L.
  Barclay (1873)

Harvard College Library

Studies of Criminal Responsibility & Limited Responsibility by Charles Folsom
  (1842–1907)

Massachusetts State Archives

Cape Cod Confidential

Jordan Dane

Louise Holmburg

Garry Rodgers

Kemberlee Shortland

Sally Blanchard-O'Brien, Vermont State Archives

Tara Giles, Salmon Press

Boston Public Library

Britney Overton, Minot-Sleeper Library

LT Brandon Esip, Bourne Police Department

Joanie Gearin, National Archives at Boston

Suzanne Hoey, Massachusetts Trial Court, Barnstable Law Library

Carol Riley, Lincoln Public Library

Massachusetts State Board of Lunacy and Charity (c. 1886)

Wicked Yankee

Sturgis Library, Barnstable

Barbara Robarts, John W. Weeks Memorial Library

Serial Killers by Joel Norris

The New England Journal of Medicine Archives

Massachusetts Medical Society

New England Surgical Society
The Sexual Criminal by J. Paul de River (c. 1949)
The Criminality of Women by Otto Pollak (c. 1950)
When She was Bad by Patricia Pearson
Science Catches the Criminal by Henry Morton Robinson (c. 1932)
The Roots of Crime by Edward Glover (c. 1960)
Psychopathia Sexualis by Dr. Richard Von Krafft-Ebing (c. 1886)
Women Who Kill by Ann Jones
The Boston Medical and Surgical Journal (c. 1902)
Massachusetts Superior Judicial Library Archives
Sarah Parke, Acquisitions Editor, Globe Pequot

Lastly, a heartfelt thank you to my husband, Bob, and the rest of my family for dealing with the long hours spent at my desk or on the road, my lack of attention at times, and for always being my loudest cheerleaders. I love you all.

OTHER BOOKS
BY SUE COLETTA

FICTION

MAYHEM SERIES
Wings of Mayhem (Book 1)
Blessed Mayhem (Book 2)
Silent Mayhem (Book 3)

MAYHEM SERIES CROSSOVER NOVELLAS
HACKED
Fractured Lives

GRAFTON COUNTY SERIES
MARRED (Book 1)
CLEAVED (Book 2)
SCATHED (Book 3)
RACKED (Book 4)

NON-FICTION
Crime Writer's Research
60 Ways to Murder (Your Characters)

STORY COLLECTIONS
The Rendering
Murder, USA

ABOUT THE AUTHOR

Sue Coletta is an award-winning crime writer. For three years running, Feedspot named her *Murder Blog* as one of the "Best 50 Crime Blogs on the Net" (*Murder Blog* sits at #5). Sue also blogs at the Kill Zone, a multi-award-winning writing blog. In addition to blogging, she's the communications manager for the Serial Killer Project and Forensic Science, both groups founded by New York homicide detective and cold case expert Joe Giacolone. Sue also founded #ACrimeChat on Twitter to help crime writers add realism to fiction. She is an active member of Mystery Writers of America, Sisters in Crime, and International Thriller Writers. Sue lives in the Lakes Region of New Hampshire (Alexandria) and writes two serial killer thriller series published by Tirgearr Publishing.